Archie® Americana Series™

BEST OF THE SIXTIES

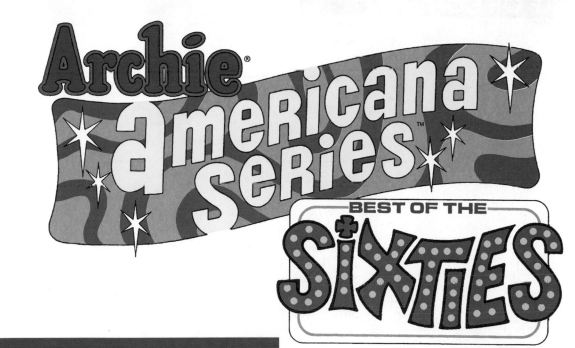

ARCHIE COMIC PUBLICATIONS, INC.

MICHAEL I. SILBERKLEIT
Chairman and Co-Publisher

RICHARD H. GOLDWATER
President and Co-Publisher

VICTOR GORELICK
Vice President /
Managing Editor

FRED MAUSSER
Vice President /
Director of Circulation

Americana Series Editor: **PAUL CASTIGLIA**

Americana Series Art Director: **JOSEPH PEPITONE**

Front Cover Illustration: **REX W. LINDSEY**

Cover colored by: **HEROIC AGE**

Production Manager: **CARYN ANTONIUK**

Production: **NANCI DAKESIAN AND KELLY FLEMING**

Archie characters created by **JOHN L. GOLDWATER**

Archie Americana Series, BEST OF THE SIXTIES, Volume 3, 1995. Printed in the U.S.A. Published by Archie Comic Publications, Inc., 325 Fayette Avenue, Mamaroneck, New York 10543.

ISBN 1-879794-02-0

TABLE OF CONTENTS

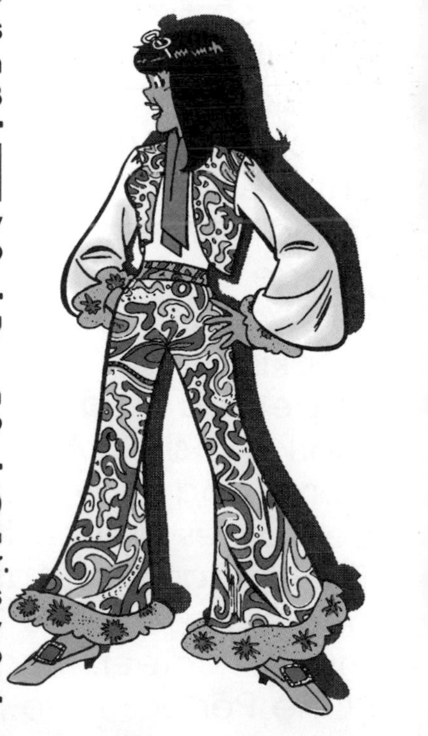

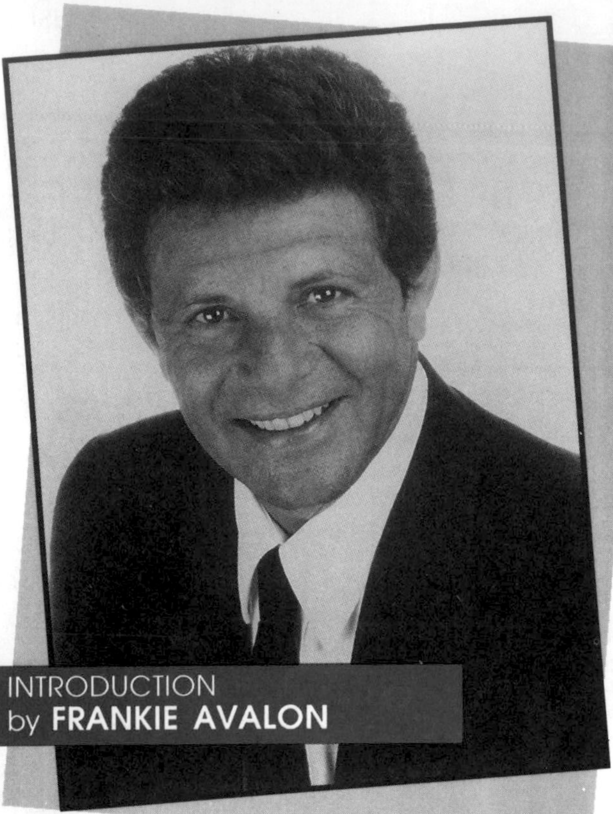

INTRODUCTION
by **FRANKIE AVALON**

Revisiting the sixties through the eyes of Archie and his gang is a great pleasure for me as it is so much like reliving that most exciting time in my career. "Sensational" is certainly the way the sixties were for me -- at least, until Beatlemania took over the music business. I had my first hit "Dede Dinah" in 1958, followed by "Venus" and "Bobby Sox to Stockings" in 1959. By 1960, I appeared frequently on Dick Clark's TV show **American Bandstand** and played many concert dates around the country. The hits came one after another and I was at the top of my musical career. "Togetherness," "One Perfect Love," "Who Else But You," "You Are Mine" and "A Miracle" were playing on every teenager's radio from 1960 to 1963.

The dress code for boys was crewcuts and letter sweaters and the talk was about physical fitness and having a car of your own. The girls were concerned with the proper age to wear high-heeled shoes and when to start wearing nylons. Both boys and girls were deeply concerned about how to deal with acne. It was right out of the pages of Archie Comics! Will life ever be so innocent?

By 1962, rock and roll was associated with clean-cut teen idols-- who would've been right at home sharing comic book adventures alongside Archie and his equally clean-cut pals. **American Bandstand** originated in Philadelphia and I guess it is fair to say that I was the first of the Philly teen idols, all of whom made regular appearances. Almost all teenagers of the time, boys and girls alike, watched the show to see their favorite stars including Bobby Rydell, Bobby Darin, Bobby Vee, Fabian, Pat Boone and Brenda Lee.

Teenagers dressed and behaved like young adults, mirroring the television shows of the time such as **The Adventures of Ozzie and**

Harriet, **Leave It To Beaver** and **The Dick Van Dyke Show**.

The girl who set the standard for girlhood in the sixties was Annette Funicello. She had a successful singing and acting career of her own but together she and I were part of the most popular series of movies to be produced in Hollywood in the sixties. These were the beach movies, which became such hits with the kids in America and the rest of the world. Starting with **Beach Party** in 1963, American International Pictures made and released **Muscle Beach Party**, **Bikini Beach**, **Beach Blanket Bingo** and many more.

I had an acting career before and after these beach movies. I appeared in **The Alamo** with John Wayne, as well as **Voyage To The Bottom of the Sea**, **The Carpetbaggers** and **Grease**. But the beach pictures catapulted me to a phenomenal level of popularity. A popular saying among girls at the time was "get your tan and get your man." The beach movies were a strong cultural influence on all teenagers, just as Archie Comics influences pre-teens. Both set standards on how boys and girls dress, behave and have fun.

These beach pictures popularized the sport of surfing and ushered in a new wave of music characterized by The Beach Boys. Years before the music video, the beach pictures introduced hits of the day as the plots were written to allow Annette and me to break into a song without the slightest pretext. **Muscle Beach Party**'s title tune was partly written by Brian Wilson of The Beach Boys. And while it is true that the sixties are remembered by many as a time of protest and turmoil, for me it will always remain a time when young people were optimistic and enthusiastic about life and the future, a time when family values were the norm as was having good, clean fun. My music and movies reflected these values -- the same wholesome, family-oriented fun that Archie Comics portrays. To me, the beach pictures are like Archie Comics in that Betty, Veronica and Archie mirror the same qualities as characters portrayed by Annette, me and whoever played the role of competing love interest.

So grab your surfboards and catch a wave with me, the "Big Kahuna," back to the **Best Of The Sixties** with Archie and his friends!

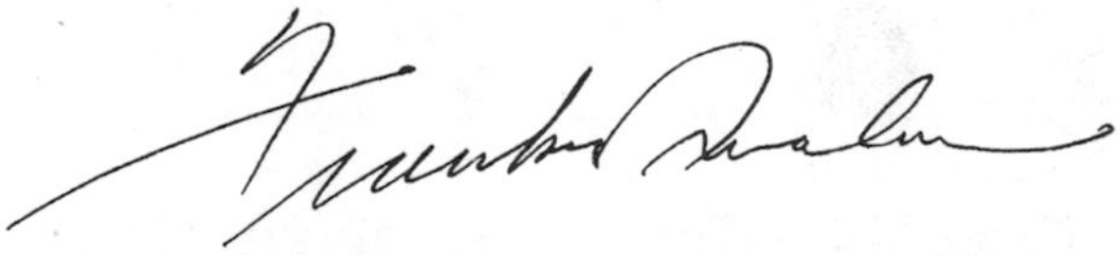

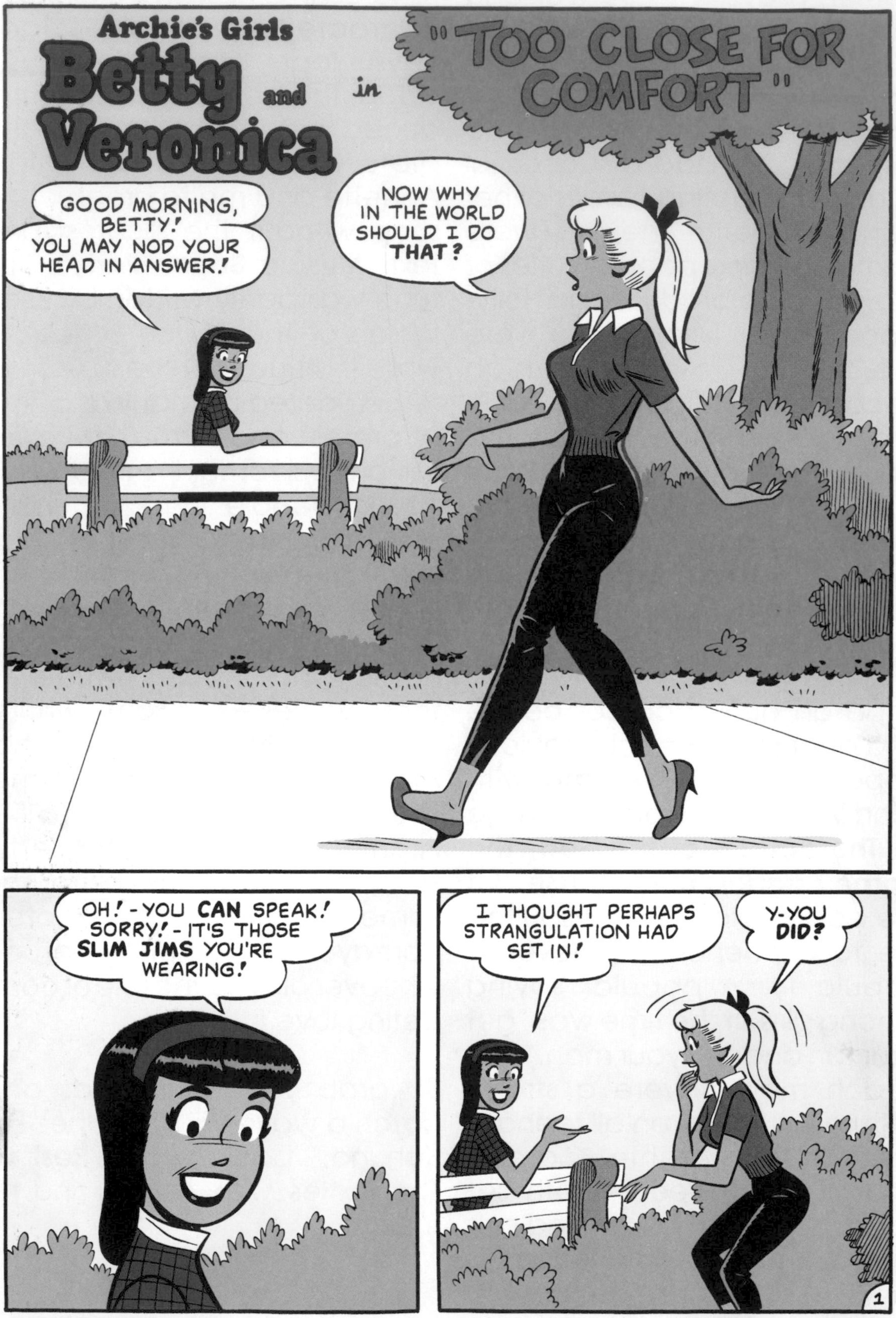
Archie's Girls Betty and Veronica in
"TOO CLOSE FOR COMFORT"
GOOD MORNING, BETTY! YOU MAY NOD YOUR HEAD IN ANSWER!
NOW WHY IN THE WORLD SHOULD I DO THAT?
OH! - YOU CAN SPEAK! SORRY! - IT'S THOSE SLIM JIMS YOU'RE WEARING!
I THOUGHT PERHAPS STRANGULATION HAD SET IN!
Y-YOU DID?
1

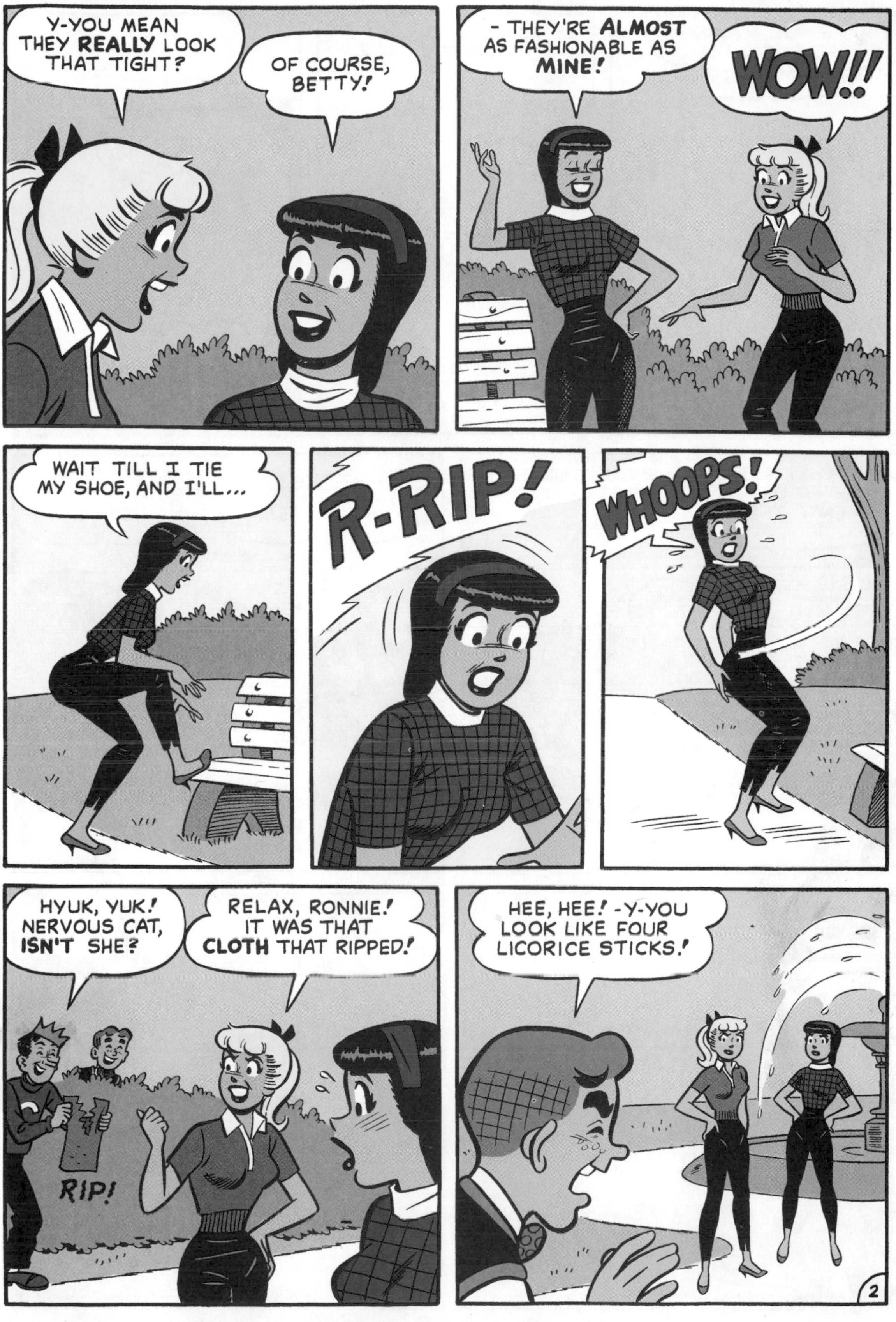
Y-YOU MEAN THEY REALLY LOOK THAT TIGHT?
OF COURSE, BETTY!
- THEY'RE ALMOST AS FASHIONABLE AS MINE!
WOW!!
WAIT TILL I TIE MY SHOE, AND I'LL...
R-RIP!
WHOOPS!
HYUK, YUK! NERVOUS CAT, ISN'T SHE?
RELAX, RONNIE! IT WAS THAT CLOTH THAT RIPPED!
RIP!
HEE, HEE! -Y-YOU LOOK LIKE FOUR LICORICE STICKS!
2

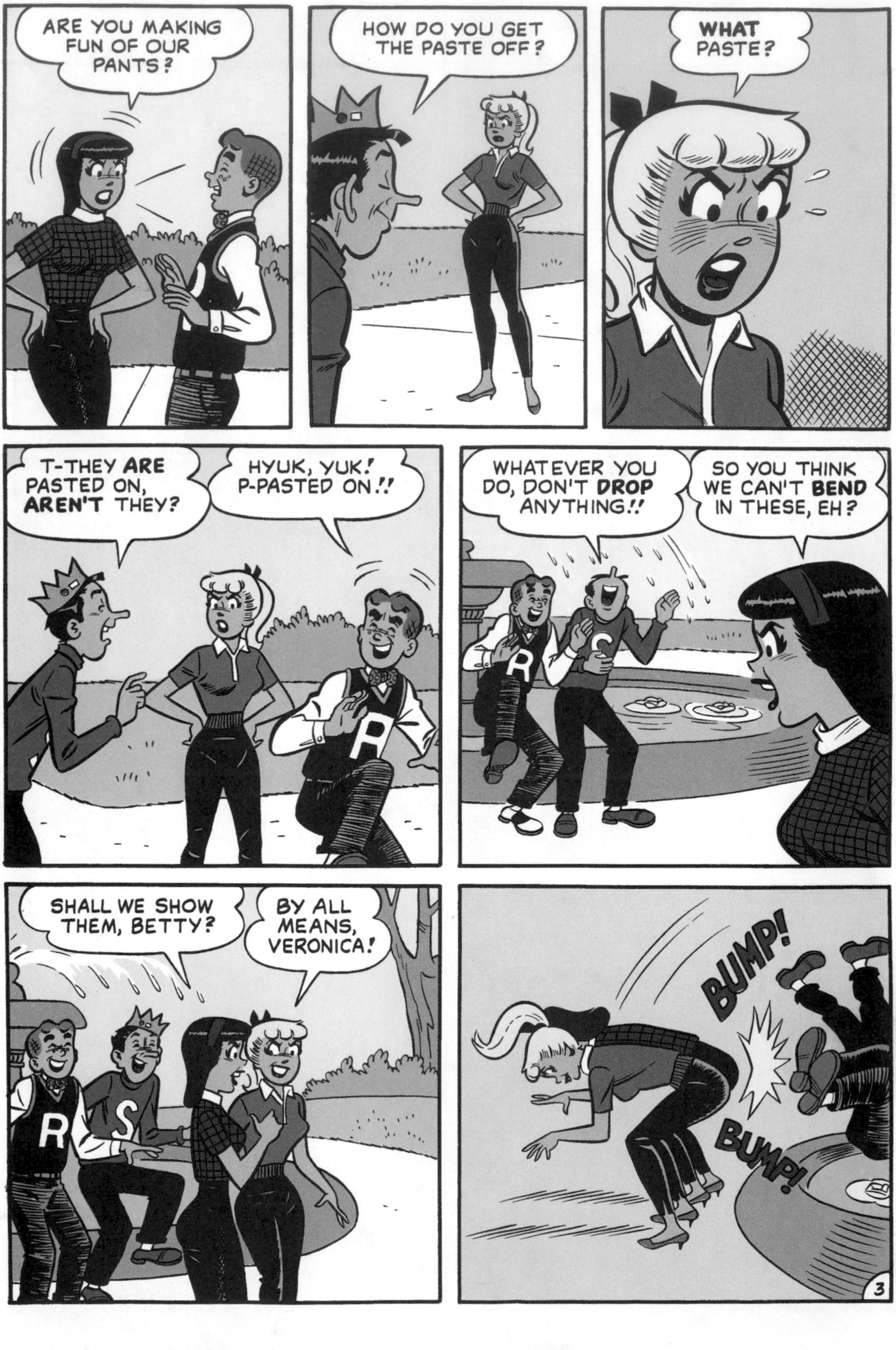
ARE YOU MAKING FUN OF OUR PANTS?
HOW DO YOU GET THE PASTE OFF?
WHAT PASTE?
T-THEY ARE PASTED ON, AREN'T THEY?
HYUK, YUK! P-PASTED ON!!
WHATEVER YOU DO, DON'T DROP ANYTHING!!
SO YOU THINK WE CAN'T BEND IN THESE, EH?
SHALL WE SHOW THEM, BETTY?
BY ALL MEANS, VERONICA!
BUMP!
BUMP!
BUMP!
3

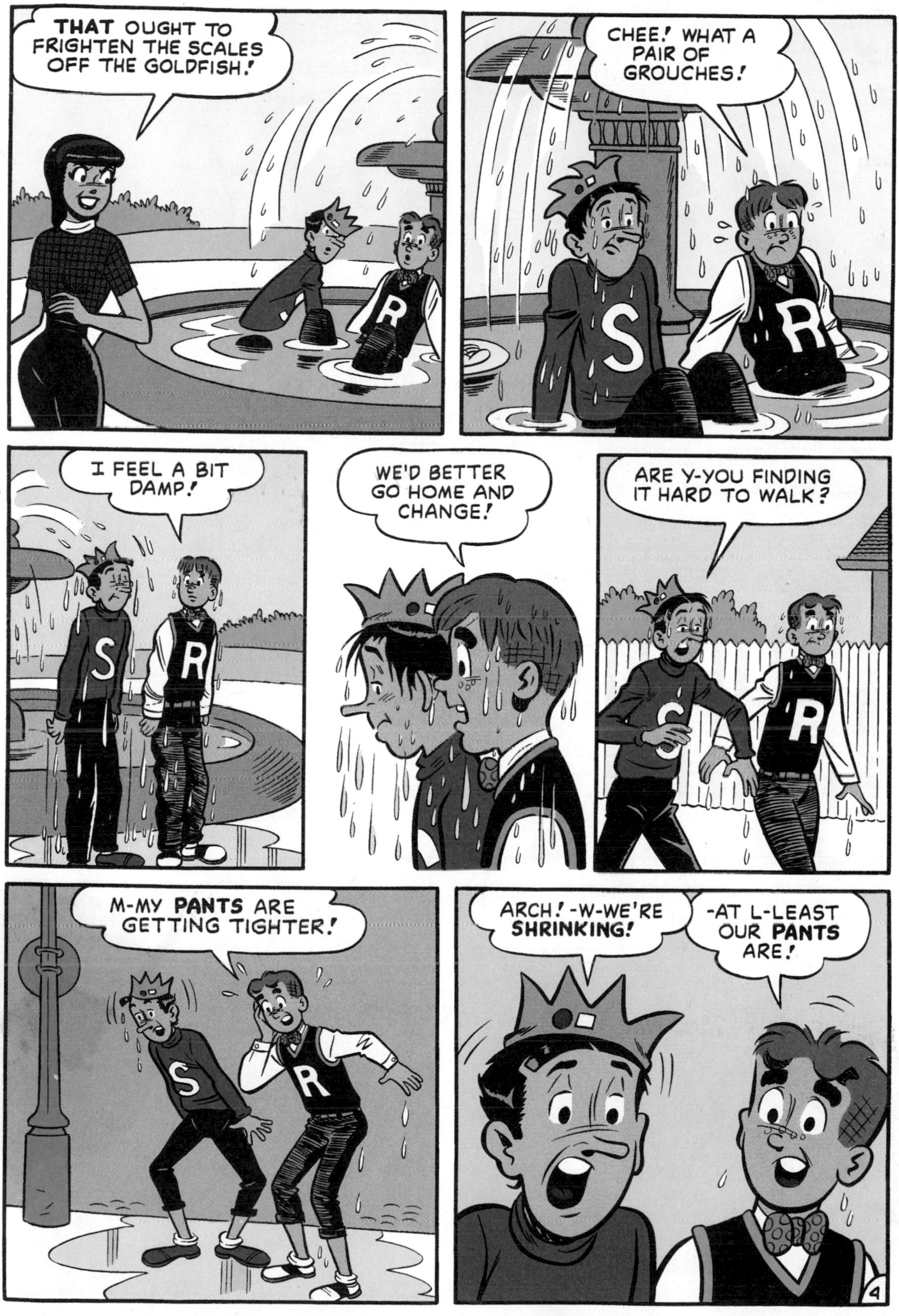
THAT OUGHT TO FRIGHTEN THE SCALES OFF THE GOLDFISH!
CHEE! WHAT A PAIR OF GROUCHES!
I FEEL A BIT DAMP!
WE'D BETTER GO HOME AND CHANGE!
ARE Y-YOU FINDING IT HARD TO WALK?
M-MY PANTS ARE GETTING TIGHTER!
ARCH! -W-WE'RE SHRINKING!
-AT L-LEAST OUR PANTS ARE!
4

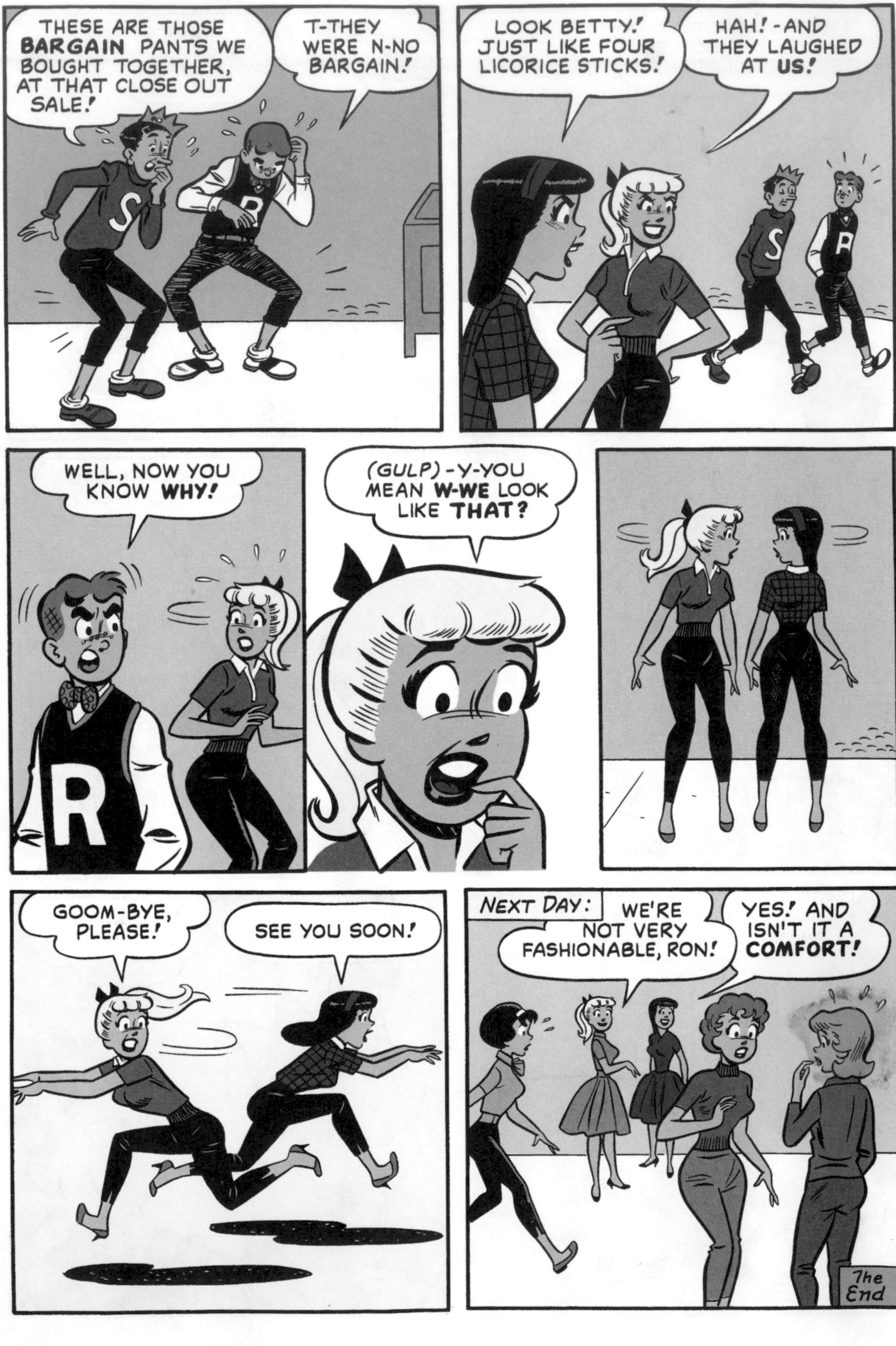
THESE ARE THOSE BARGAIN PANTS WE BOUGHT TOGETHER, AT THAT CLOSE OUT SALE!
T-THEY WERE N-NO BARGAIN!
LOOK BETTY! JUST LIKE FOUR LICORICE STICKS!
HAH! -AND THEY LAUGHED AT US!
WELL, NOW YOU KNOW WHY!
(GULP) -Y-YOU MEAN W-WE LOOK LIKE THAT?
GOOM-BYE, PLEASE!
SEE YOU SOON!
NEXT DAY:
WE'RE NOT VERY FASHIONABLE, RON!
YES! AND ISN'T IT A COMFORT!
The End

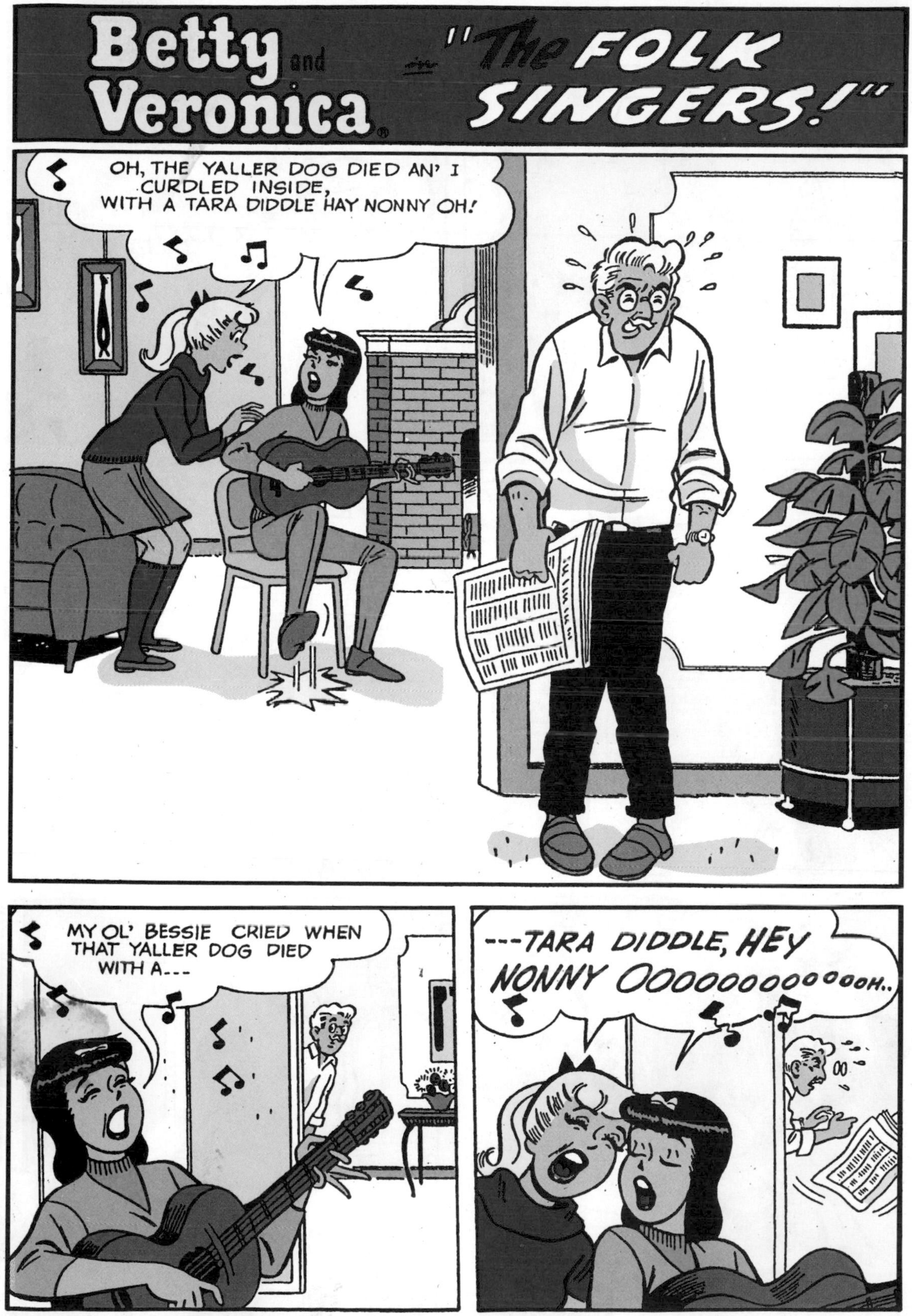
Betty and Veronica
in "The FOLK SINGERS!"
OH, THE YALLER DOG DIED AN' I CURDLED INSIDE, WITH A TARA DIDDLE HAY NONNY OH!
MY OL' BESSIE CRIED WHEN THAT YALLER DOG DIED WITH A---
---TARA DIDDLE, HEY NONNY OOOOOOOOOOOOOOH..

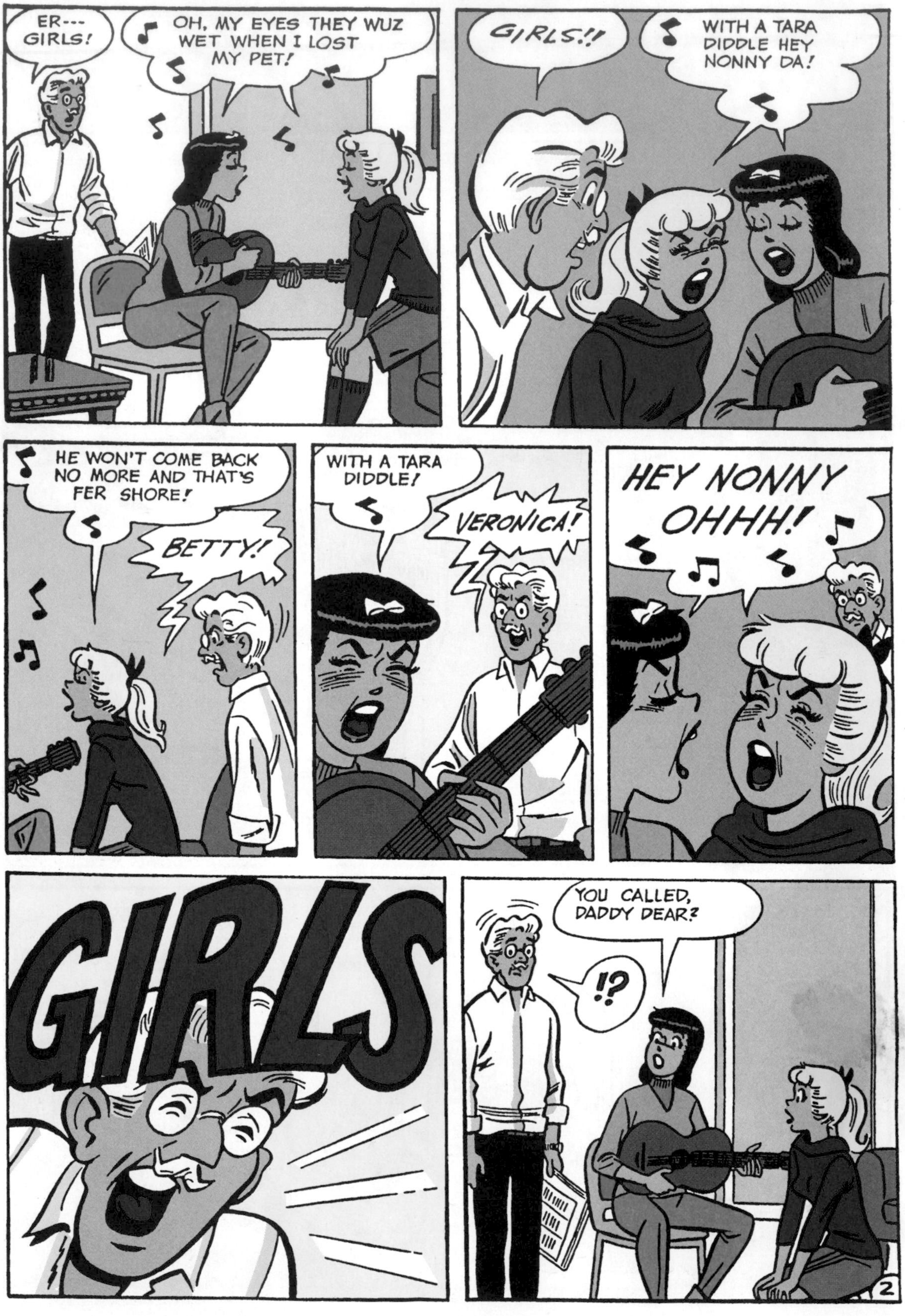
ER--- GIRLS!
OH, MY EYES THEY WUZ WET WHEN I LOST MY PET!
GIRLS!!
WITH A TARA DIDDLE HEY NONNY DA!
HE WON'T COME BACK NO MORE AND THAT'S FER SHORE!
BETTY!
WITH A TARA DIDDLE!
VERONICA!
HEY NONNY OHHH!
GIRLS
YOU CALLED, DADDY DEAR?
!?
2

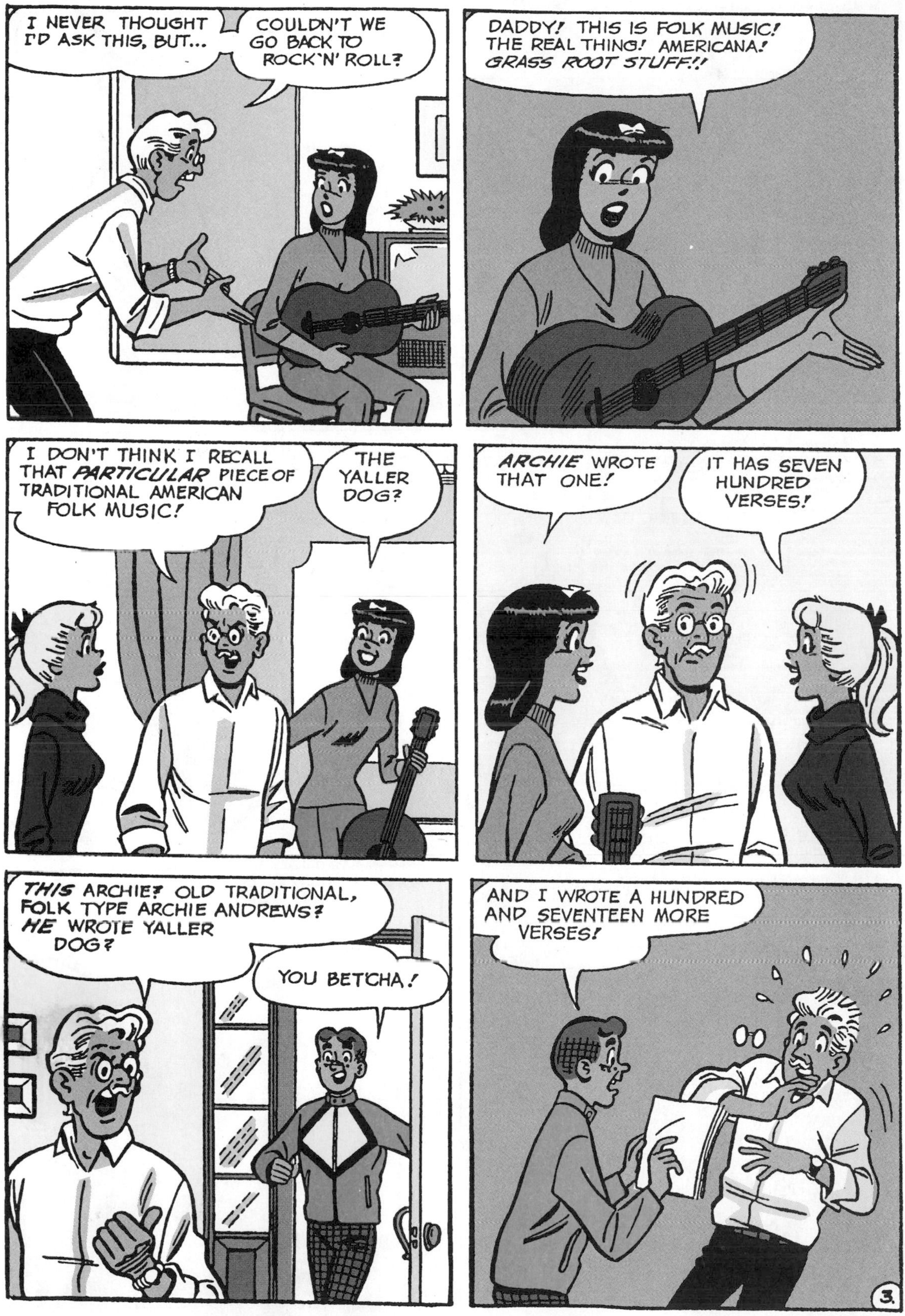
I NEVER THOUGHT I'D ASK THIS, BUT...
COULDN'T WE GO BACK TO ROCK'N' ROLL?
DADDY! THIS IS FOLK MUSIC! THE REAL THING! AMERICANA! GRASS ROOT STUFF!!
I DON'T THINK I RECALL THAT PARTICULAR PIECE OF TRADITIONAL AMERICAN FOLK MUSIC!
THE YALLER DOG?
ARCHIE WROTE THAT ONE!
IT HAS SEVEN HUNDRED VERSES!
THIS ARCHIE? OLD TRADITIONAL, FOLK TYPE ARCHIE ANDREWS? HE WROTE YALLER DOG?
YOU BET'CHA!
AND I WROTE A HUNDRED AND SEVENTEEN MORE VERSES!
3.

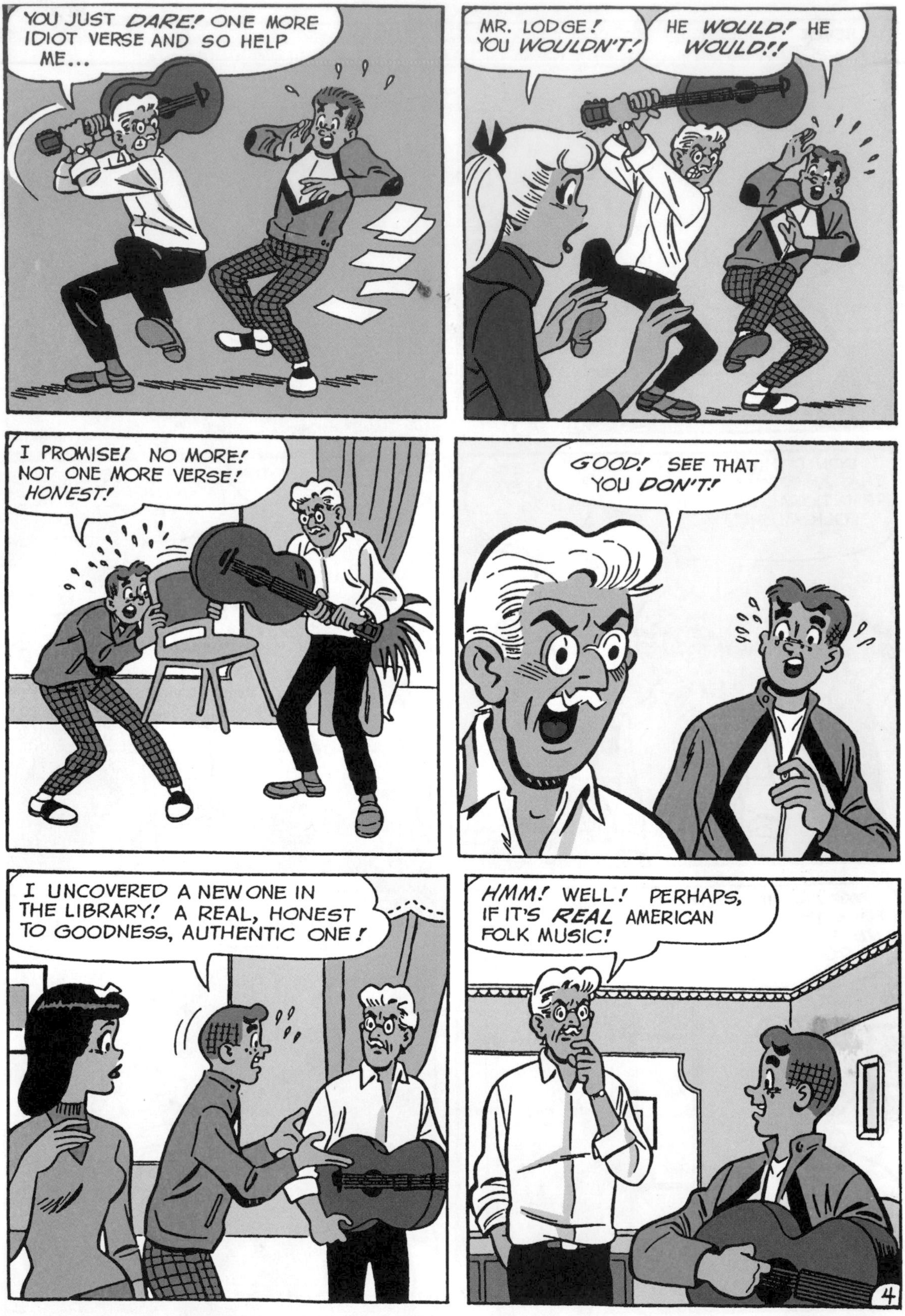
YOU JUST DARE! ONE MORE IDIOT VERSE AND SO HELP ME...
MR. LODGE! YOU WOULDN'T!
HE WOULD! HE WOULD!!
I PROMISE! NO MORE! NOT ONE MORE VERSE! HONEST!
GOOD! SEE THAT YOU DON'T!
I UNCOVERED A NEW ONE IN THE LIBRARY! A REAL, HONEST TO GOODNESS, AUTHENTIC ONE!
HMM! WELL! PERHAPS, IF IT'S REAL AMERICAN FOLK MUSIC!
4

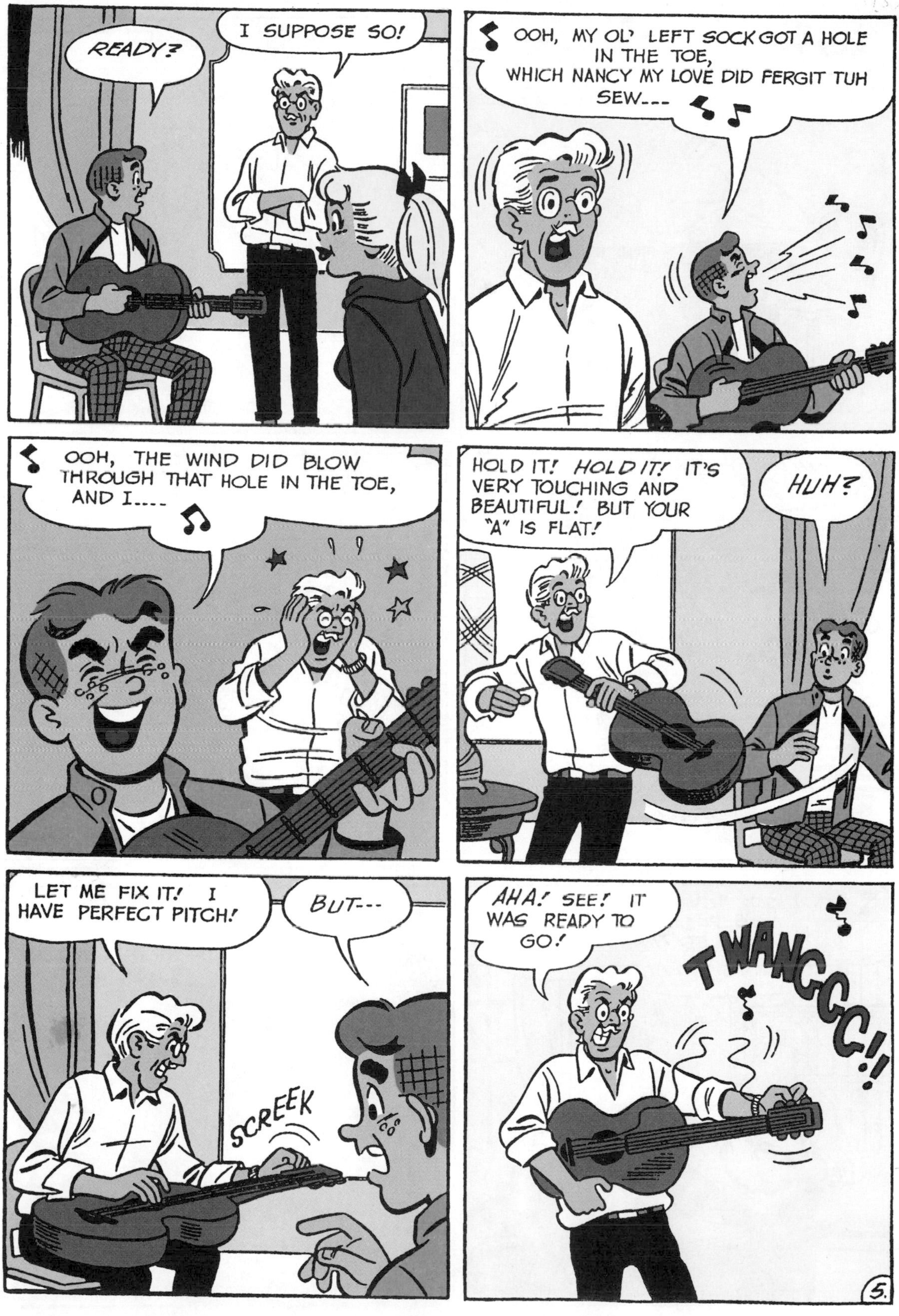
READY?
I SUPPOSE SO!
OOH, MY OL' LEFT SOCK GOT A HOLE IN THE TOE, WHICH NANCY MY LOVE DID FERGIT TUH SEW...
OOH, THE WIND DID BLOW THROUGH THAT HOLE IN THE TOE, AND I....
HOLD IT! HOLD IT! IT'S VERY TOUCHING AND BEAUTIFUL! BUT YOUR "A" IS FLAT!
HUH?
LET ME FIX IT! I HAVE PERFECT PITCH!
BUT---
SCREEK
AHA! SEE! IT WAS READY TO GO!
TWANGCC!!
5.

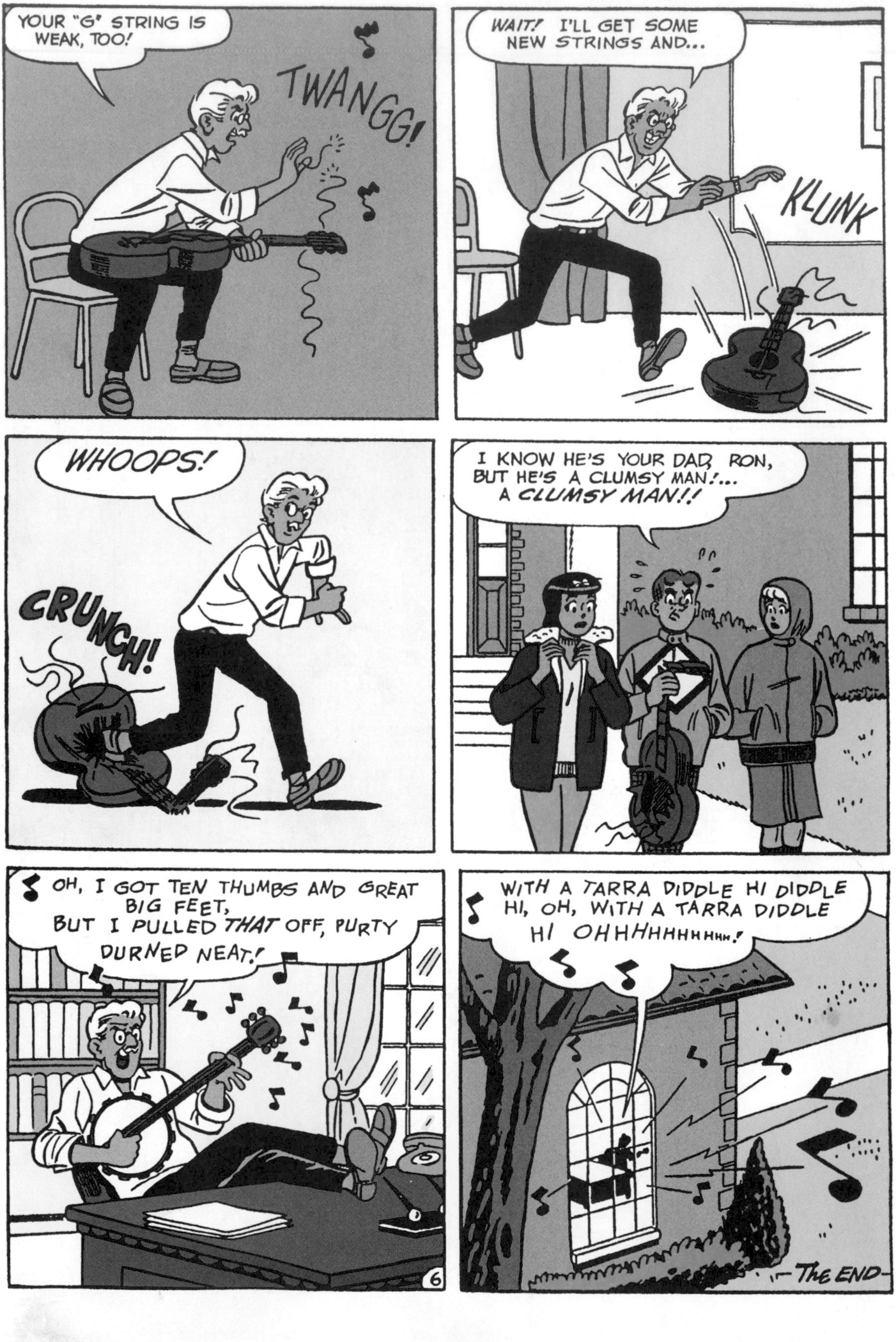
YOUR "G" STRING IS WEAK, TOO!
TWANGG!
WAIT! I'LL GET SOME NEW STRINGS AND...
KLUNK
WHOOPS!
CRUNCH!
I KNOW HE'S YOUR DAD, RON, BUT HE'S A CLUMSY MAN!... A CLUMSY MAN!!
OH, I GOT TEN THUMBS AND GREAT BIG FEET, BUT I PULLED THAT OFF, PURTY DURNED NEAT!
6
WITH A TARRA DIDDLE HI DIDDLE HI, OH, WITH A TARRA DIDDLE HI OHHHHHHHHHH!
THE END

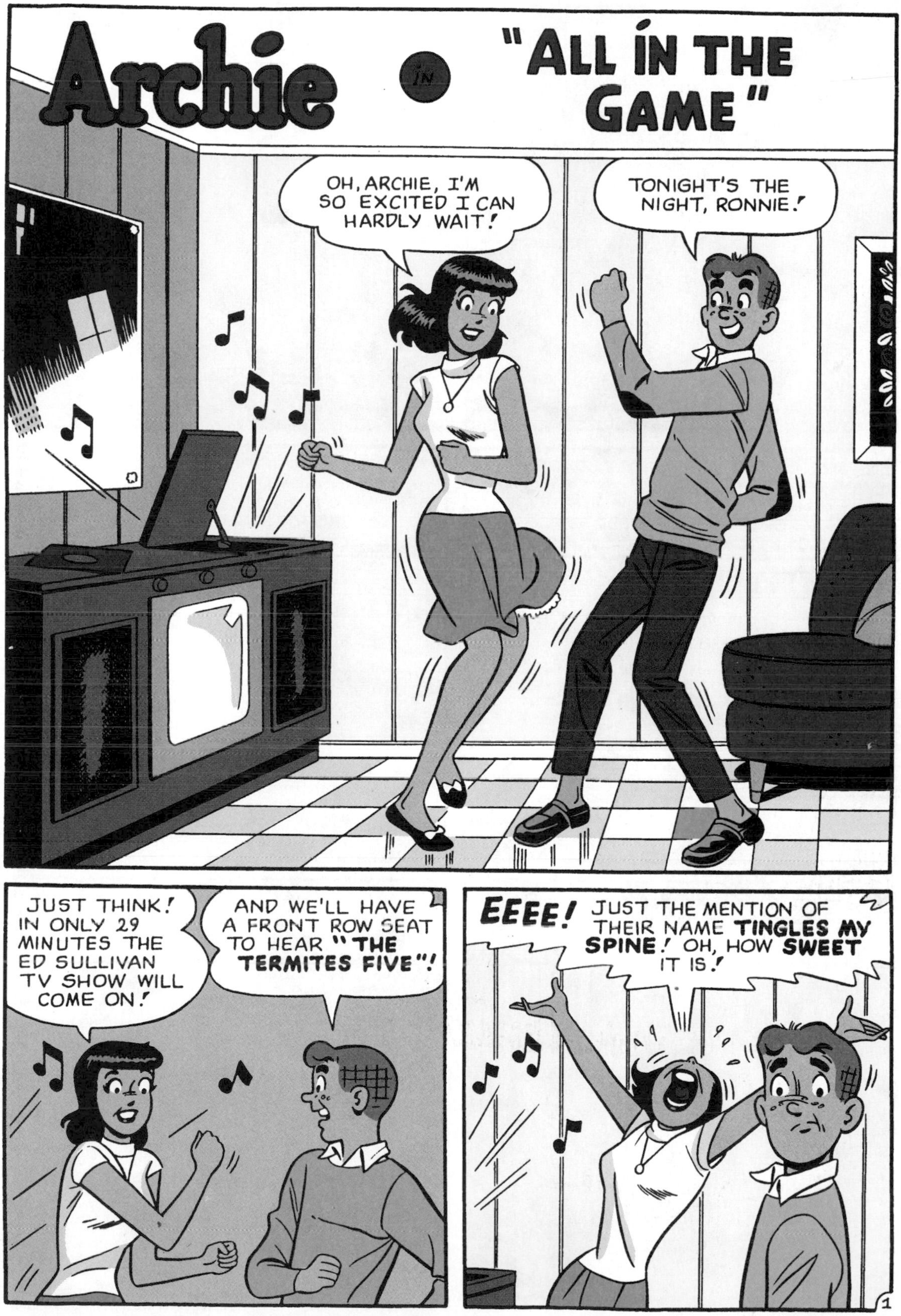
Archie IN "ALL IN THE GAME"
OH, ARCHIE, I'M SO EXCITED I CAN HARDLY WAIT!
TONIGHT'S THE NIGHT, RONNIE!
JUST THINK! IN ONLY 29 MINUTES THE ED SULLIVAN TV SHOW WILL COME ON!
AND WE'LL HAVE A FRONT ROW SEAT TO HEAR "THE TERMITES FIVE"!
EEEE! JUST THE MENTION OF THEIR NAME TINGLES MY SPINE! OH, HOW SWEET IT IS!
1

ORIGINALLY PRESENTED IN **LAUGH #162**, SEPTEMBER, 1964

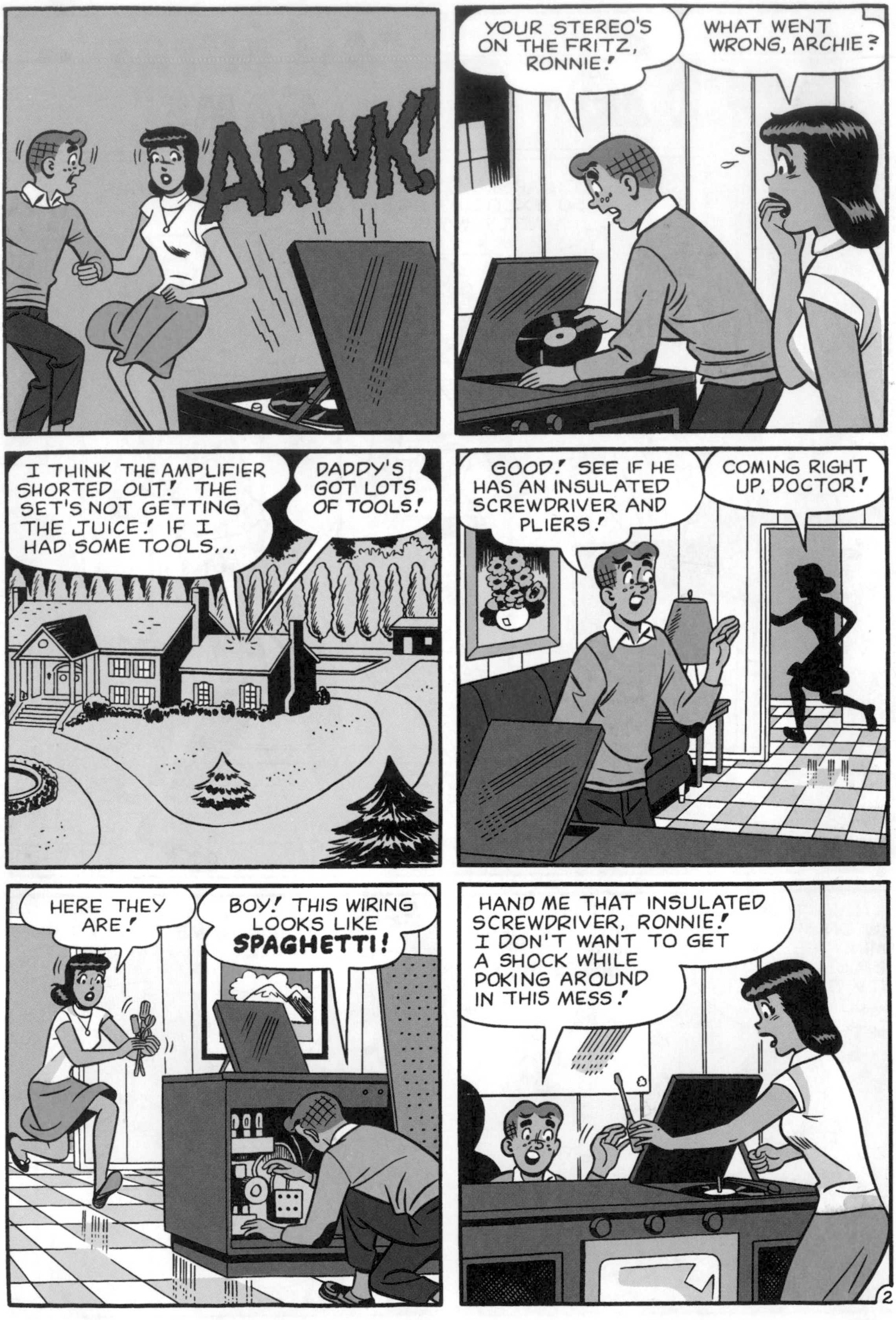
ARWK!
YOUR STEREO'S ON THE FRITZ, RONNIE!
WHAT WENT WRONG, ARCHIE?
I THINK THE AMPLIFIER SHORTED OUT! THE SET'S NOT GETTING THE JUICE! IF I HAD SOME TOOLS...
DADDY'S GOT LOTS OF TOOLS!
GOOD! SEE IF HE HAS AN INSULATED SCREWDRIVER AND PLIERS!
COMING RIGHT UP, DOCTOR!
HERE THEY ARE!
BOY! THIS WIRING LOOKS LIKE **SPAGHETTI!**
HAND ME THAT INSULATED SCREWDRIVER, RONNIE! I DON'T WANT TO GET A SHOCK WHILE POKING AROUND IN THIS MESS!
2

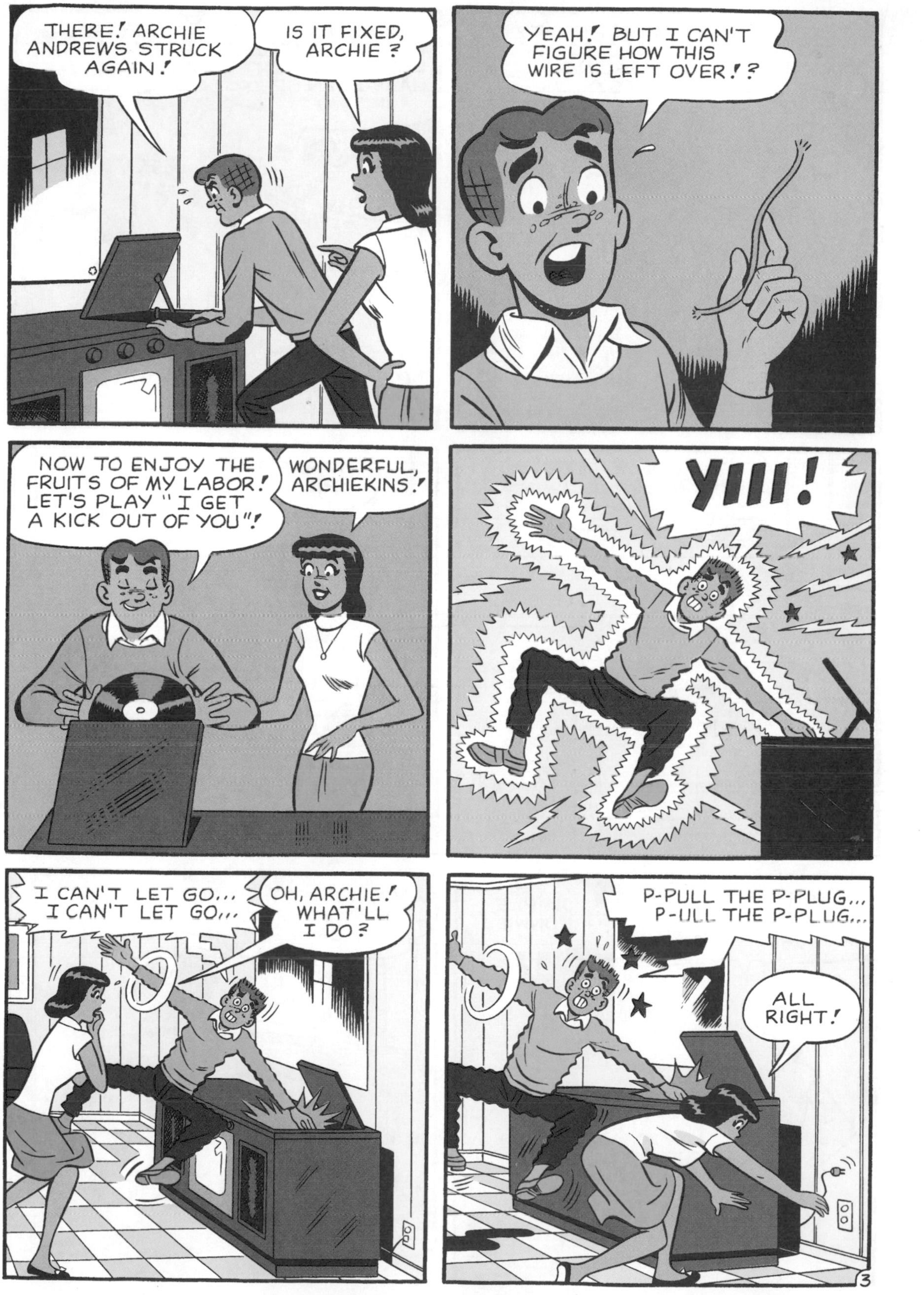
THERE! ARCHIE ANDREWS STRUCK AGAIN!
IS IT FIXED, ARCHIE?
YEAH! BUT I CAN'T FIGURE HOW THIS WIRE IS LEFT OVER!?
NOW TO ENJOY THE FRUITS OF MY LABOR! LET'S PLAY "I GET A KICK OUT OF YOU"!
WONDERFUL, ARCHIEKINS!
YIII!
I CAN'T LET GO... I CAN'T LET GO...
OH, ARCHIE! WHAT'LL I DO?
P-PULL THE P-PLUG... P-ULL THE P-PLUG...
ALL RIGHT!
3

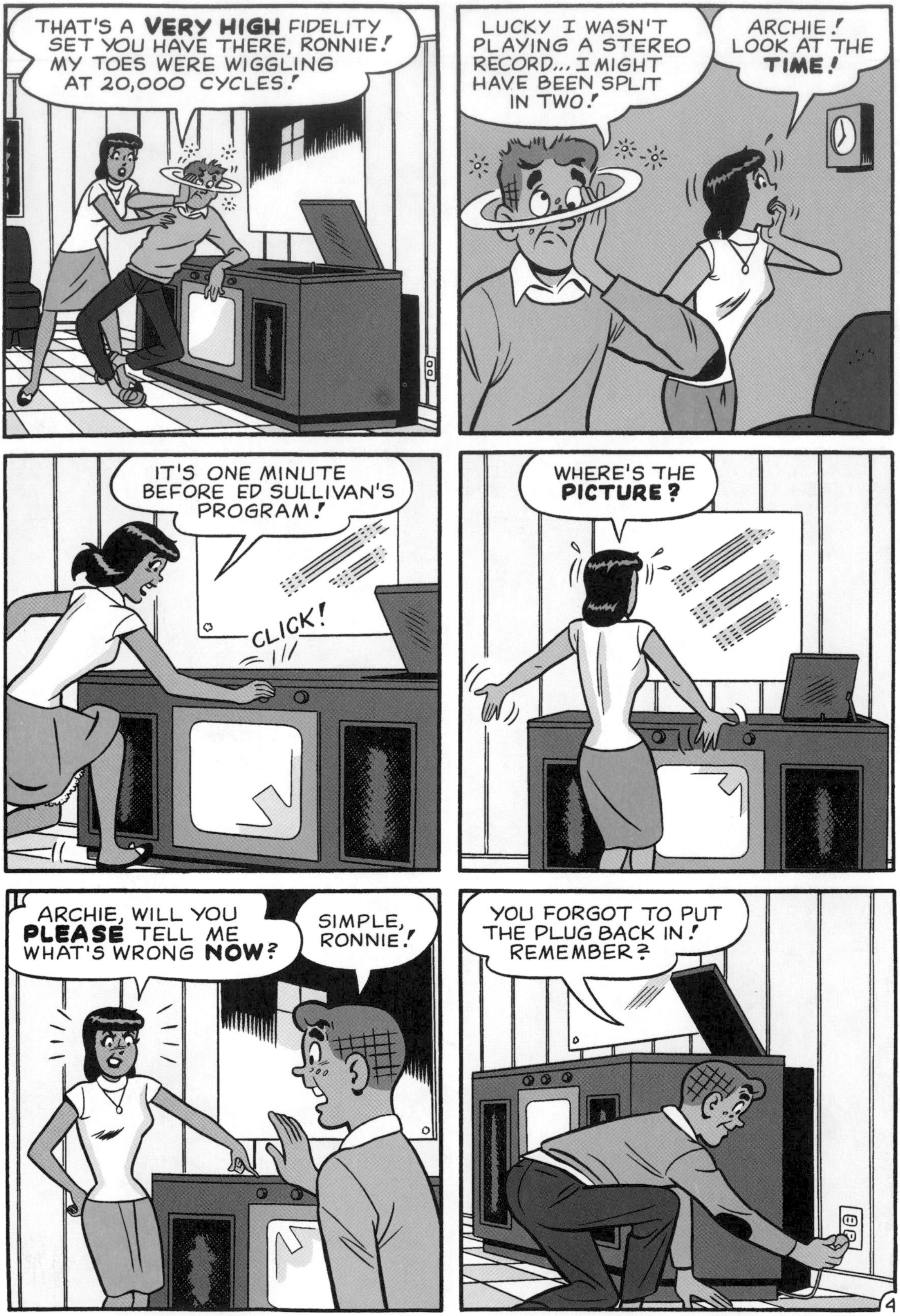
THAT'S A **VERY HIGH** FIDELITY SET YOU HAVE THERE, RONNIE! MY TOES WERE WIGGLING AT 20,000 CYCLES!
LUCKY I WASN'T PLAYING A STEREO RECORD... I MIGHT HAVE BEEN SPLIT IN TWO!
ARCHIE! LOOK AT THE **TIME**!
IT'S ONE MINUTE BEFORE ED SULLIVAN'S PROGRAM!
CLICK!
WHERE'S THE **PICTURE**?
ARCHIE, WILL YOU **PLEASE** TELL ME WHAT'S WRONG **NOW**?
SIMPLE, RONNIE!
YOU FORGOT TO PUT THE PLUG BACK IN! REMEMBER?
4

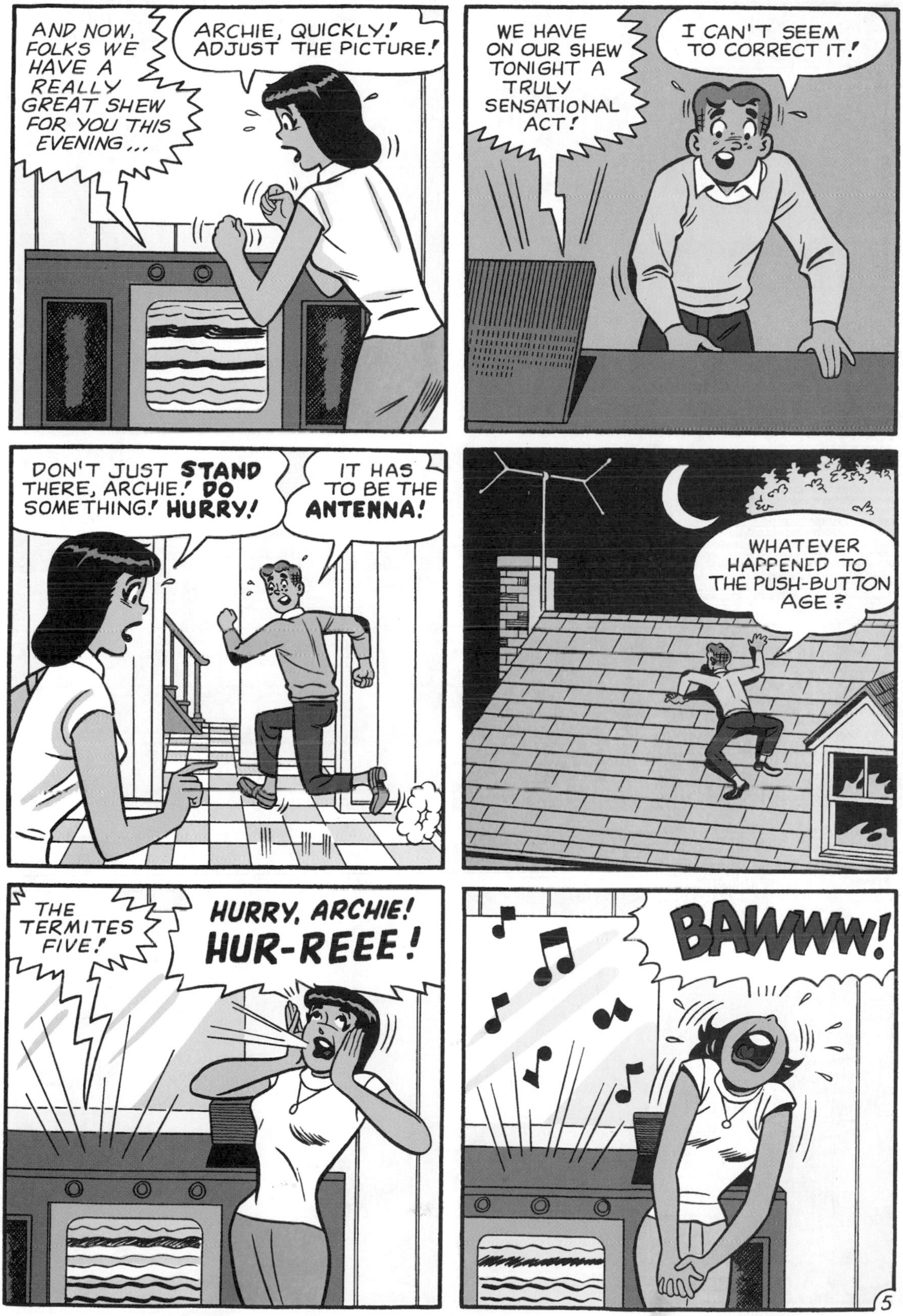
AND NOW, FOLKS WE HAVE A REALLY GREAT SHEW FOR YOU THIS EVENING...
ARCHIE, QUICKLY! ADJUST THE PICTURE!
WE HAVE ON OUR SHEW TONIGHT A TRULY SENSATIONAL ACT!
I CAN'T SEEM TO CORRECT IT!
DON'T JUST STAND THERE, ARCHIE! DO SOMETHING! HURRY!
IT HAS TO BE THE ANTENNA!
WHATEVER HAPPENED TO THE PUSH-BUTTON AGE?
THE TERMITES FIVE!
HURRY, ARCHIE! HUR-REEE!
BAWWW!
5

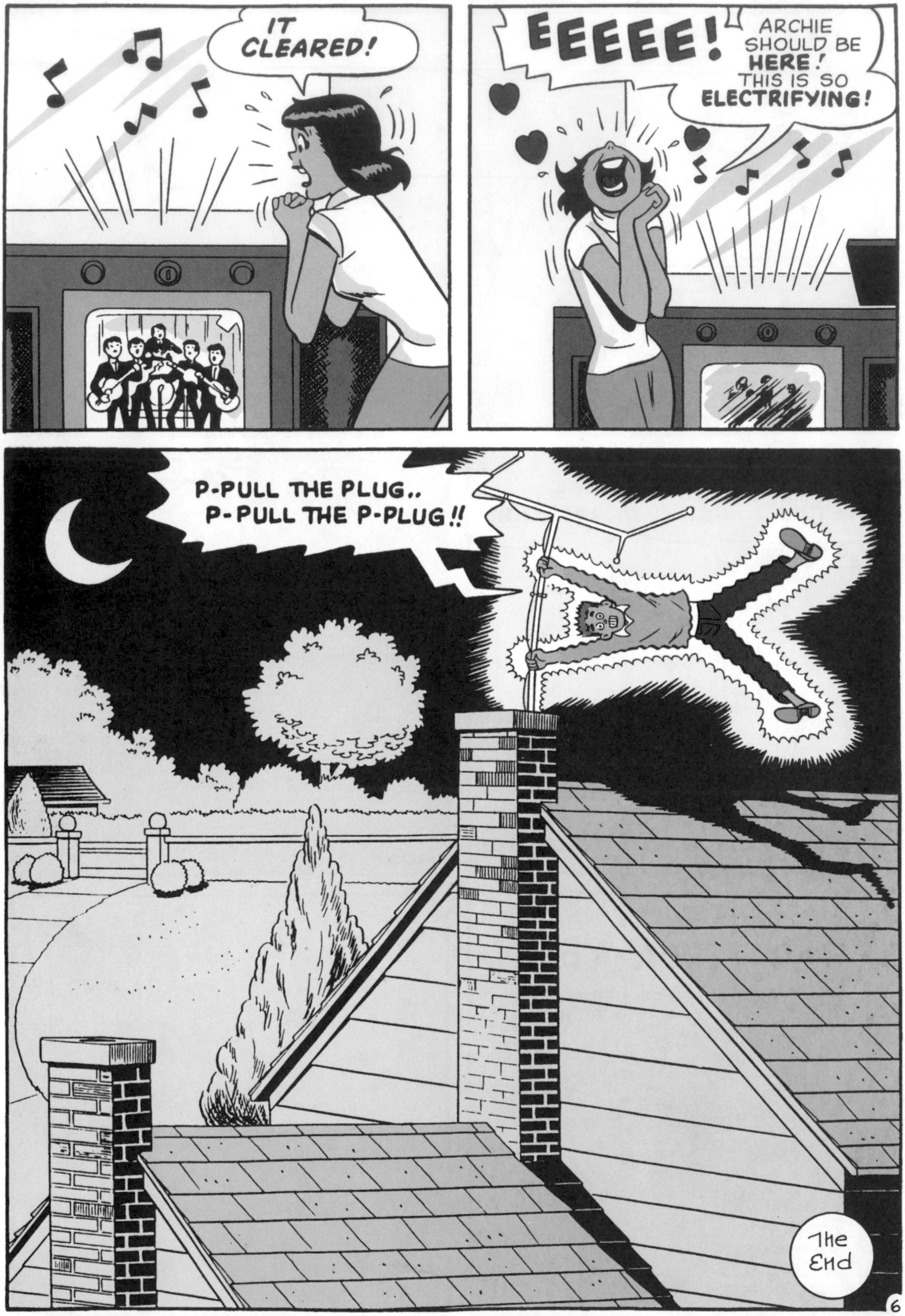
IT CLEARED!
EEEEE!
ARCHIE SHOULD BE HERE! THIS IS SO ELECTRIFYING!
P-PULL THE PLUG.. P-PULL THE P-PLUG!!
The End
6

Betty and Veronica in "BOP THAT BEETLE"

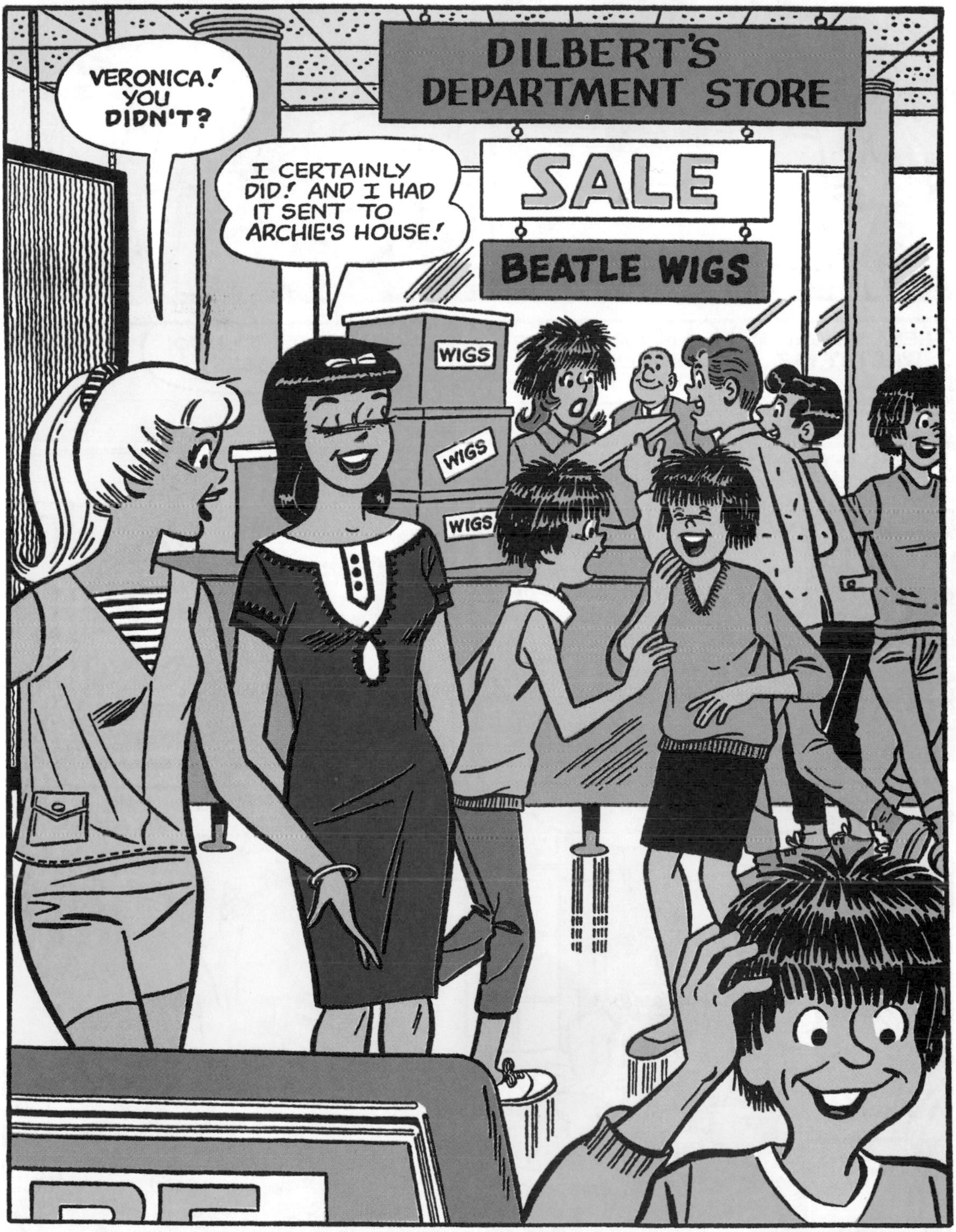
DILBERT'S DEPARTMENT STORE
SALE
BEATLE WIGS
VERONICA! YOU DIDN'T?
I CERTAINLY DID! AND I HAD IT SENT TO ARCHIE'S HOUSE!
WIGS
WIGS
WIGS

ORIGINALLY PRESENTED IN **BETTY & VERONICA #105**, SEPTEMBER, 1964

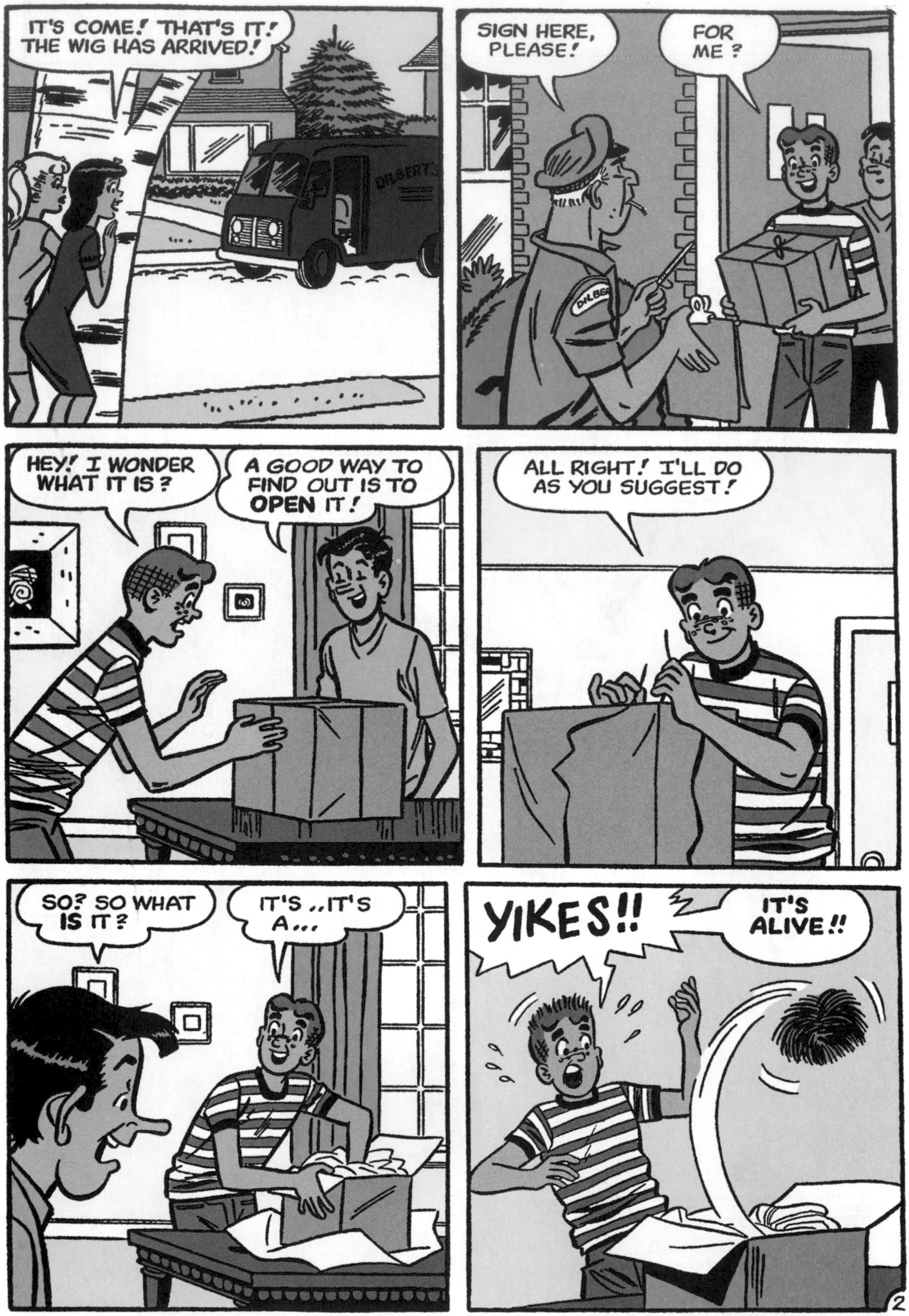
IT'S COME! THAT'S IT! THE WIG HAS ARRIVED!
DILBERT'S
SIGN HERE, PLEASE!
FOR ME ?
HEY! I WONDER WHAT IT IS ?
A GOOD WAY TO FIND OUT IS TO OPEN IT!
ALL RIGHT! I'LL DO AS YOU SUGGEST!
SO? SO WHAT IS IT?
IT'S ..IT'S A...
YIKES!!
IT'S ALIVE!!
2

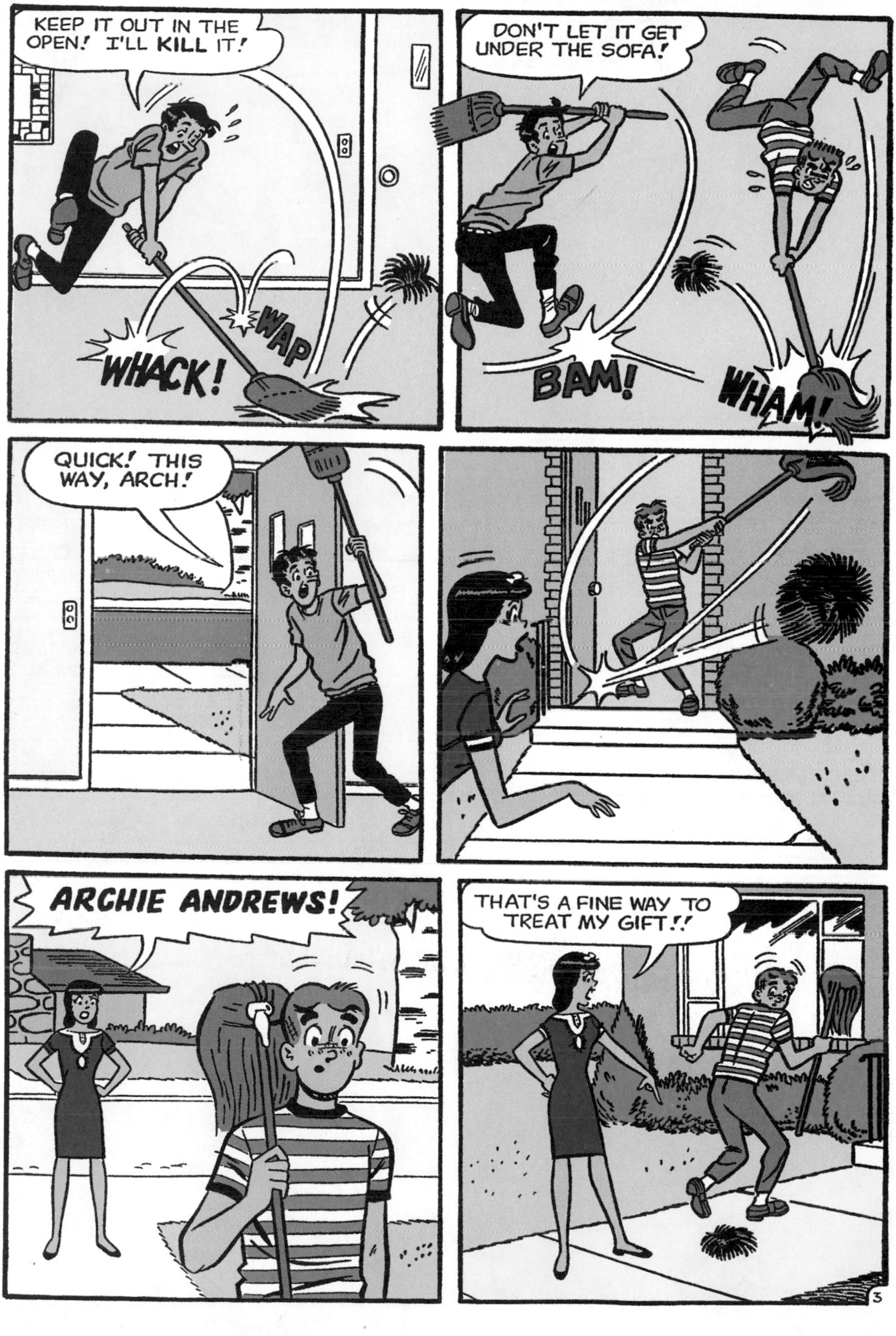
KEEP IT OUT IN THE OPEN! I'LL KILL IT!
WHACK!
WAP
DON'T LET IT GET UNDER THE SOFA!
BAM!
WHAM!
QUICK! THIS WAY, ARCH!
ARCHIE ANDREWS!
THAT'S A FINE WAY TO TREAT MY GIFT!!
3

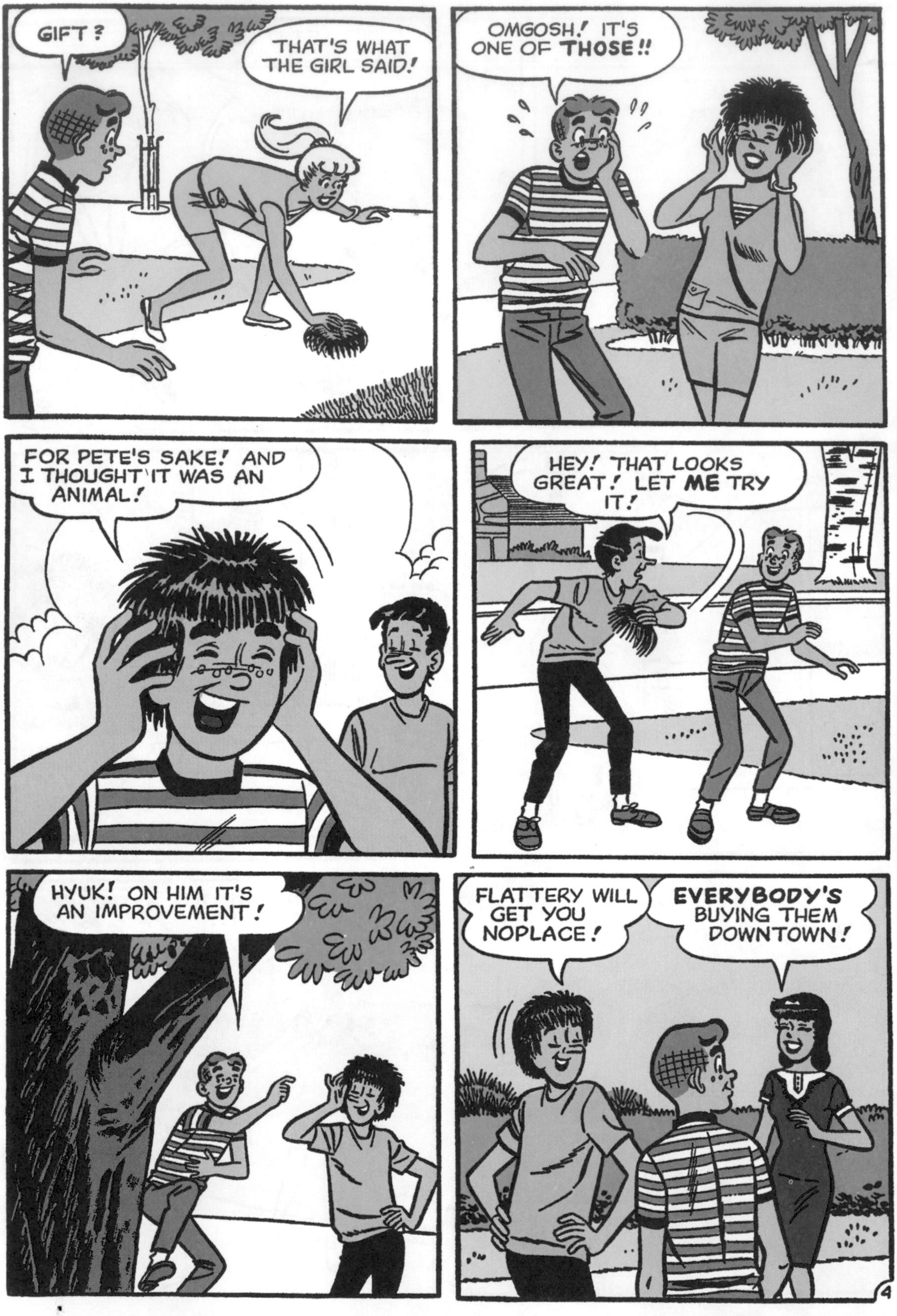
GIFT ?
THAT'S WHAT THE GIRL SAID!
OMGOSH! IT'S ONE OF THOSE!!
FOR PETE'S SAKE! AND I THOUGHT IT WAS AN ANIMAL!
HEY! THAT LOOKS GREAT! LET ME TRY IT!
HYUK! ON HIM IT'S AN IMPROVEMENT!
FLATTERY WILL GET YOU NOPLACE!
EVERYBODY'S BUYING THEM DOWNTOWN!
4

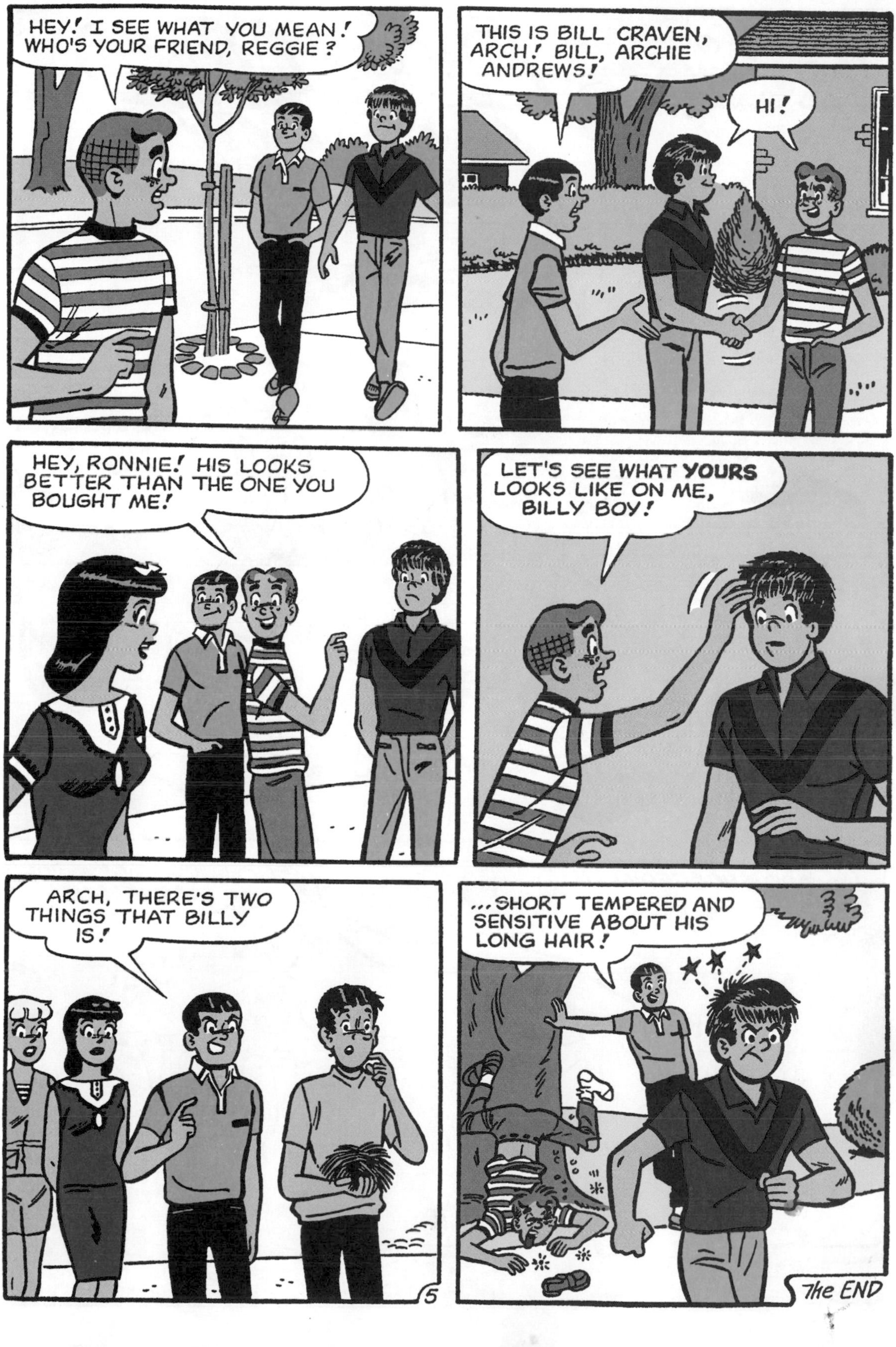
HEY! I SEE WHAT YOU MEAN! WHO'S YOUR FRIEND, REGGIE?
THIS IS BILL CRAVEN, ARCH! BILL, ARCHIE ANDREWS!
HI!
HEY, RONNIE! HIS LOOKS BETTER THAN THE ONE YOU BOUGHT ME!
LET'S SEE WHAT **YOURS** LOOKS LIKE ON ME, BILLY BOY!
ARCH, THERE'S TWO THINGS THAT BILLY IS!
5
...SHORT TEMPERED AND SENSITIVE ABOUT HIS LONG HAIR!
The END

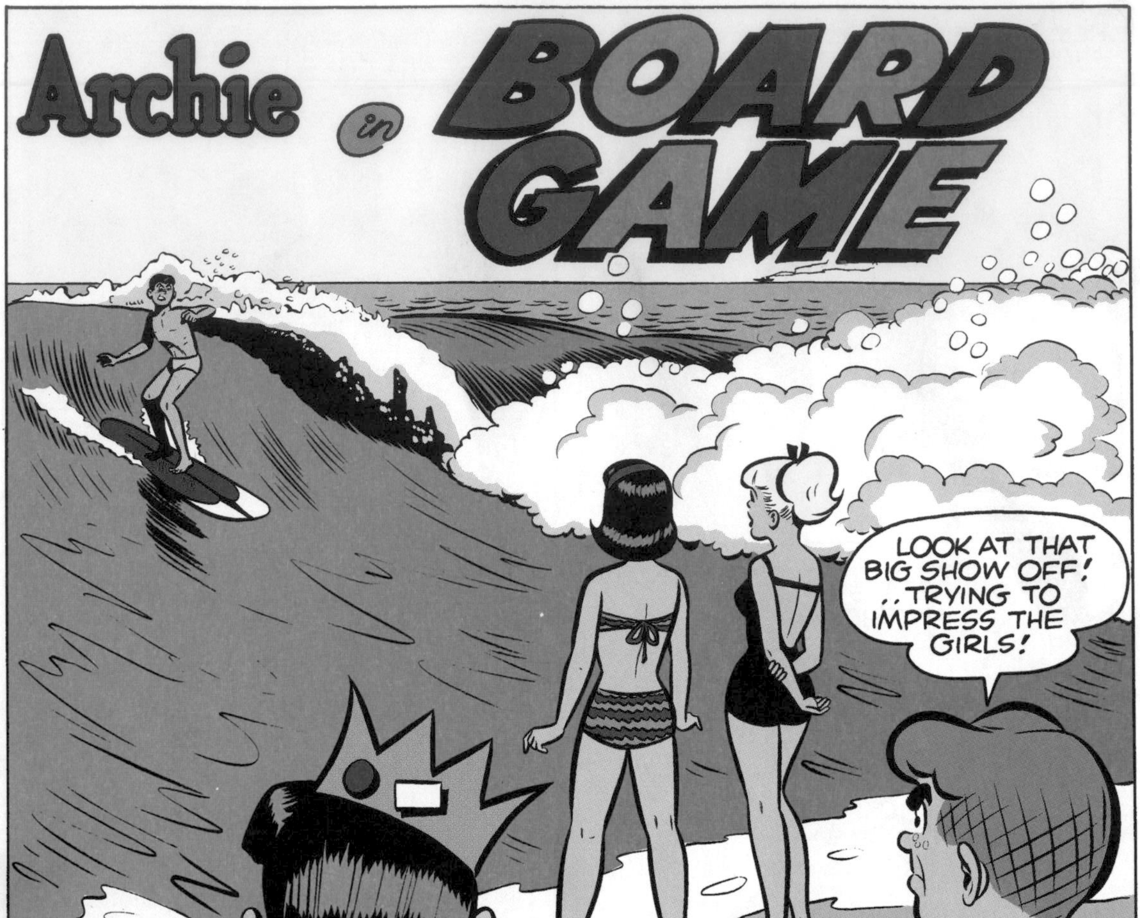
Archie in BOARD GAME
LOOK AT THAT BIG SHOW OFF! ..TRYING TO IMPRESS THE GIRLS!

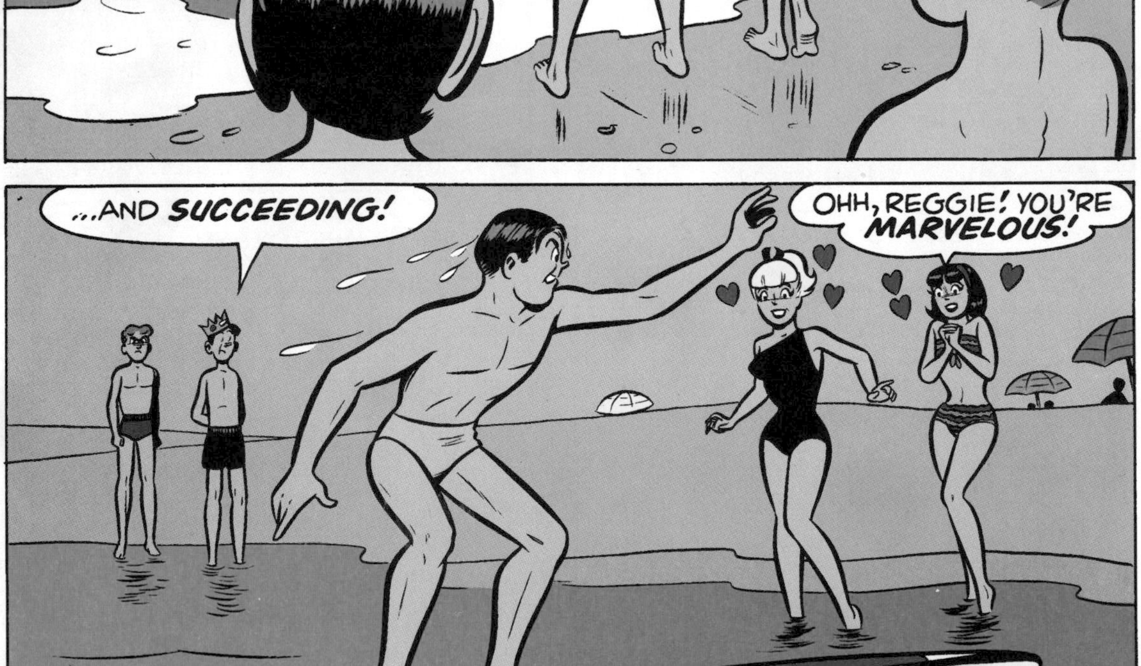
...AND SUCCEEDING!
OHH, REGGIE! YOU'RE MARVELOUS!

ORIGINALLY PRESENTED IN **ARCHIE #167**, SEPTEMBER, 1966

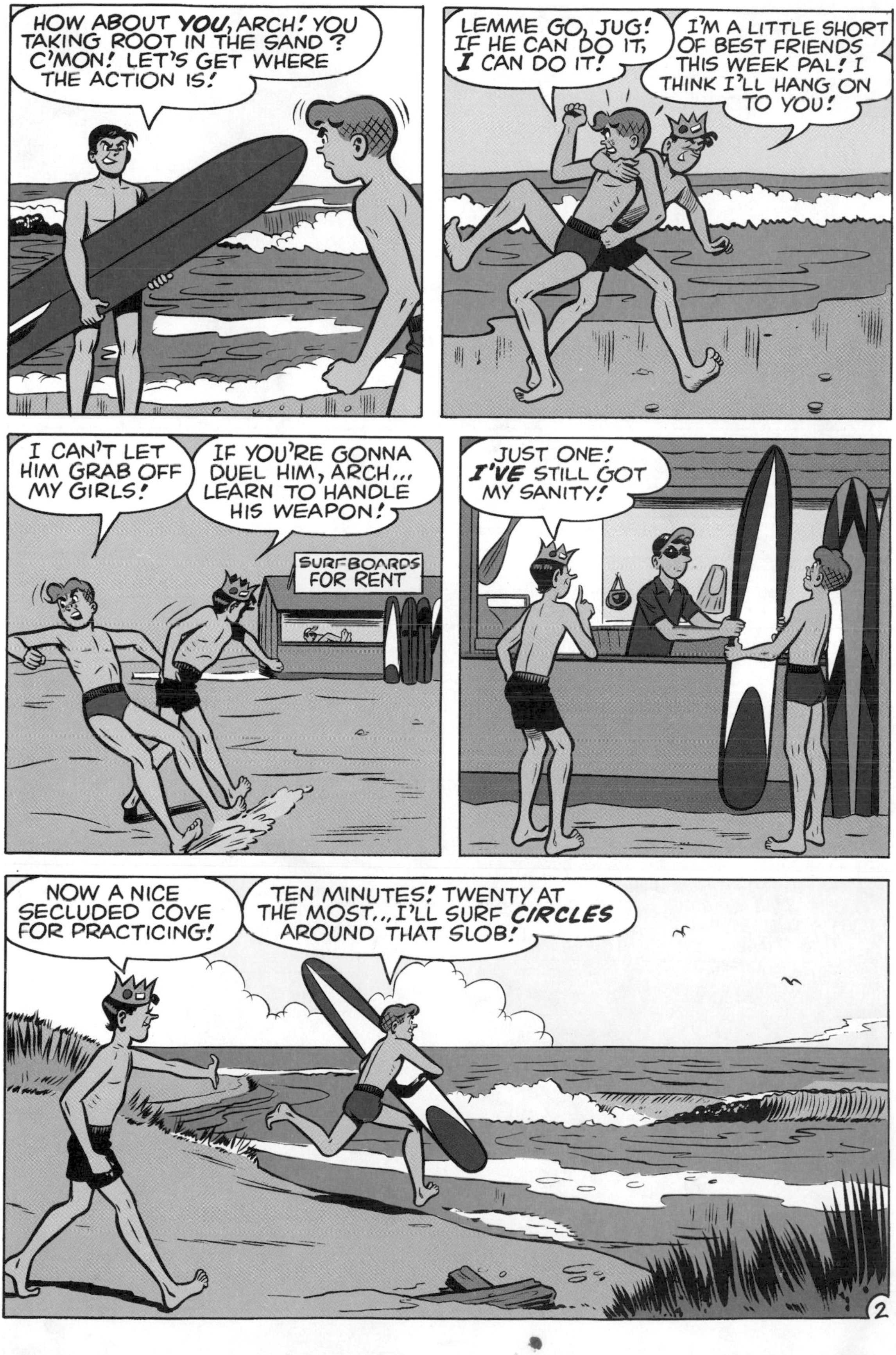
HOW ABOUT YOU, ARCH! YOU TAKING ROOT IN THE SAND? C'MON! LET'S GET WHERE THE ACTION IS!
LEMME GO, JUG! IF HE CAN DO IT, I CAN DO IT!
I'M A LITTLE SHORT OF BEST FRIENDS THIS WEEK PAL! I THINK I'LL HANG ON TO YOU!
I CAN'T LET HIM GRAB OFF MY GIRLS!
IF YOU'RE GONNA DUEL HIM, ARCH... LEARN TO HANDLE HIS WEAPON!
SURFBOARDS FOR RENT
JUST ONE! I'VE STILL GOT MY SANITY!
NOW A NICE SECLUDED COVE FOR PRACTICING!
TEN MINUTES! TWENTY AT THE MOST... I'LL SURF CIRCLES AROUND THAT SLOB!
2

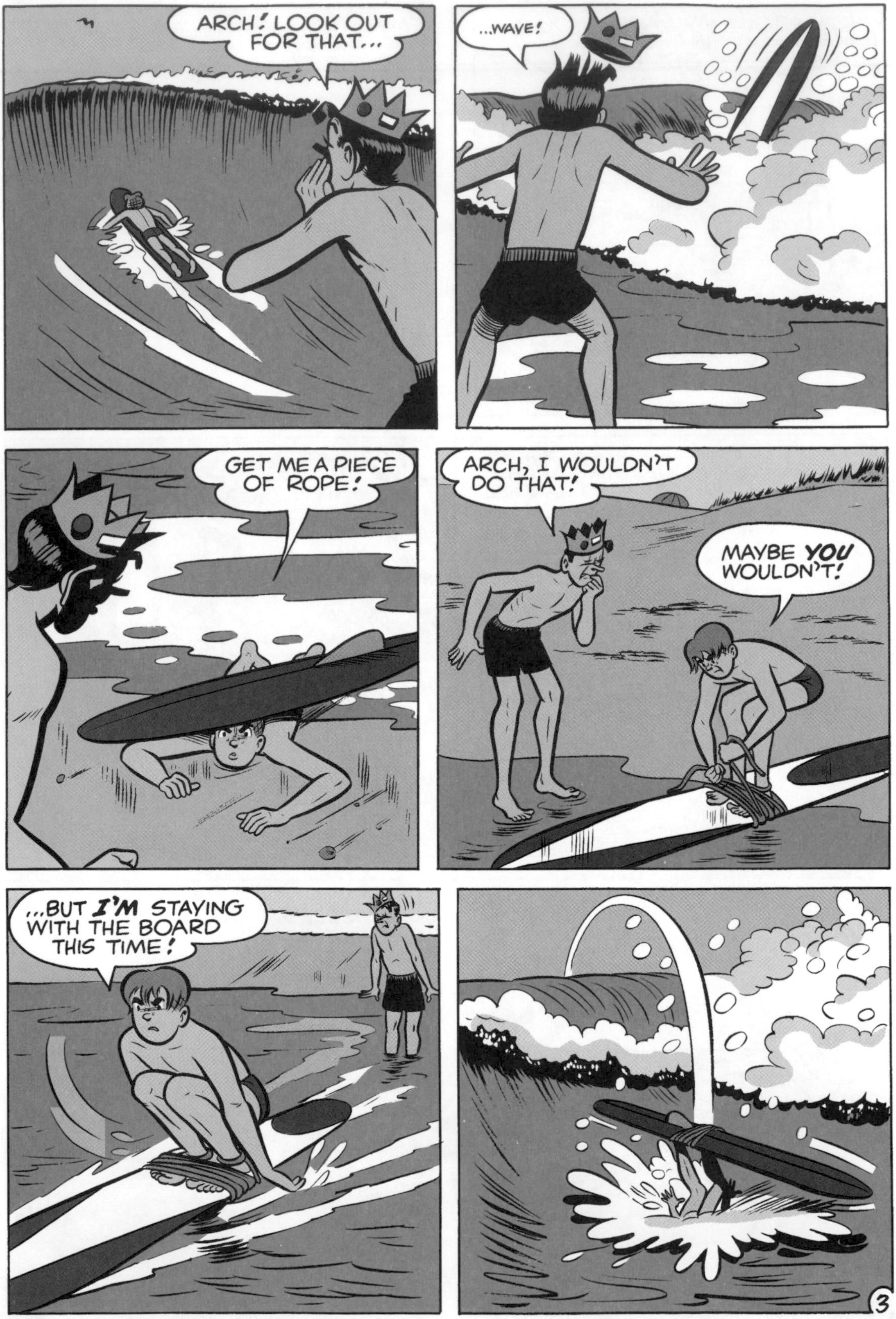
ARCH! LOOK OUT FOR THAT...
...WAVE!
GET ME A PIECE OF ROPE!
ARCH, I WOULDN'T DO THAT!
MAYBE YOU WOULDN'T!
...BUT I'M STAYING WITH THE BOARD THIS TIME!
3

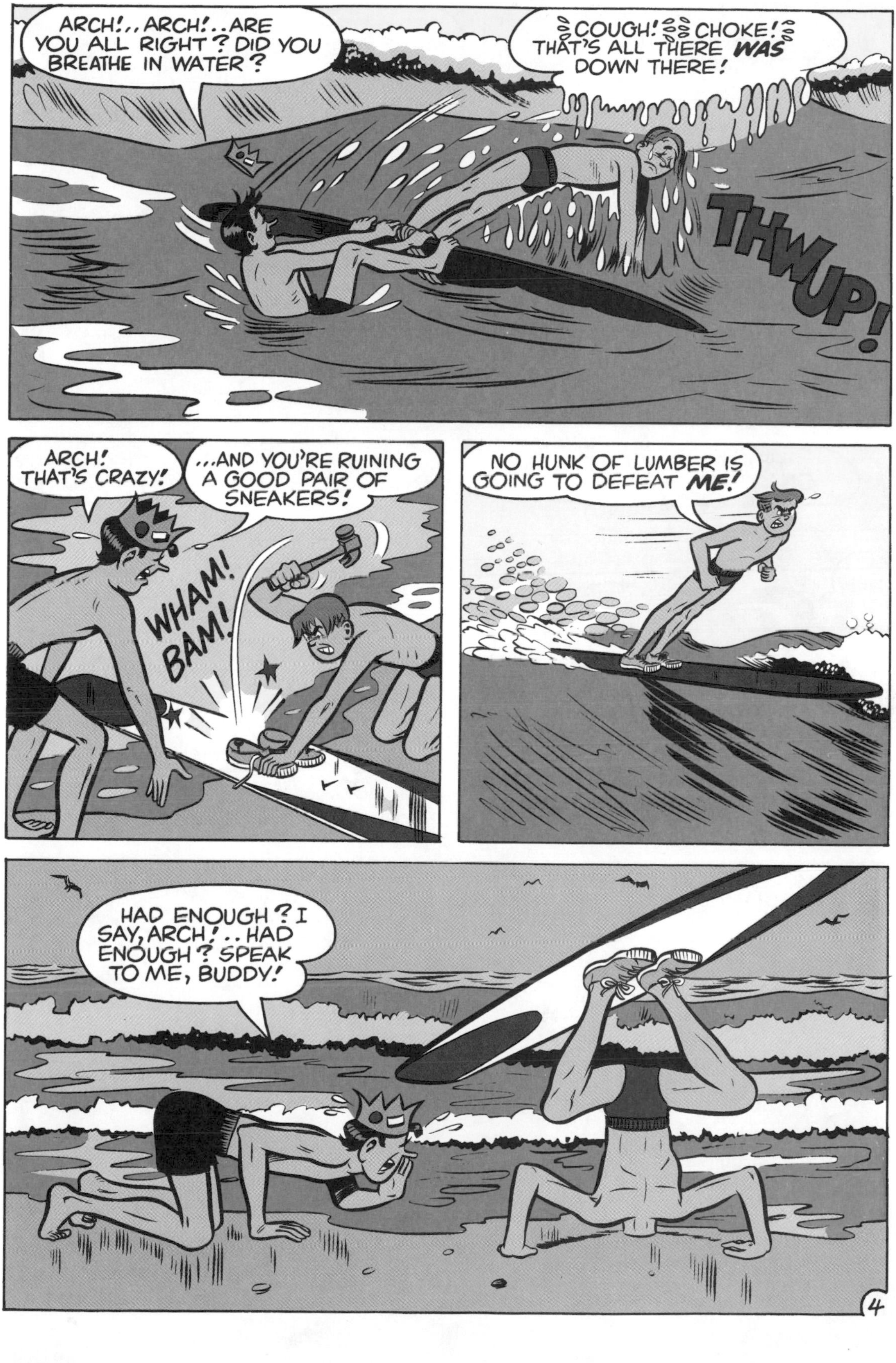
ARCH!.. ARCH!.. ARE YOU ALL RIGHT? DID YOU BREATHE IN WATER?
COUGH! CHOKE! THAT'S ALL THERE WAS DOWN THERE!
THWUP!
ARCH! THAT'S CRAZY!
...AND YOU'RE RUINING A GOOD PAIR OF SNEAKERS!
WHAM! BAM!
NO HUNK OF LUMBER IS GOING TO DEFEAT ME!
HAD ENOUGH? I SAY, ARCH!.. HAD ENOUGH? SPEAK TO ME, BUDDY!
4

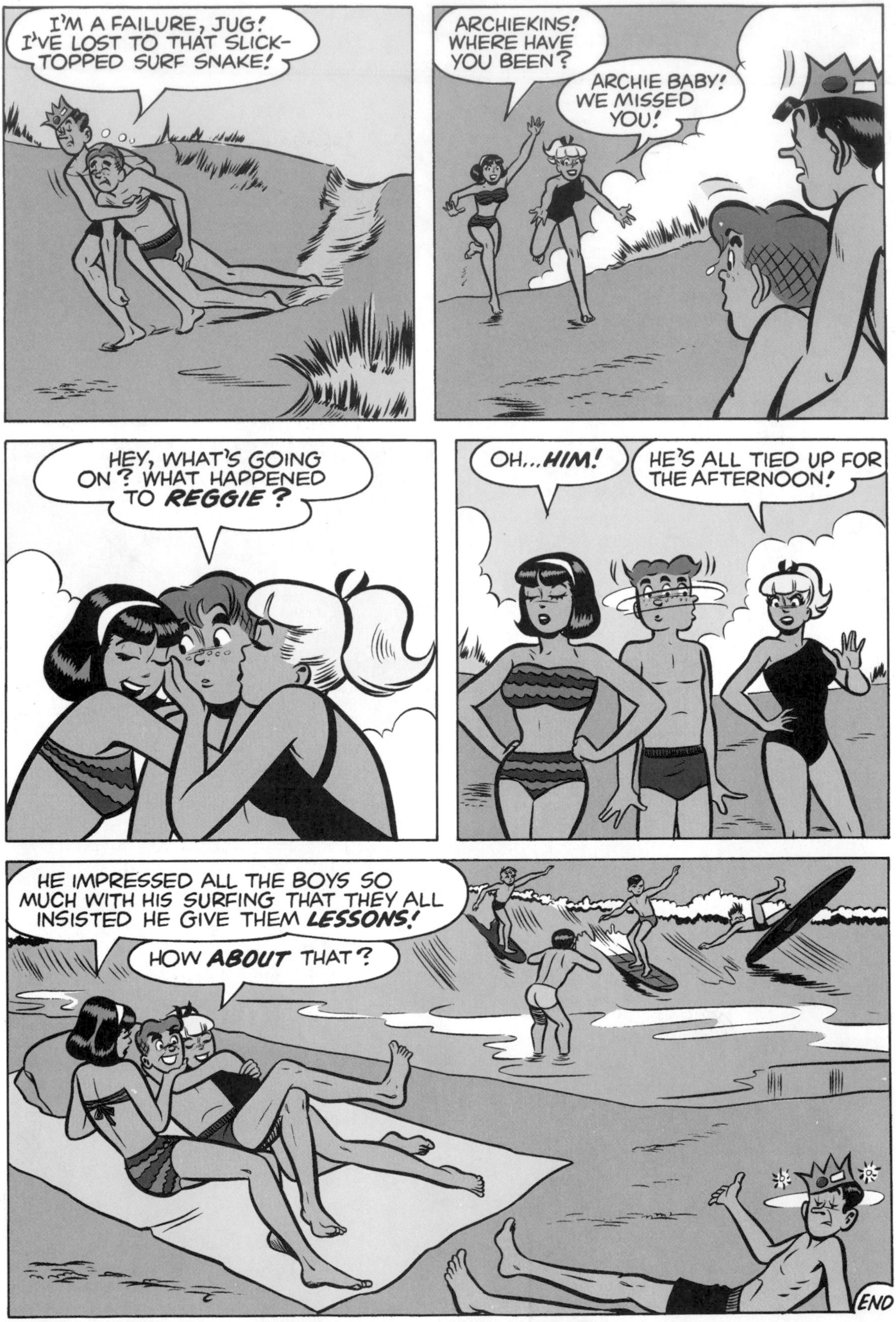
I'M A FAILURE, JUG! I'VE LOST TO THAT SLICK-TOPPED SURF SNAKE!
ARCHIEKINS! WHERE HAVE YOU BEEN?
ARCHIE BABY! WE MISSED YOU!
HEY, WHAT'S GOING ON? WHAT HAPPENED TO **REGGIE**?
OH,...**HIM**!
HE'S ALL TIED UP FOR THE AFTERNOON!
HE IMPRESSED ALL THE BOYS SO MUCH WITH HIS SURFING THAT THEY ALL INSISTED HE GIVE THEM **LESSONS**!
HOW **ABOUT** THAT?
END

A GALLERY OF CLASSIC 60'S COVER GAGS

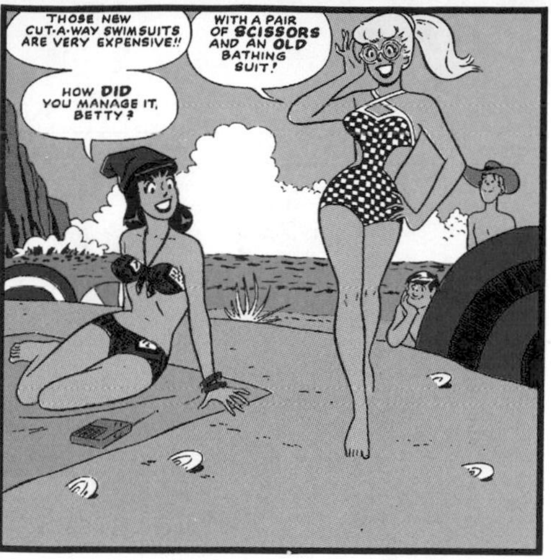
THOSE NEW CUT-A-WAY SWIMSUITS ARE VERY EXPENSIVE!!
HOW DID YOU MANAGE IT, BETTY?
WITH A PAIR OF SCISSORS AND AN OLD BATHING SUIT!

B&V SUMMER FUN #34
SEPT., 1965

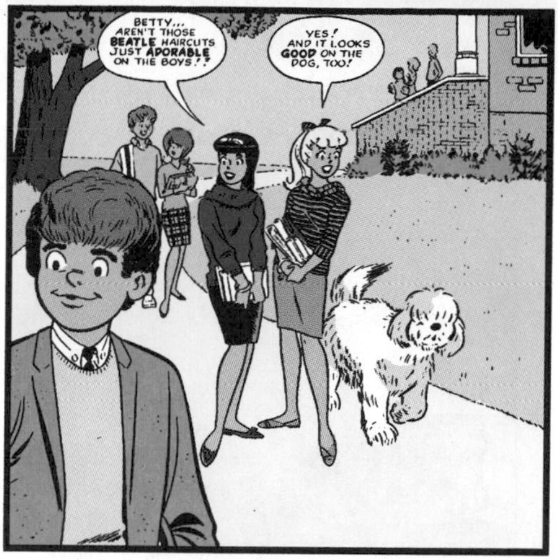
BETTY... AREN'T THOSE BEATLE HAIRCUTS JUST ADORABLE ON THE BOYS?
YES! AND IT LOOKS GOOD ON THE DOG, TOO!

LAUGH #160
JULY, 1960

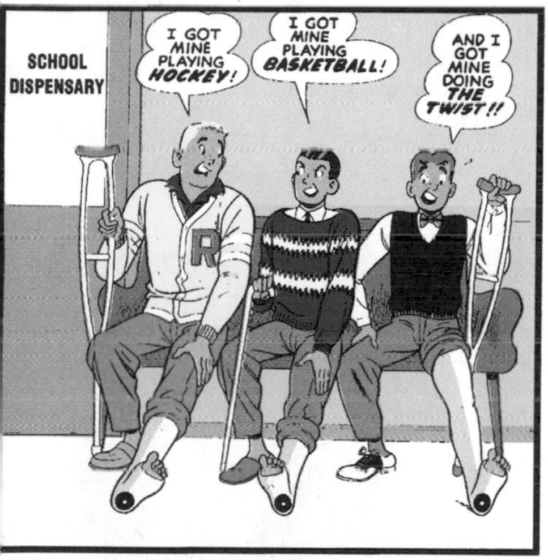
SCHOOL DISPENSARY
I GOT MINE PLAYING HOCKEY!
I GOT MINE PLAYING BASKETBALL!
AND I GOT MINE DOING THE TWIST!!

LAUGH #134
MAY 1962

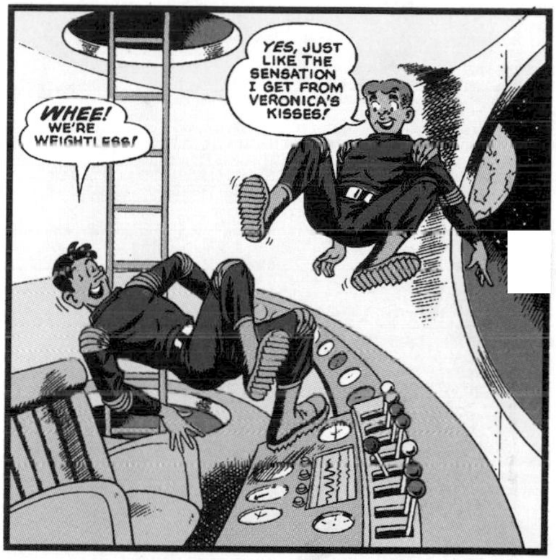
WHEE! WE'RE WEIGHTLESS!
YES, JUST LIKE THE SENSATION I GET FROM VERONICA'S KISSES!

LAUGH #139
OCT., 1962

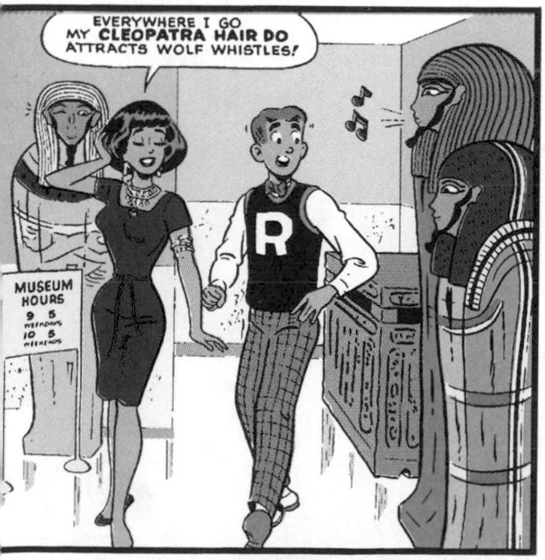
EVERYWHERE I GO MY CLEOPATRA HAIR DO ATTRACTS WOLF WHISTLES!
MUSEUM HOURS

LAUGH #148
JULY, 1963

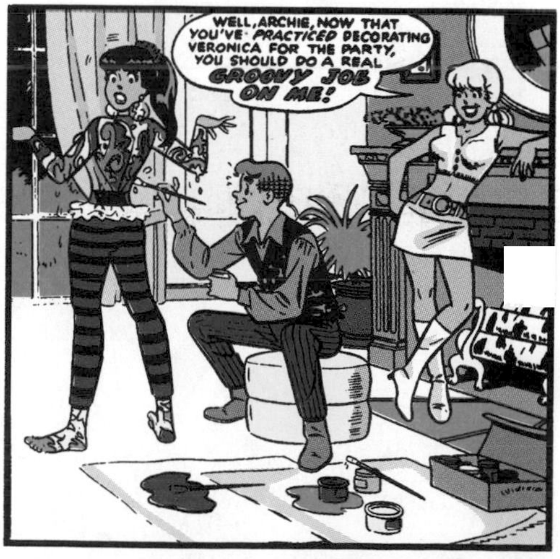
WELL, ARCHIE, NOW THAT YOU'VE PRACTICED DECORATING VERONICA FOR THE PARTY, YOU SHOULD DO A REAL GROOVY JOB ON ME!

B&V SPECTACULAR #153
JUNE, 1968

Betty and Veronica in "DRAG DRAMA"

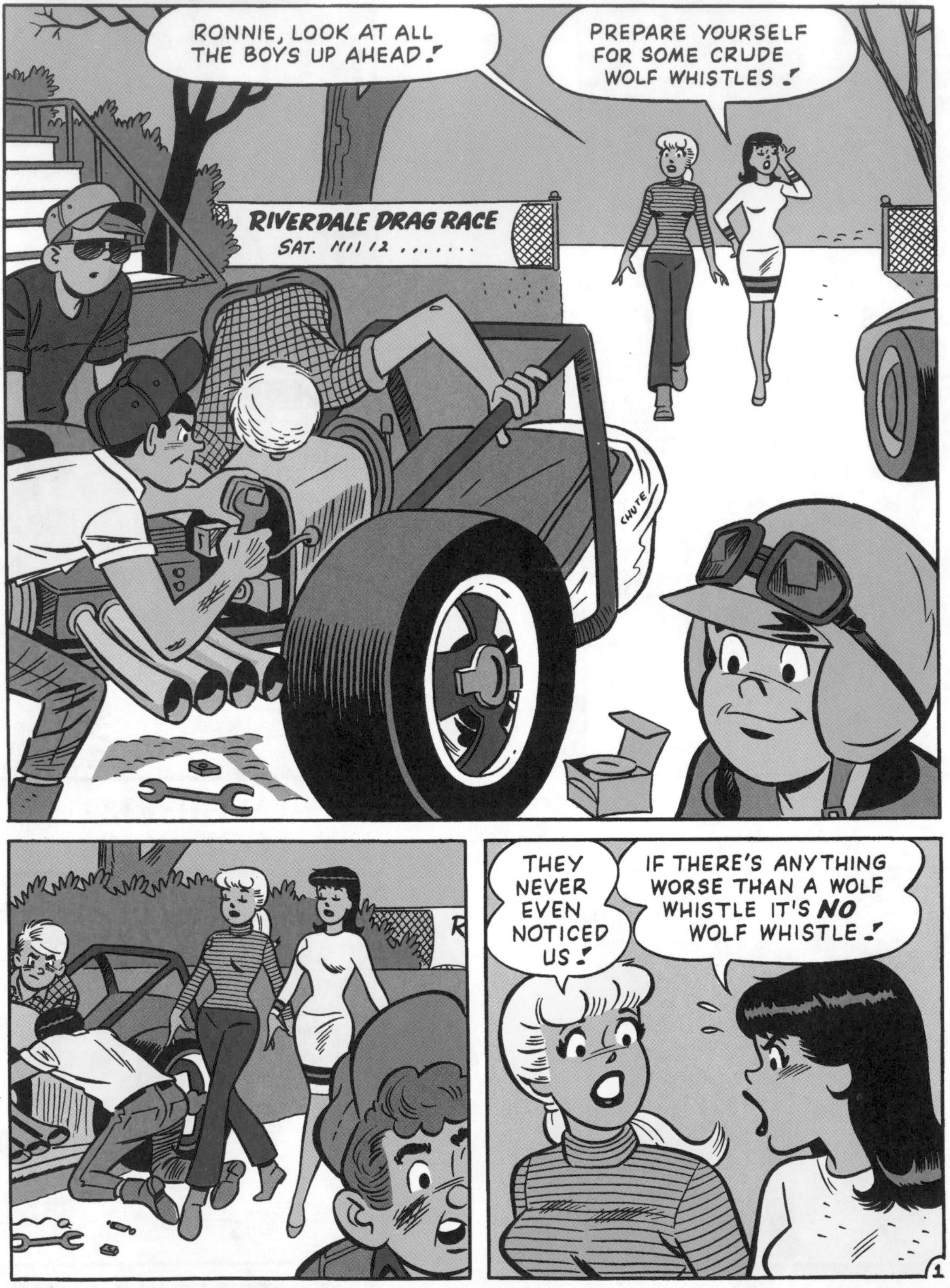
RONNIE, LOOK AT ALL THE BOYS UP AHEAD!
PREPARE YOURSELF FOR SOME CRUDE WOLF WHISTLES!
RIVERDALE DRAG RACE
SAT.
CHUTE
THEY NEVER EVEN NOTICED US!
IF THERE'S ANYTHING WORSE THAN A WOLF WHISTLE IT'S ***NO*** WOLF WHISTLE!
1

ORIGINALLY PRESENTED IN **BETTY & VERONICA #135**, MARCH, 1967

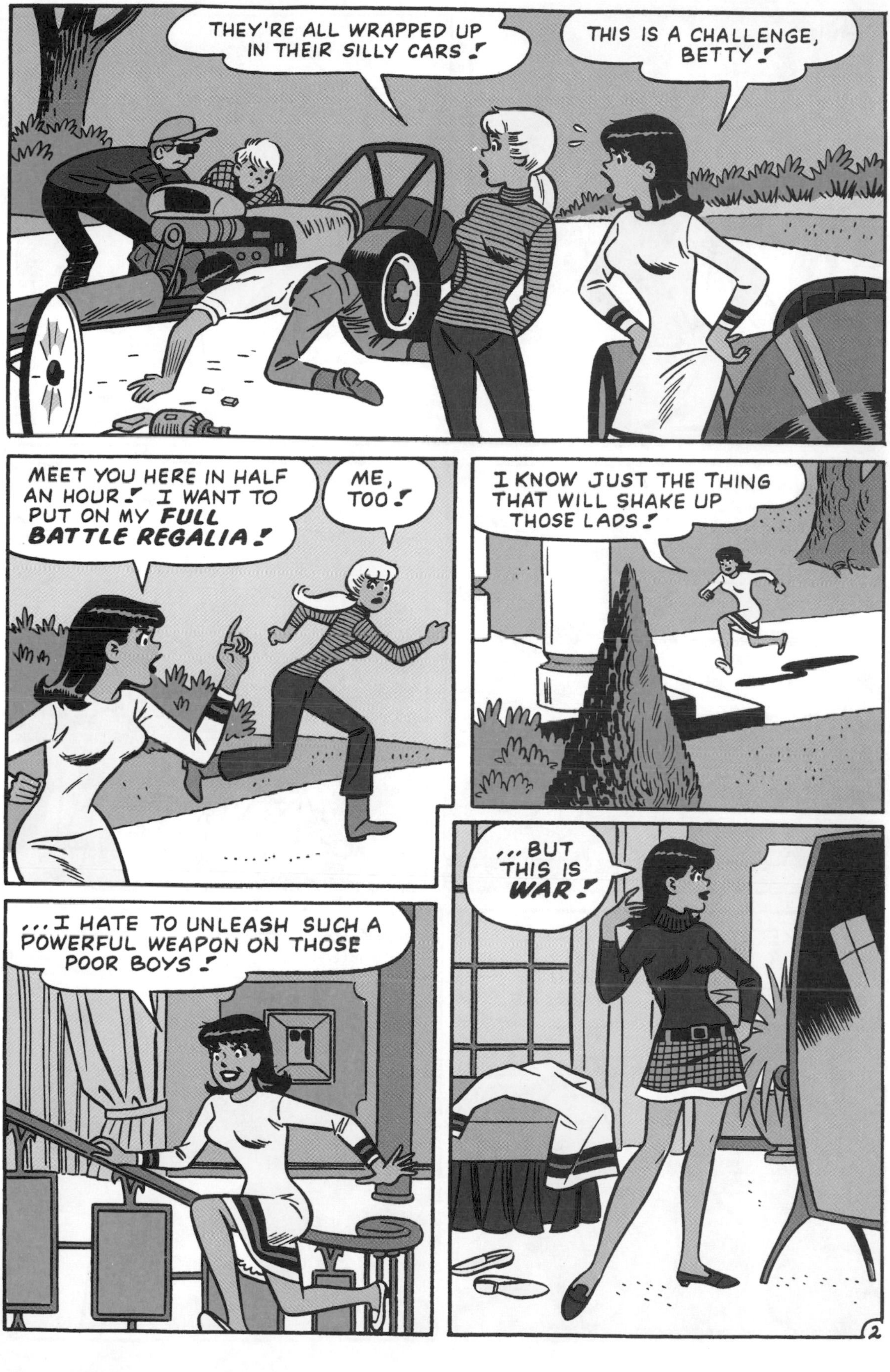
THEY'RE ALL WRAPPED UP IN THEIR SILLY CARS!
THIS IS A CHALLENGE, BETTY!
MEET YOU HERE IN HALF AN HOUR! I WANT TO PUT ON MY FULL BATTLE REGALIA!
ME, TOO!
I KNOW JUST THE THING THAT WILL SHAKE UP THOSE LADS!
...I HATE TO UNLEASH SUCH A POWERFUL WEAPON ON THOSE POOR BOYS!
...BUT THIS IS WAR!
2

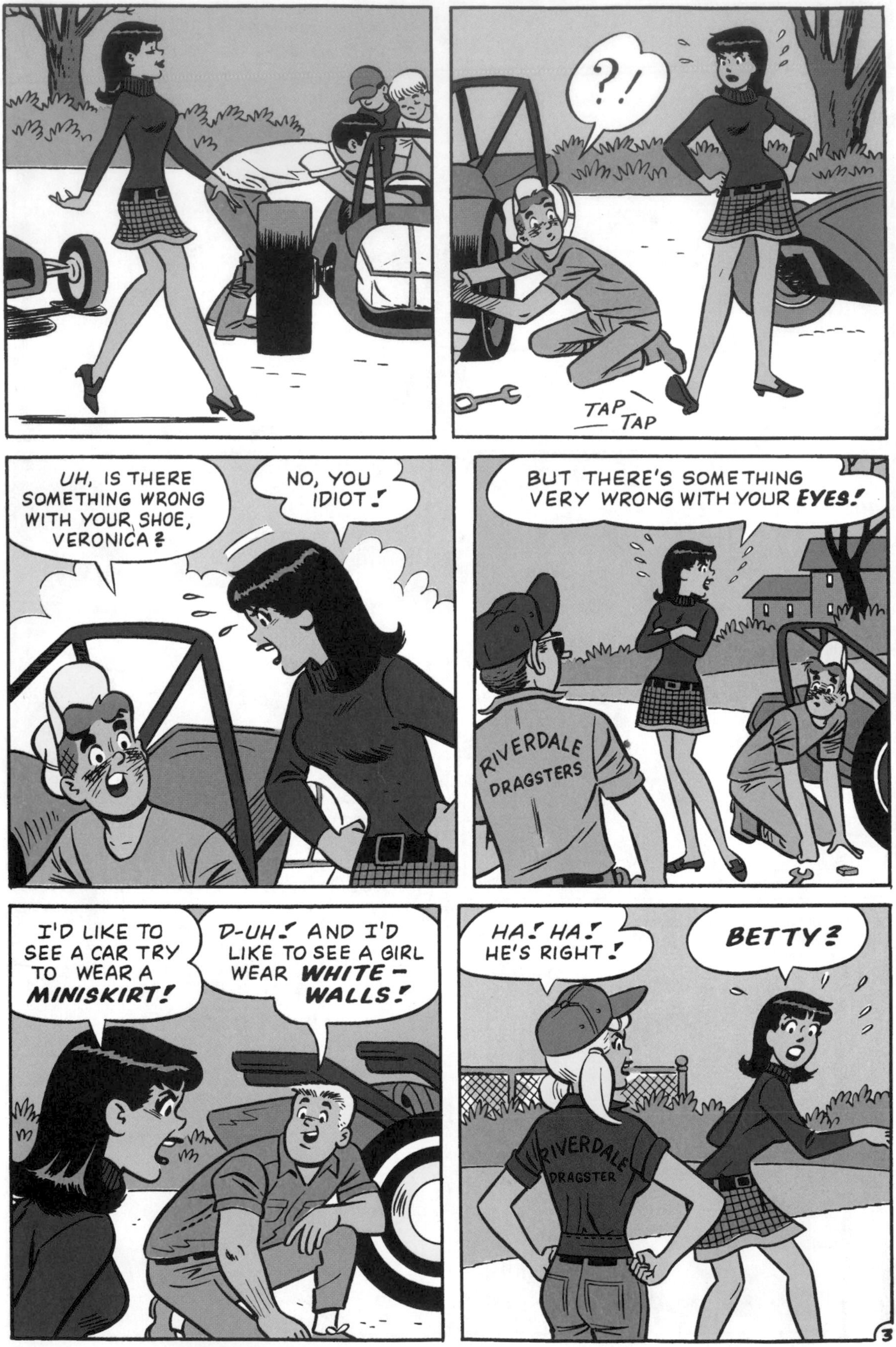
?!
TAP TAP
UH, IS THERE SOMETHING WRONG WITH YOUR SHOE, VERONICA?
NO, YOU IDIOT!
BUT THERE'S SOMETHING VERY WRONG WITH YOUR EYES!
RIVERDALE DRAGSTERS
I'D LIKE TO SEE A CAR TRY TO WEAR A MINISKIRT!
D-UH! AND I'D LIKE TO SEE A GIRL WEAR WHITE-WALLS!
HA! HA! HE'S RIGHT!
BETTY?
RIVERDALE DRAGSTER
3

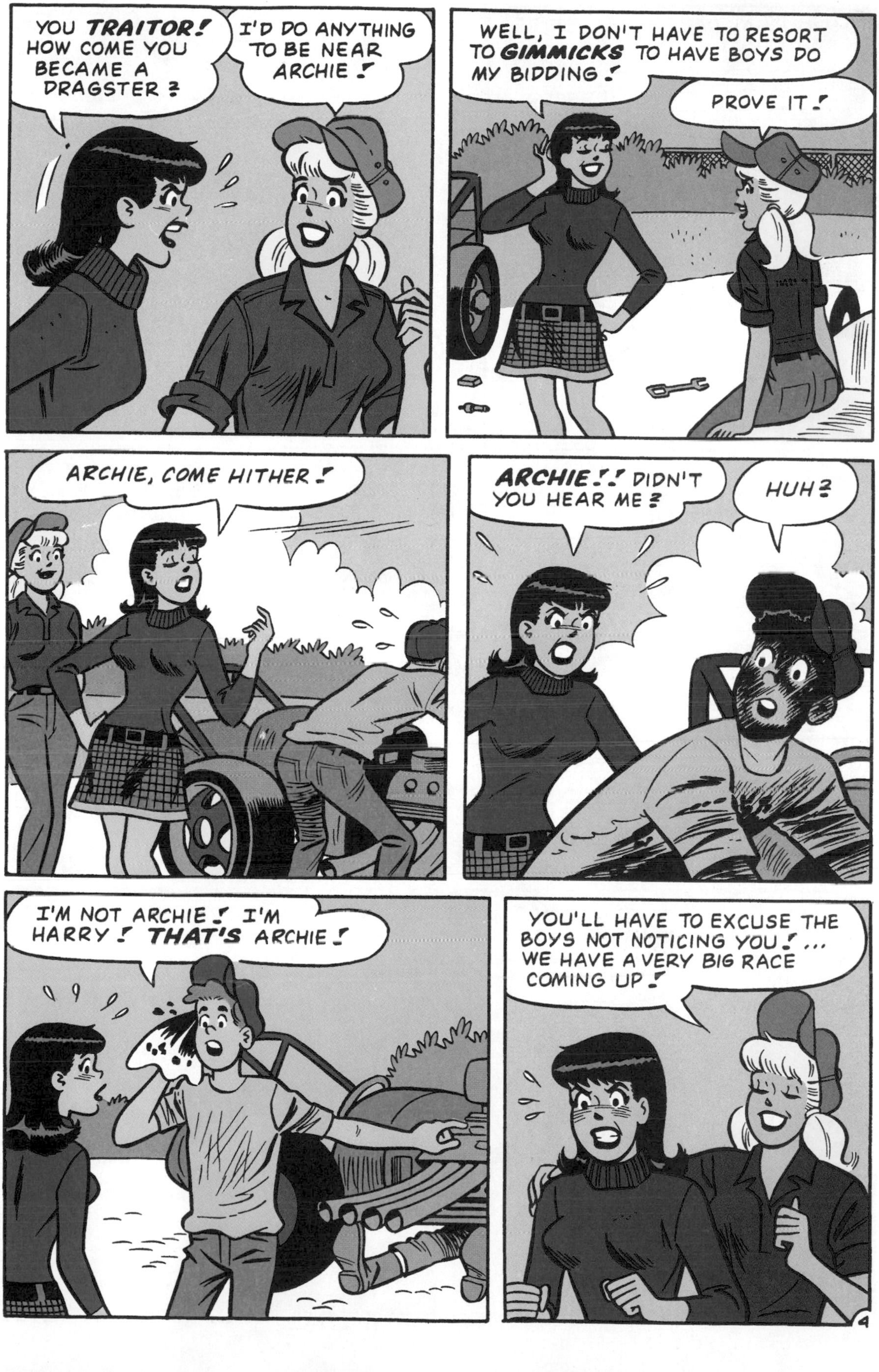
YOU TRAITOR! HOW COME YOU BECAME A DRAGSTER?
I'D DO ANYTHING TO BE NEAR ARCHIE!
WELL, I DON'T HAVE TO RESORT TO GIMMICKS TO HAVE BOYS DO MY BIDDING!
PROVE IT!
ARCHIE, COME HITHER!
ARCHIE!! DIDN'T YOU HEAR ME?
HUH?
I'M NOT ARCHIE! I'M HARRY! THAT'S ARCHIE!
YOU'LL HAVE TO EXCUSE THE BOYS NOT NOTICING YOU! ... WE HAVE A VERY BIG RACE COMING UP!
4

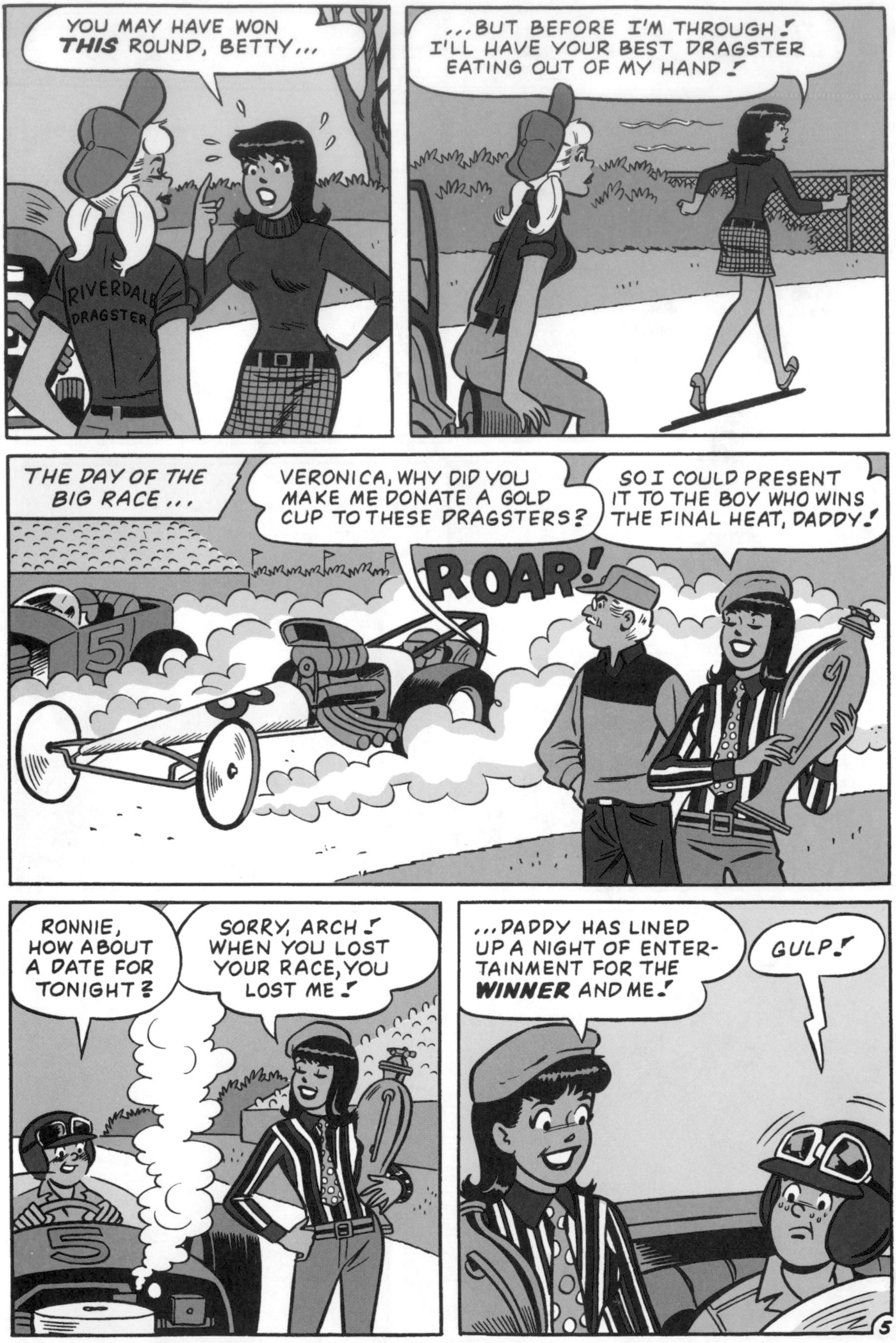
YOU MAY HAVE WON THIS ROUND, BETTY...
RIVERDALE DRAGSTER
...BUT BEFORE I'M THROUGH! I'LL HAVE YOUR BEST DRAGSTER EATING OUT OF MY HAND!
THE DAY OF THE BIG RACE...
VERONICA, WHY DID YOU MAKE ME DONATE A GOLD CUP TO THESE DRAGSTERS?
SO I COULD PRESENT IT TO THE BOY WHO WINS THE FINAL HEAT, DADDY!
ROAR!
RONNIE, HOW ABOUT A DATE FOR TONIGHT?
SORRY, ARCH! WHEN YOU LOST YOUR RACE, YOU LOST ME!
...DADDY HAS LINED UP A NIGHT OF ENTER-TAINMENT FOR THE WINNER AND ME!
GULP!
5

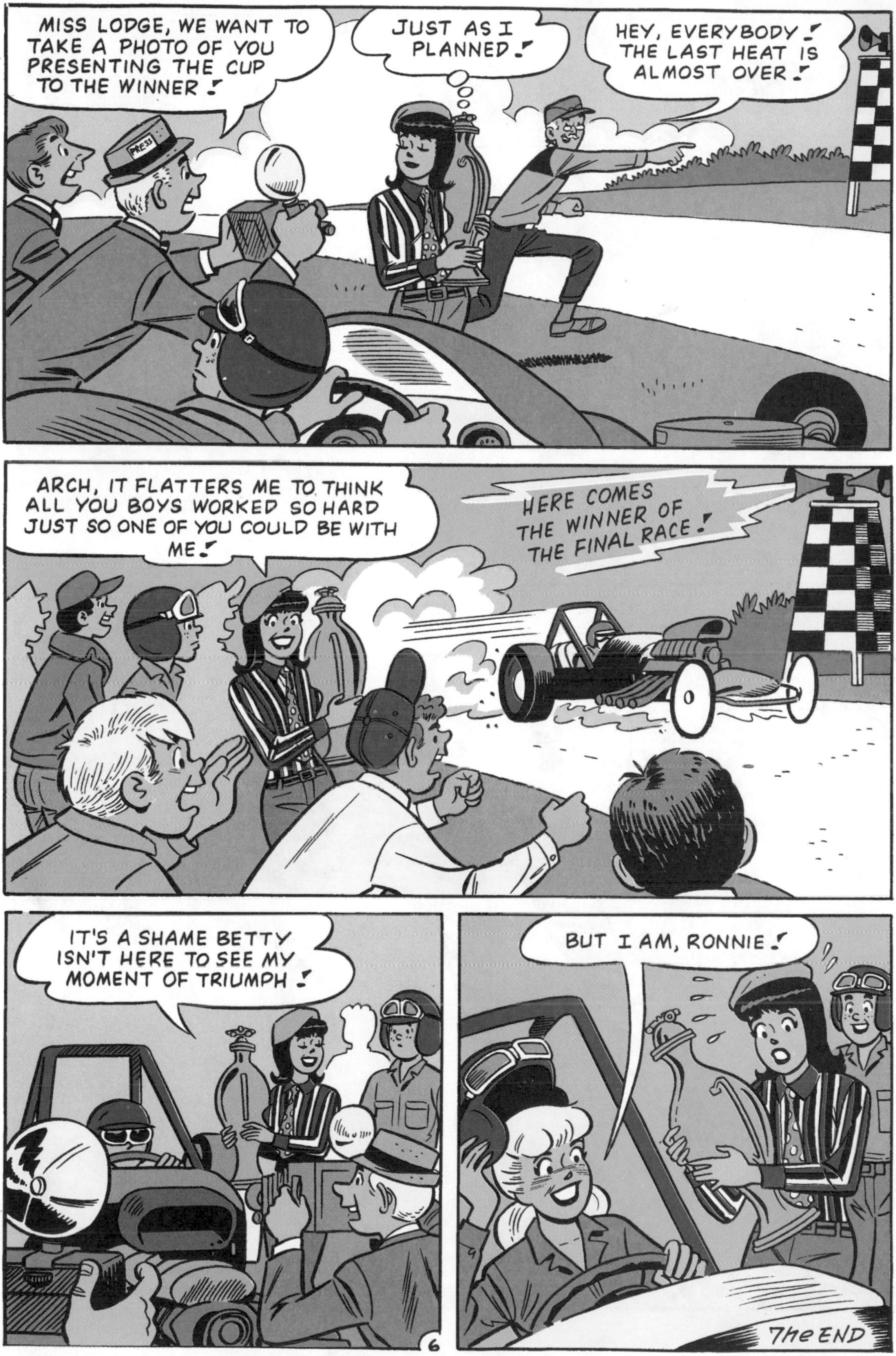
MISS LODGE, WE WANT TO TAKE A PHOTO OF YOU PRESENTING THE CUP TO THE WINNER!
JUST AS I PLANNED!
HEY, EVERYBODY! THE LAST HEAT IS ALMOST OVER!
PRESS
ARCH, IT FLATTERS ME TO THINK ALL YOU BOYS WORKED SO HARD JUST SO ONE OF YOU COULD BE WITH ME!
HERE COMES THE WINNER OF THE FINAL RACE!
IT'S A SHAME BETTY ISN'T HERE TO SEE MY MOMENT OF TRIUMPH!
BUT I AM, RONNIE!
6
The END

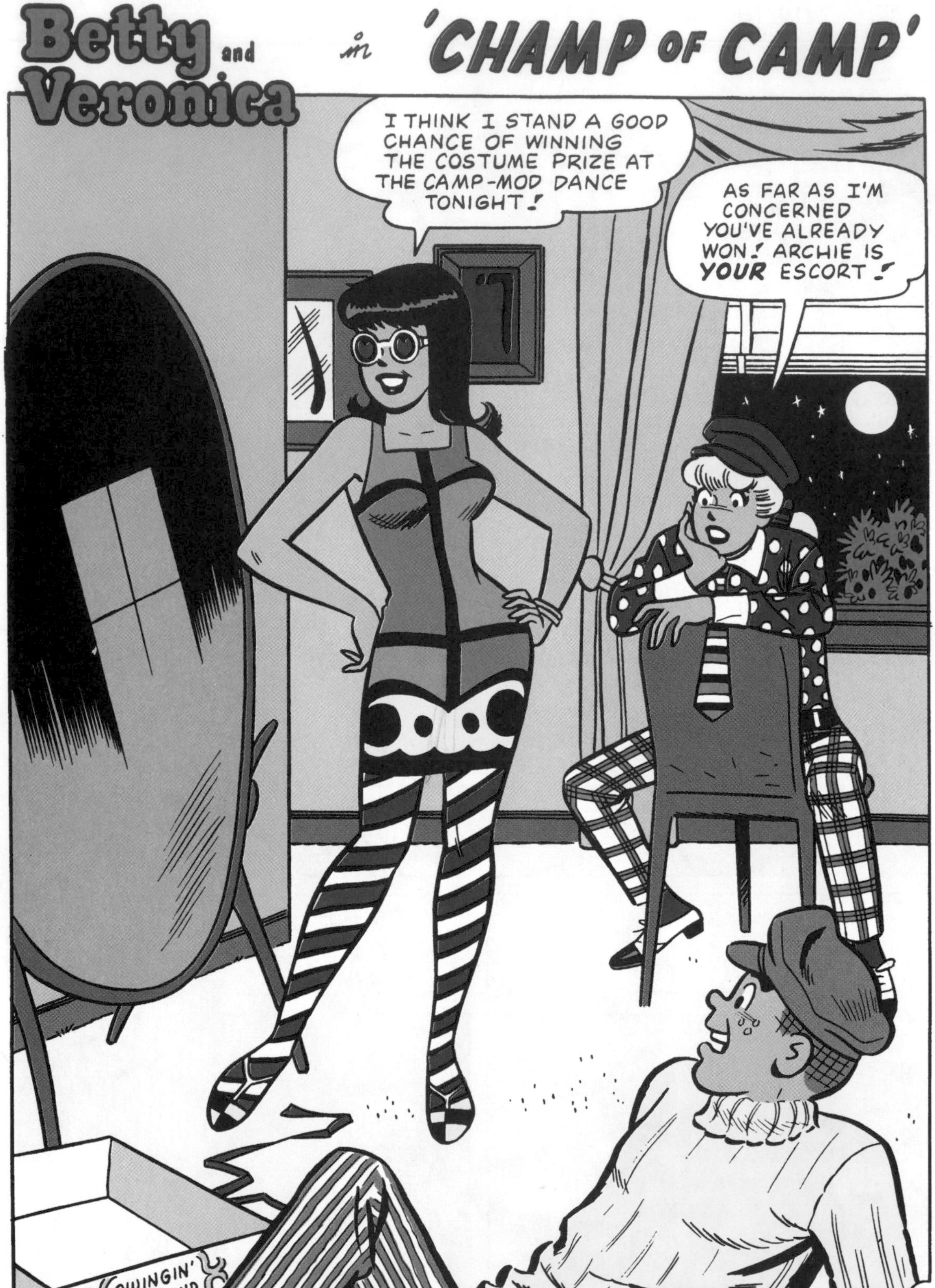
Betty and Veronica in 'CHAMP OF CAMP'
I THINK I STAND A GOOD CHANCE OF WINNING THE COSTUME PRIZE AT THE CAMP-MOD DANCE TONIGHT!
AS FAR AS I'M CONCERNED YOU'VE ALREADY WON! ARCHIE IS YOUR ESCORT!
SWINGIN' ENGLAND
1

ORIGINALLY PRESENTED IN **BETTY & VERONICA #138**, JUNE, 1967

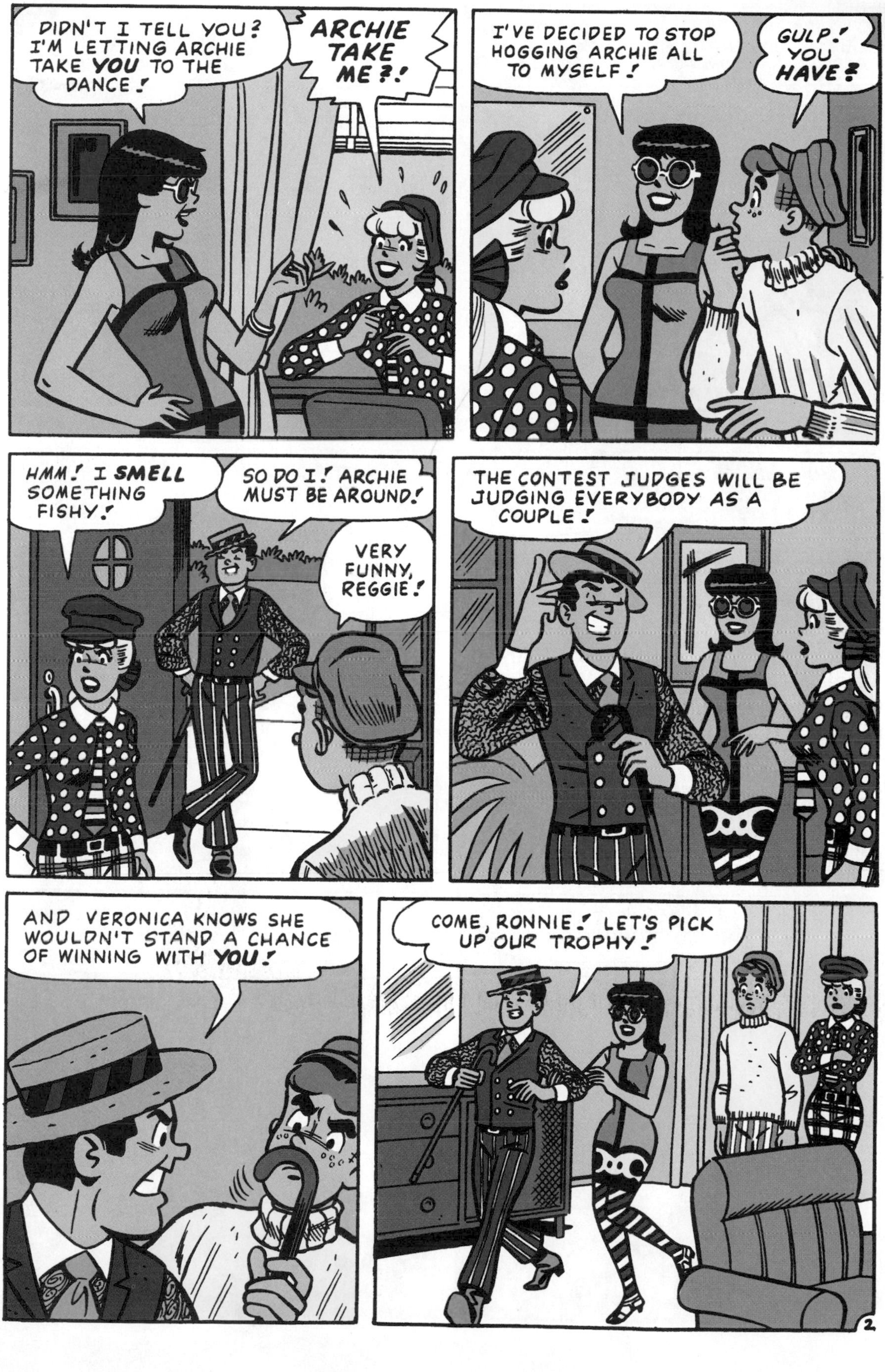
DIDN'T I TELL YOU? I'M LETTING ARCHIE TAKE YOU TO THE DANCE!
ARCHIE TAKE ME?!
I'VE DECIDED TO STOP HOGGING ARCHIE ALL TO MYSELF!
GULP! YOU HAVE?
HMM! I SMELL SOMETHING FISHY!
SO DO I! ARCHIE MUST BE AROUND!
VERY FUNNY, REGGIE!
THE CONTEST JUDGES WILL BE JUDGING EVERYBODY AS A COUPLE!
AND VERONICA KNOWS SHE WOULDN'T STAND A CHANCE OF WINNING WITH YOU!
COME, RONNIE! LET'S PICK UP OUR TROPHY!
2

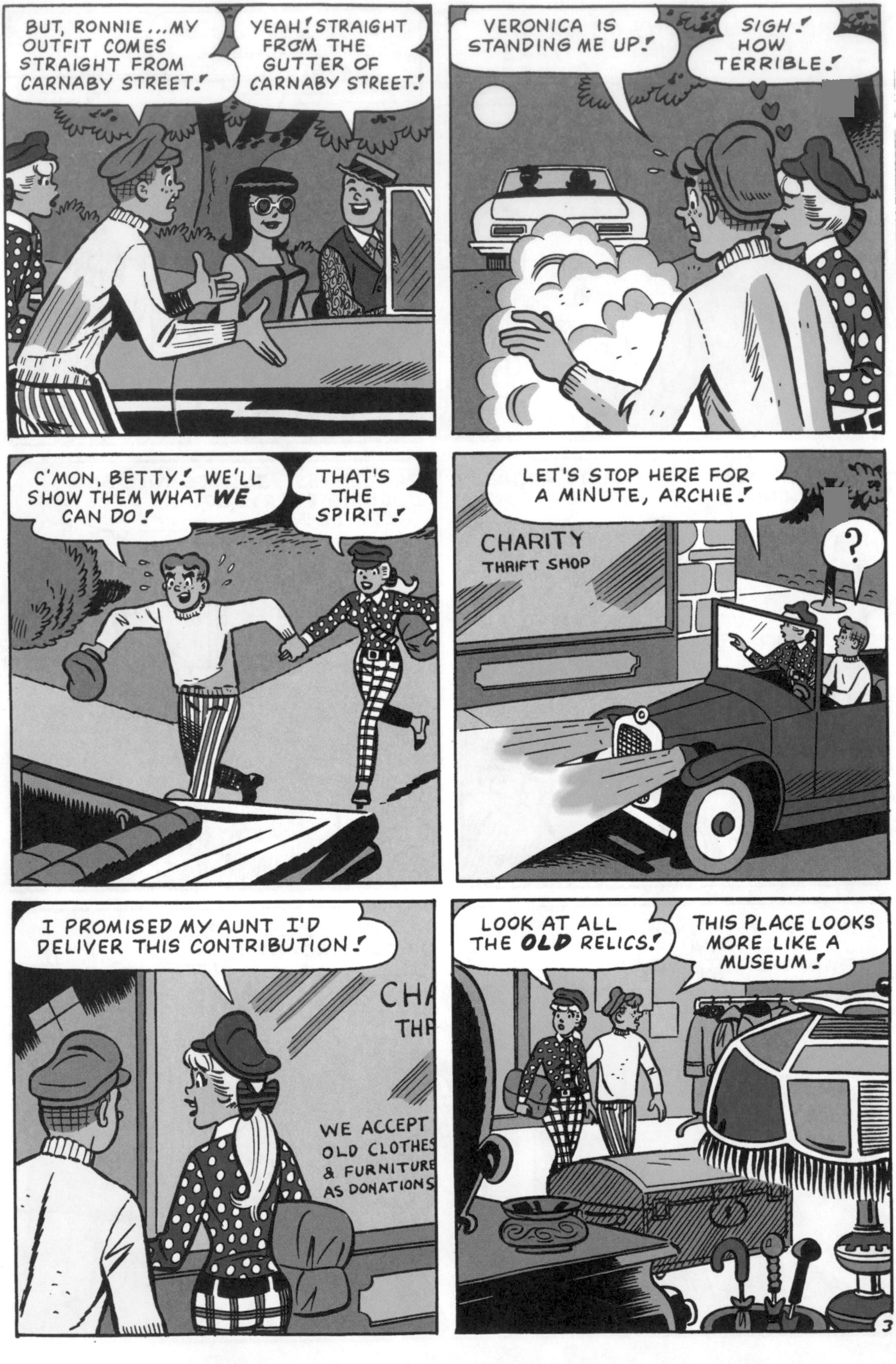
BUT, RONNIE ... MY OUTFIT COMES STRAIGHT FROM CARNABY STREET!
YEAH! STRAIGHT FROM THE GUTTER OF CARNABY STREET!
VERONICA IS STANDING ME UP!
SIGH! HOW TERRIBLE!
C'MON, BETTY! WE'LL SHOW THEM WHAT WE CAN DO!
THAT'S THE SPIRIT!
LET'S STOP HERE FOR A MINUTE, ARCHIE!
CHARITY
THRIFT SHOP
?
I PROMISED MY AUNT I'D DELIVER THIS CONTRIBUTION!
CHA
THR
WE ACCEPT
OLD CLOTHES
& FURNITURE
AS DONATIONS
LOOK AT ALL THE OLD RELICS!
THIS PLACE LOOKS MORE LIKE A MUSEUM!
3

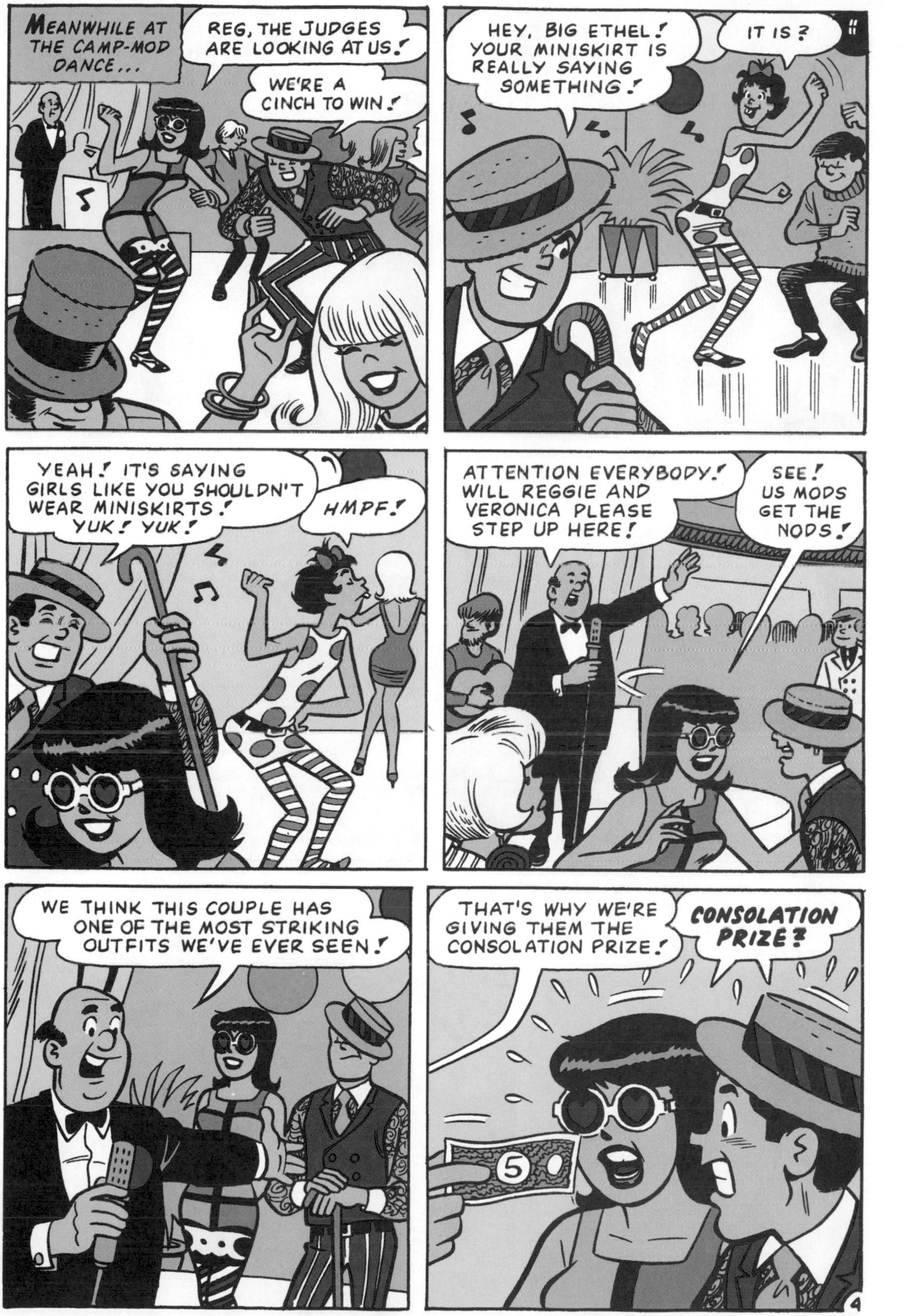
MEANWHILE AT THE CAMP-MOD DANCE...
REG, THE JUDGES ARE LOOKING AT US!
WE'RE A CINCH TO WIN!
HEY, BIG ETHEL! YOUR MINISKIRT IS REALLY SAYING SOMETHING!
IT IS?
YEAH! IT'S SAYING GIRLS LIKE YOU SHOULDN'T WEAR MINISKIRTS! YUK! YUK!
HMPF!
ATTENTION EVERYBODY! WILL REGGIE AND VERONICA PLEASE STEP UP HERE!
SEE! US MODS GET THE NODS!
WE THINK THIS COUPLE HAS ONE OF THE MOST STRIKING OUTFITS WE'VE EVER SEEN!
THAT'S WHY WE'RE GIVING THEM THE CONSOLATION PRIZE!
CONSOLATION PRIZE?
5
4

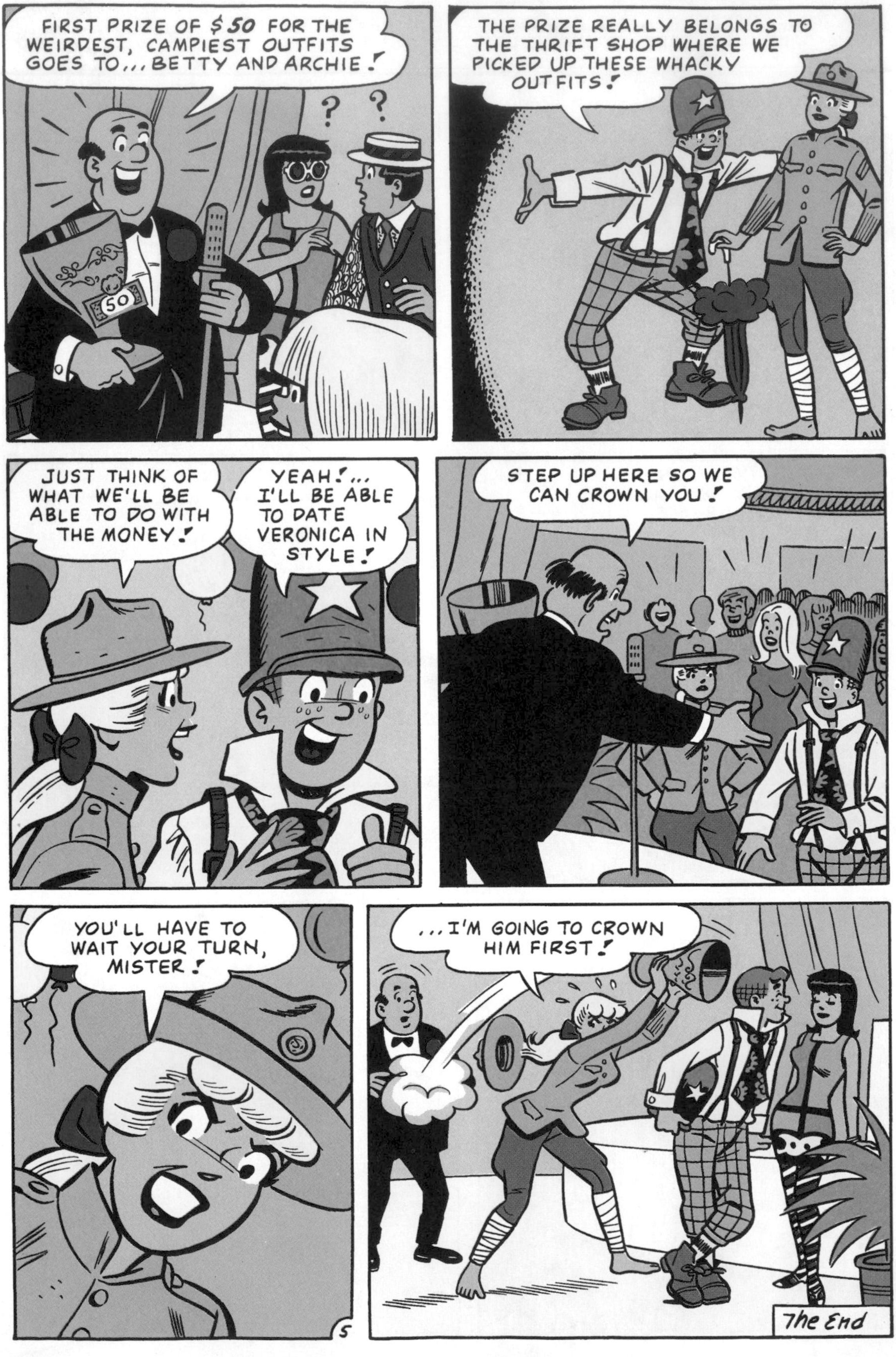
FIRST PRIZE OF $50 FOR THE WEIRDEST, CAMPIEST OUTFITS GOES TO... BETTY AND ARCHIE!
? ?
50
THE PRIZE REALLY BELONGS TO THE THRIFT SHOP WHERE WE PICKED UP THESE WHACKY OUTFITS!
JUST THINK OF WHAT WE'LL BE ABLE TO DO WITH THE MONEY!
YEAH!... I'LL BE ABLE TO DATE VERONICA IN STYLE!
STEP UP HERE SO WE CAN CROWN YOU!
YOU'LL HAVE TO WAIT YOUR TURN, MISTER!
5
...I'M GOING TO CROWN HIM FIRST!
The End

Betty and Veronica in "THE PAWN"

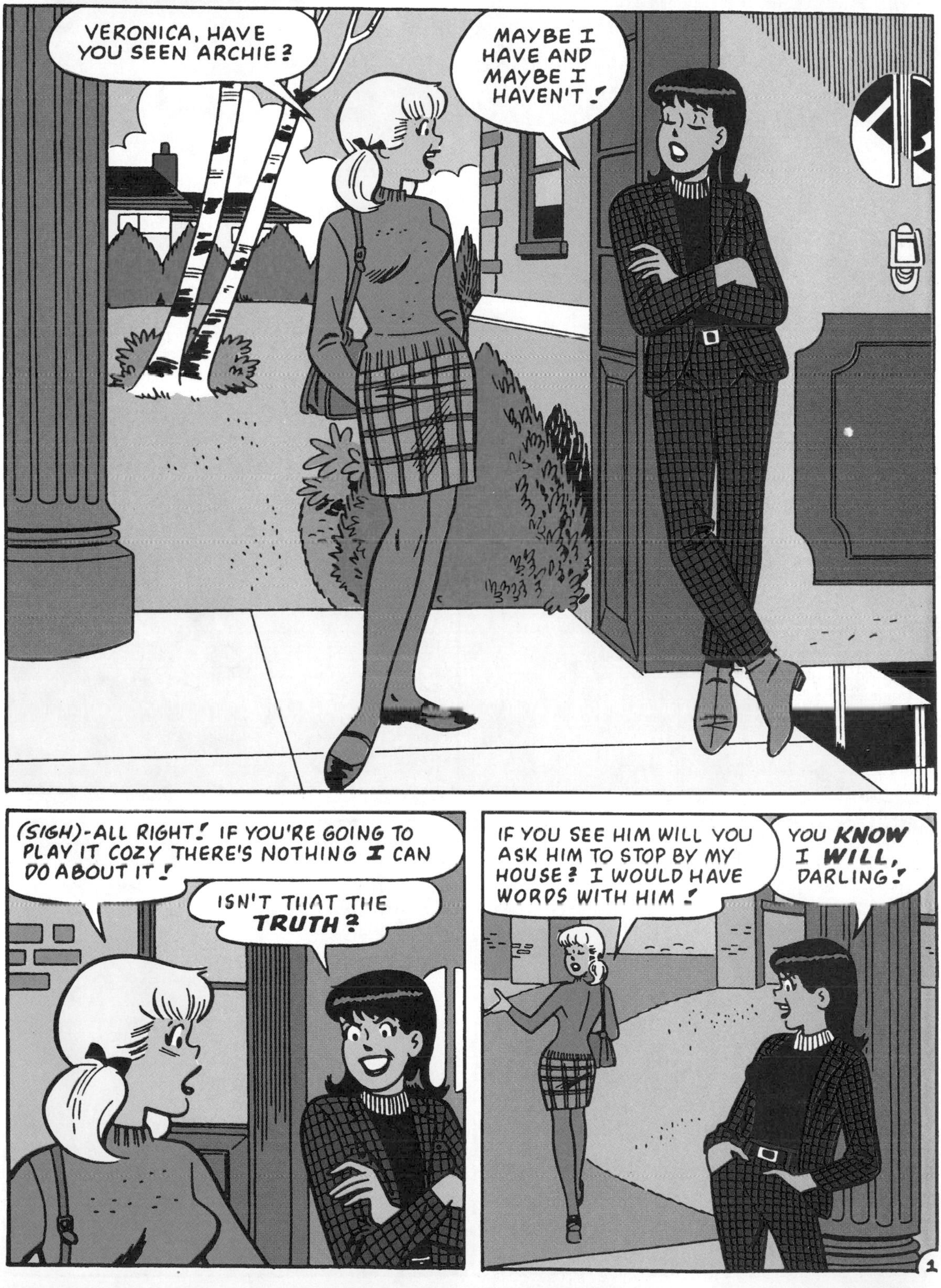
VERONICA, HAVE YOU SEEN ARCHIE?
MAYBE I HAVE AND MAYBE I HAVEN'T!
(SIGH)-ALL RIGHT! IF YOU'RE GOING TO PLAY IT COZY THERE'S NOTHING I CAN DO ABOUT IT!
ISN'T THAT THE TRUTH?
IF YOU SEE HIM WILL YOU ASK HIM TO STOP BY MY HOUSE? I WOULD HAVE WORDS WITH HIM!
YOU KNOW I WILL, DARLING!
1

ORIGINALLY PRESENTED IN **BETTY & VERONICA #138**, JUNE, 1967

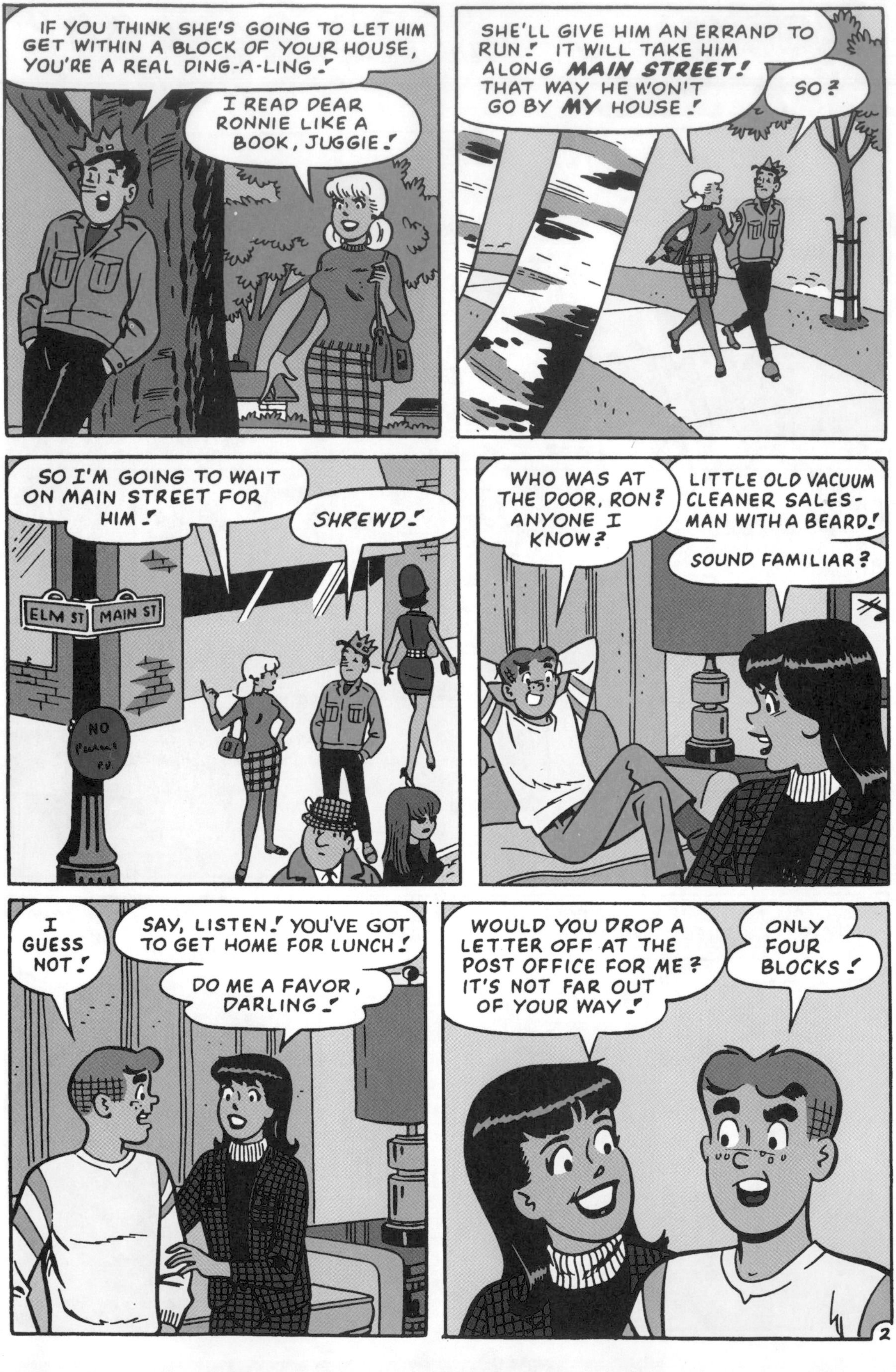
IF YOU THINK SHE'S GOING TO LET HIM GET WITHIN A BLOCK OF YOUR HOUSE, YOU'RE A REAL DING-A-LING!
I READ DEAR RONNIE LIKE A BOOK, JUGGIE!
SHE'LL GIVE HIM AN ERRAND TO RUN! IT WILL TAKE HIM ALONG MAIN STREET! THAT WAY HE WON'T GO BY MY HOUSE!
SO?
SO I'M GOING TO WAIT ON MAIN STREET FOR HIM!
SHREWD!
ELM ST
MAIN ST
WHO WAS AT THE DOOR, RON? ANYONE I KNOW?
LITTLE OLD VACUUM CLEANER SALES-MAN WITH A BEARD!
SOUND FAMILIAR?
I GUESS NOT!
SAY, LISTEN! YOU'VE GOT TO GET HOME FOR LUNCH!
DO ME A FAVOR, DARLING!
WOULD YOU DROP A LETTER OFF AT THE POST OFFICE FOR ME? IT'S NOT FAR OUT OF YOUR WAY!
ONLY FOUR BLOCKS!
2

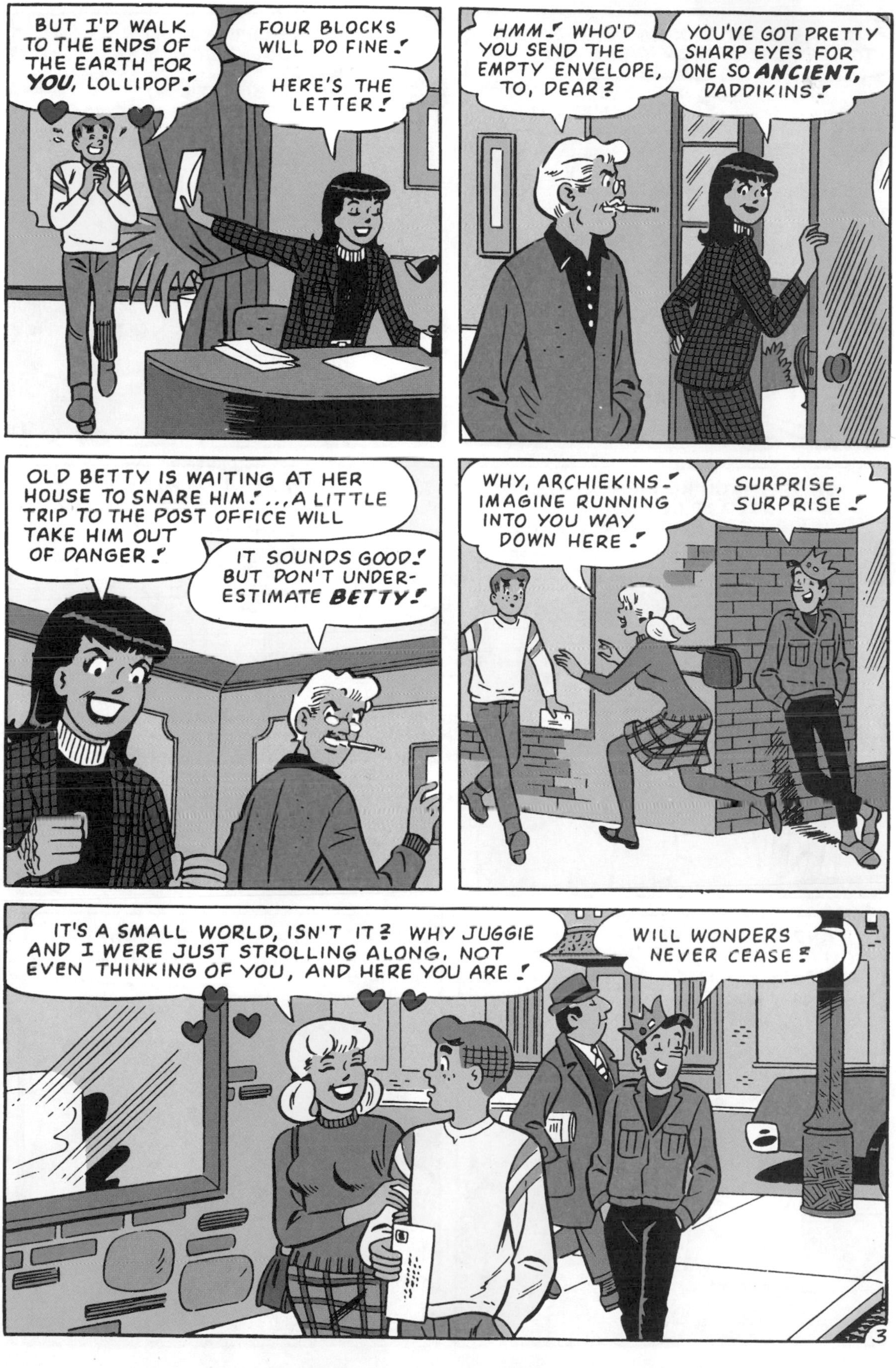
BUT I'D WALK TO THE ENDS OF THE EARTH FOR YOU, LOLLIPOP!
FOUR BLOCKS WILL DO FINE!
HERE'S THE LETTER!
HMM! WHO'D YOU SEND THE EMPTY ENVELOPE, TO, DEAR?
YOU'VE GOT PRETTY SHARP EYES FOR ONE SO ANCIENT, DADDIKINS!
OLD BETTY IS WAITING AT HER HOUSE TO SNARE HIM! ...A LITTLE TRIP TO THE POST OFFICE WILL TAKE HIM OUT OF DANGER!
IT SOUNDS GOOD! BUT DON'T UNDER-ESTIMATE BETTY!
WHY, ARCHIEKINS! IMAGINE RUNNING INTO YOU WAY DOWN HERE!
SURPRISE, SURPRISE!
IT'S A SMALL WORLD, ISN'T IT? WHY JUGGIE AND I WERE JUST STROLLING ALONG, NOT EVEN THINKING OF YOU, AND HERE YOU ARE!
WILL WONDERS NEVER CEASE?
3

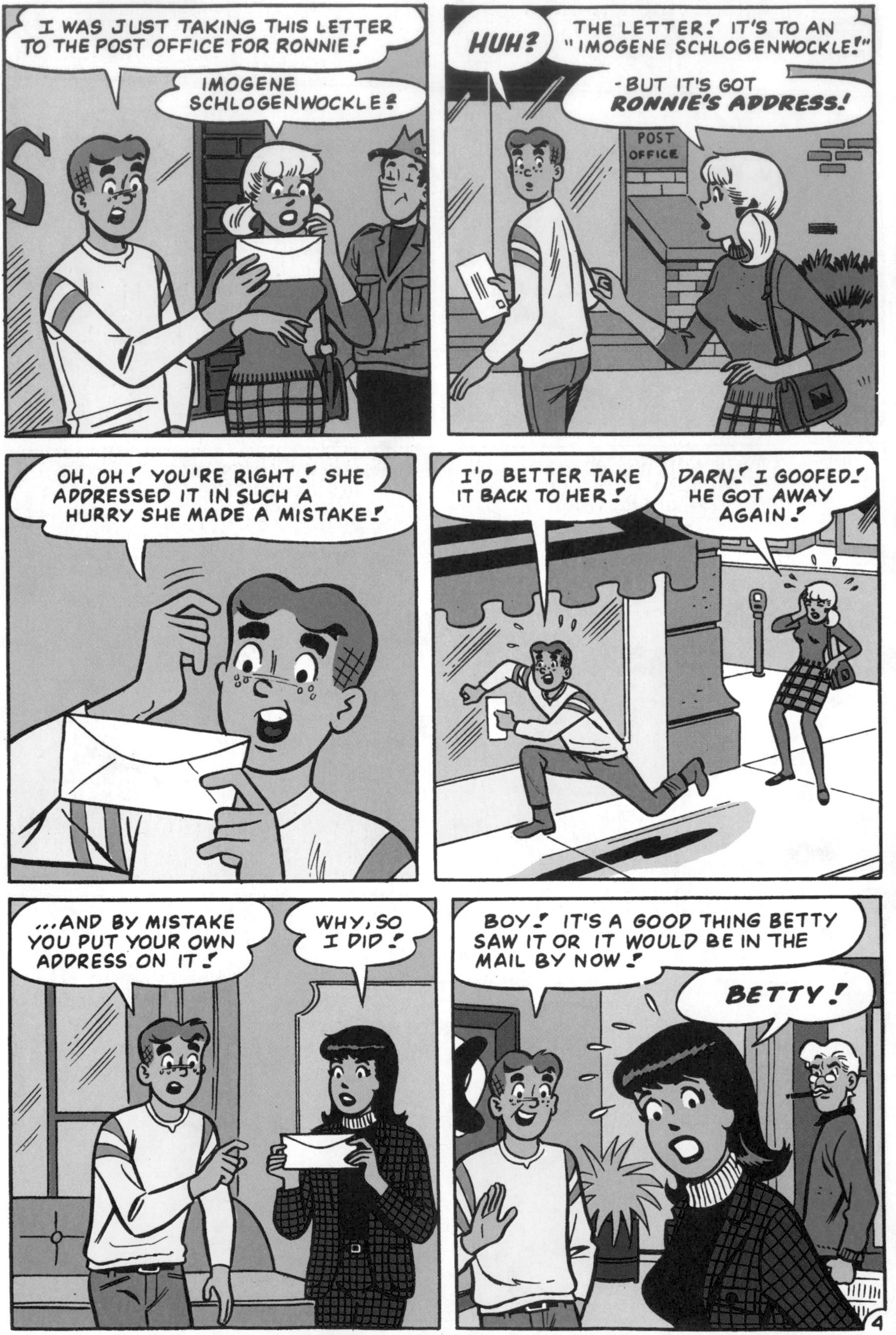
I WAS JUST TAKING THIS LETTER TO THE POST OFFICE FOR RONNIE!
IMOGENE SCHLOGENWOCKLE?
HUH?
THE LETTER! IT'S TO AN "IMOGENE SCHLOGENWOCKLE!"
-BUT IT'S GOT RONNIE'S ADDRESS!
POST OFFICE
OH, OH! YOU'RE RIGHT! SHE ADDRESSED IT IN SUCH A HURRY SHE MADE A MISTAKE!
I'D BETTER TAKE IT BACK TO HER!
DARN! I GOOFED! HE GOT AWAY AGAIN!
...AND BY MISTAKE YOU PUT YOUR OWN ADDRESS ON IT!
WHY, SO I DID!
BOY! IT'S A GOOD THING BETTY SAW IT OR IT WOULD BE IN THE MAIL BY NOW!
BETTY!
4

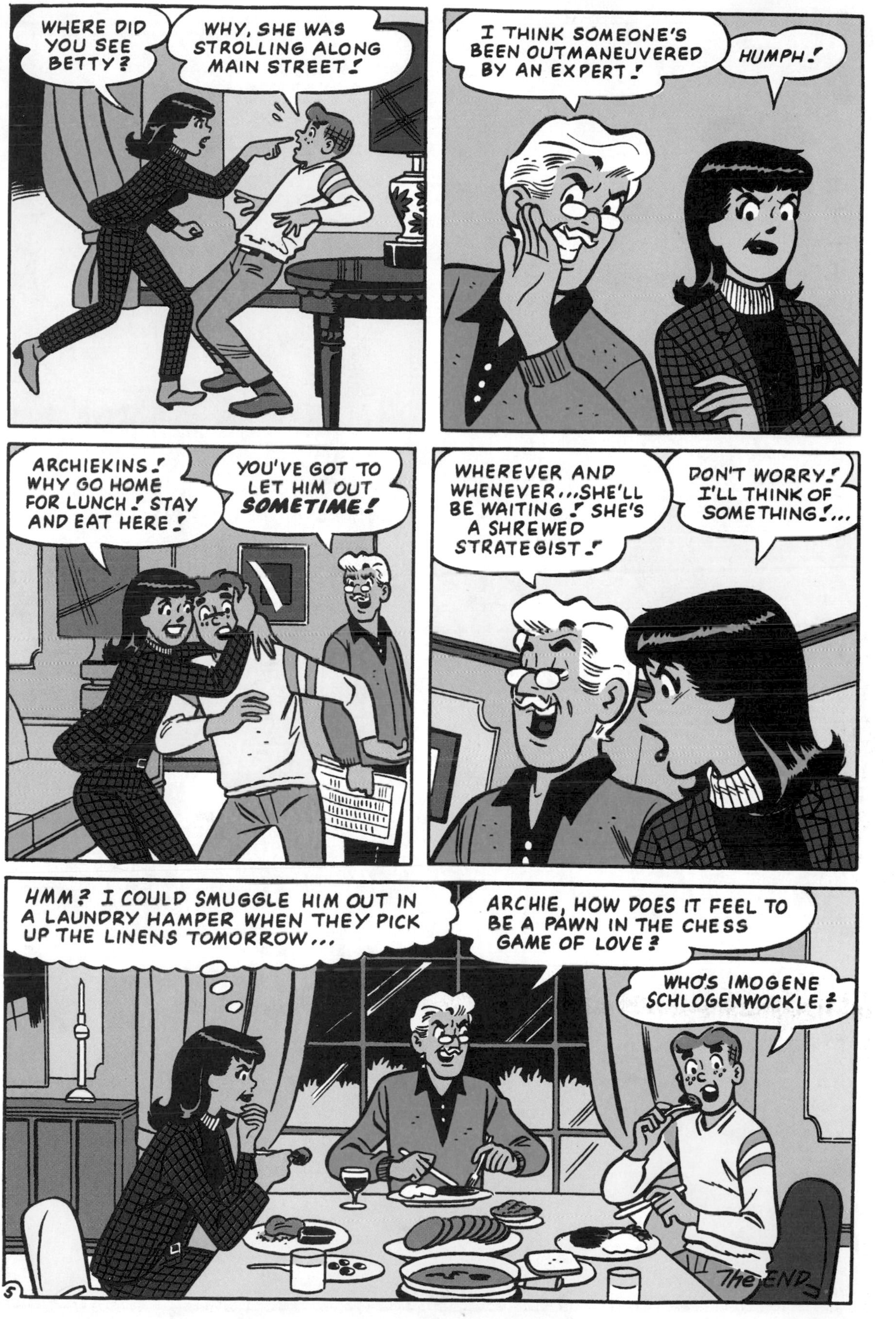
WHERE DID YOU SEE BETTY?
WHY, SHE WAS STROLLING ALONG MAIN STREET!
I THINK SOMEONE'S BEEN OUTMANEUVERED BY AN EXPERT!
HUMPH!
ARCHIEKINS! WHY GO HOME FOR LUNCH! STAY AND EAT HERE!
YOU'VE GOT TO LET HIM OUT SOMETIME!
WHEREVER AND WHENEVER...SHE'LL BE WAITING! SHE'S A SHREWED STRATEGIST!
DON'T WORRY! I'LL THINK OF SOMETHING!...
HMM? I COULD SMUGGLE HIM OUT IN A LAUNDRY HAMPER WHEN THEY PICK UP THE LINENS TOMORROW...
ARCHIE, HOW DOES IT FEEL TO BE A PAWN IN THE CHESS GAME OF LOVE?
WHO'S IMOGENE SCHLOGENWOCKLE?
5
The END

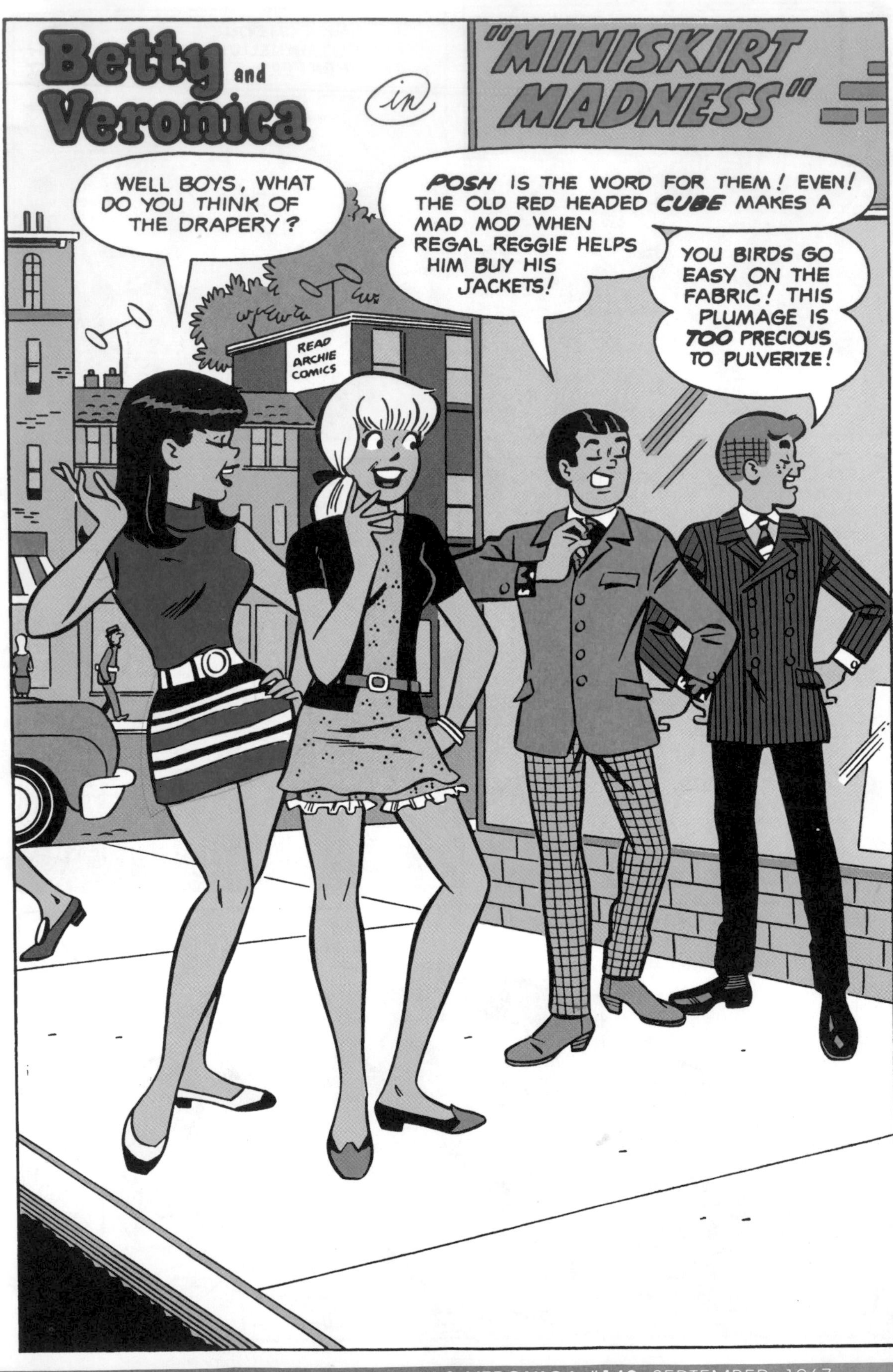
Betty and Veronica
in
"MINISKIRT MADNESS"
WELL BOYS, WHAT DO YOU THINK OF THE DRAPERY?
POSH IS THE WORD FOR THEM! EVEN! THE OLD RED HEADED CUBE MAKES A MAD MOD WHEN REGAL REGGIE HELPS HIM BUY HIS JACKETS!
YOU BIRDS GO EASY ON THE FABRIC! THIS PLUMAGE IS TOO PRECIOUS TO PULVERIZE!
READ ARCHIE COMICS

ORIGINALLY PRESENTED IN **BETTY & VERONICA #142**, SEPTEMBER, 1967

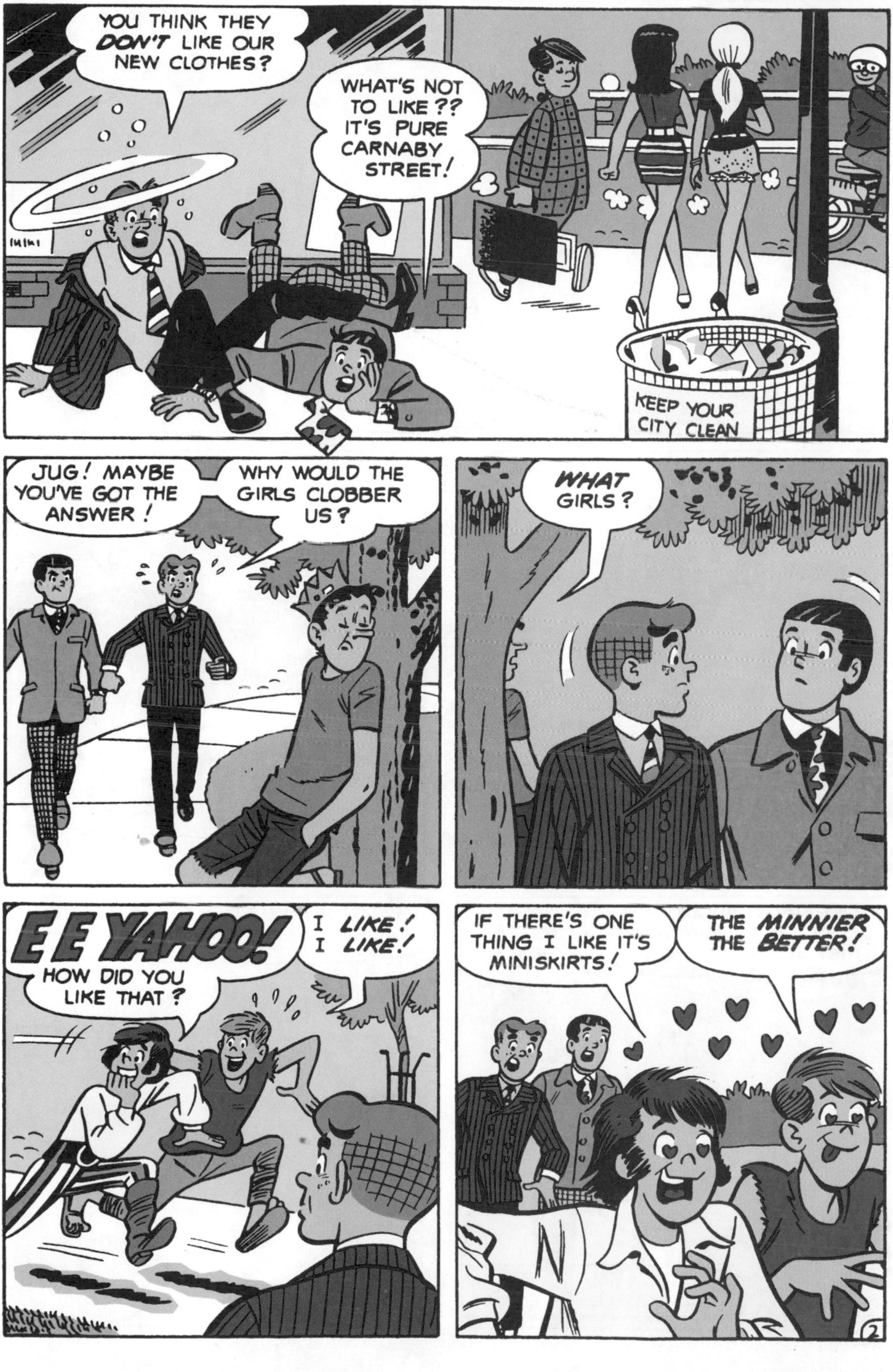
YOU THINK THEY *DON'T* LIKE OUR NEW CLOTHES?
WHAT'S NOT TO LIKE?? IT'S PURE CARNABY STREET!
KEEP YOUR CITY CLEAN
JUG! MAYBE YOU'VE GOT THE ANSWER!
WHY WOULD THE GIRLS CLOBBER US?
WHAT GIRLS?
E E YAHOO! HOW DID YOU LIKE THAT?
I *LIKE!* I *LIKE!*
IF THERE'S ONE THING I LIKE IT'S MINISKIRTS!
THE *MINNIER* THE *BETTER!*
2

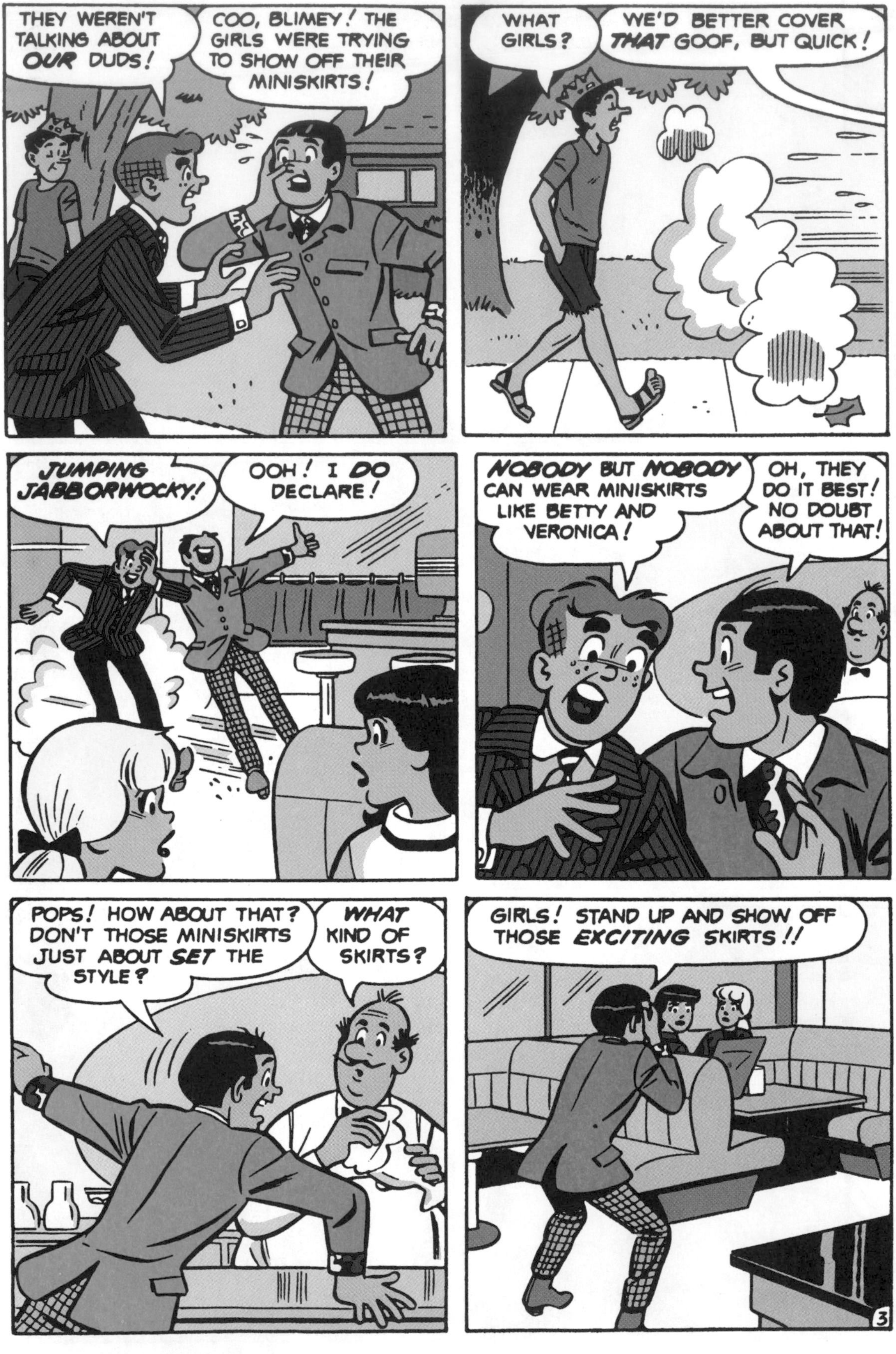
THEY WEREN'T TALKING ABOUT OUR DUDS!
COO, BLIMEY! THE GIRLS WERE TRYING TO SHOW OFF THEIR MINISKIRTS!
WHAT GIRLS?
WE'D BETTER COVER THAT GOOF, BUT QUICK!
JUMPING JABBORWOCKY!
OOH! I DO DECLARE!
NOBODY BUT NOBODY CAN WEAR MINISKIRTS LIKE BETTY AND VERONICA!
OH, THEY DO IT BEST! NO DOUBT ABOUT THAT!
POPS! HOW ABOUT THAT? DON'T THOSE MINISKIRTS JUST ABOUT SET THE STYLE?
WHAT KIND OF SKIRTS?
GIRLS! STAND UP AND SHOW OFF THOSE EXCITING SKIRTS!!
3

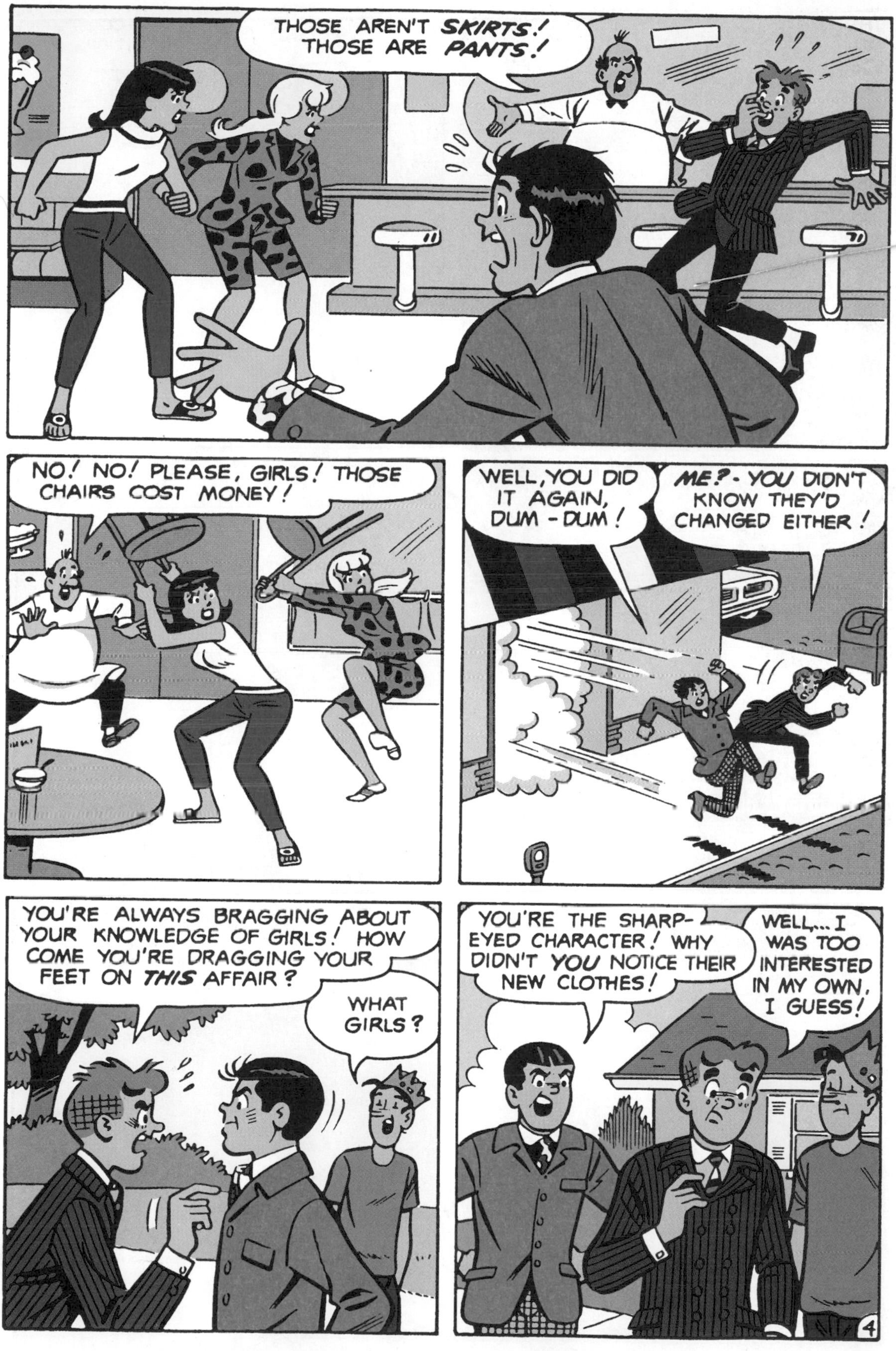
THOSE AREN'T *SKIRTS!* THOSE ARE *PANTS!*
NO! NO! PLEASE, GIRLS! THOSE CHAIRS COST MONEY!
WELL, YOU DID IT AGAIN, DUM - DUM!
ME? - *YOU* DIDN'T KNOW THEY'D CHANGED EITHER!
YOU'RE ALWAYS BRAGGING ABOUT YOUR KNOWLEDGE OF GIRLS! HOW COME YOU'RE DRAGGING YOUR FEET ON *THIS* AFFAIR?
WHAT GIRLS?
YOU'RE THE SHARP-EYED CHARACTER! WHY DIDN'T *YOU* NOTICE THEIR NEW CLOTHES!
WELL,... I WAS TOO INTERESTED IN MY OWN, I GUESS!
4

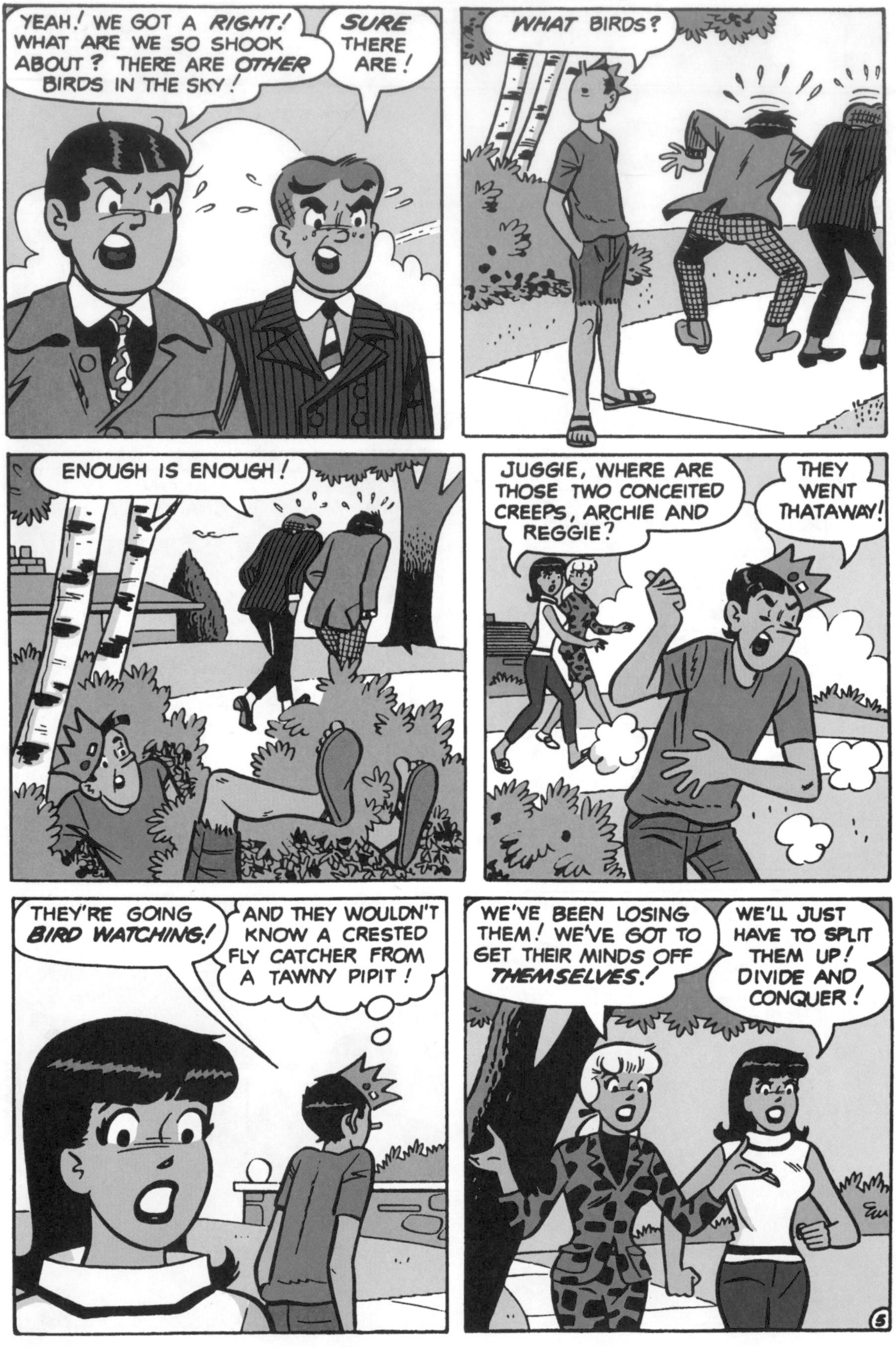
YEAH! WE GOT A RIGHT! WHAT ARE WE SO SHOOK ABOUT? THERE ARE OTHER BIRDS IN THE SKY!
SURE THERE ARE!
WHAT BIRDS?
ENOUGH IS ENOUGH!
JUGGIE, WHERE ARE THOSE TWO CONCEITED CREEPS, ARCHIE AND REGGIE?
THEY WENT THATAWAY!
THEY'RE GOING BIRD WATCHING!
AND THEY WOULDN'T KNOW A CRESTED FLY CATCHER FROM A TAWNY PIPIT!
WE'VE BEEN LOSING THEM! WE'VE GOT TO GET THEIR MINDS OFF THEMSELVES!
WE'LL JUST HAVE TO SPLIT THEM UP! DIVIDE AND CONQUER!
5

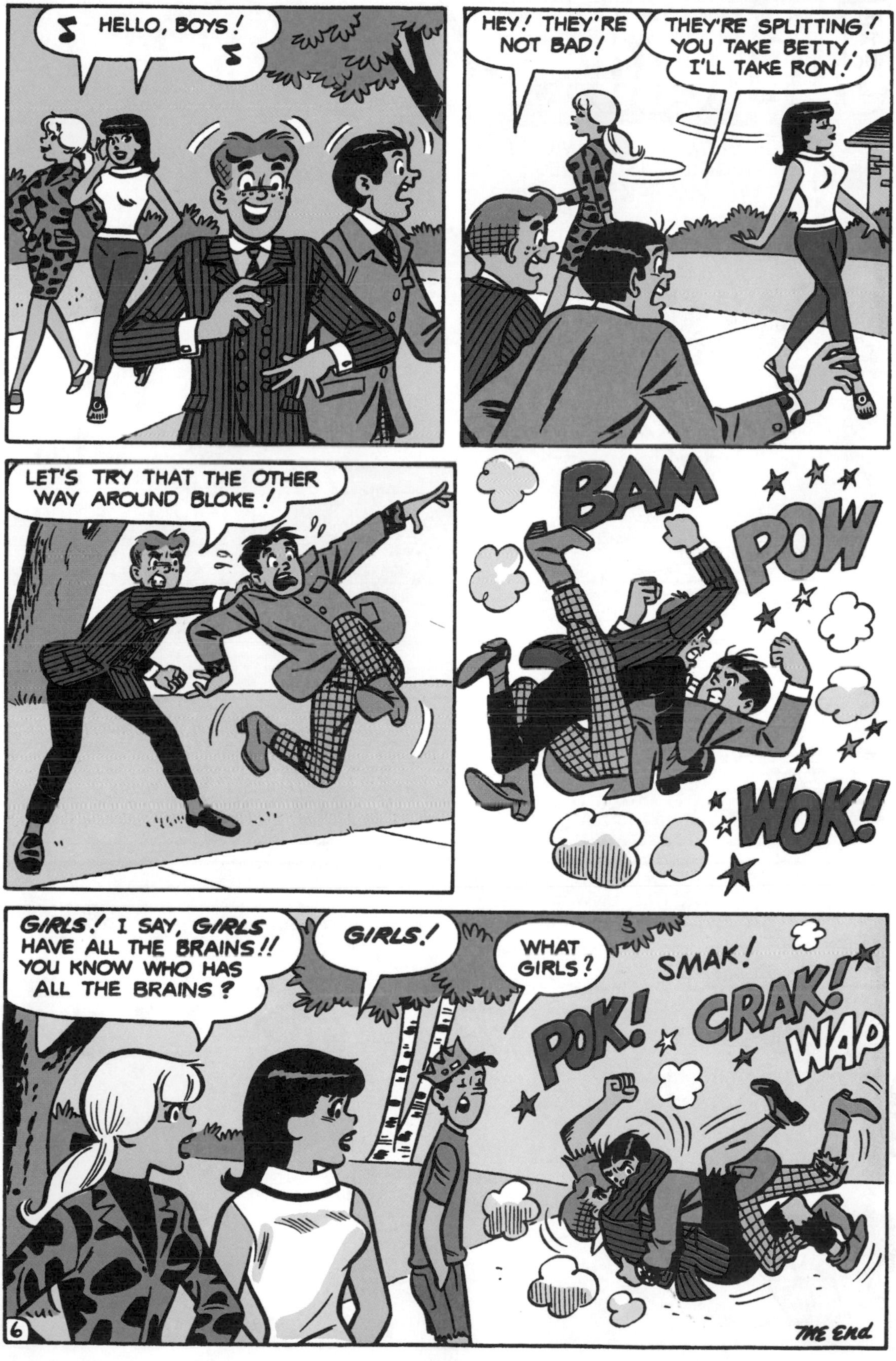
HELLO, BOYS!
HEY! THEY'RE NOT BAD!
THEY'RE SPLITTING! YOU TAKE BETTY, I'LL TAKE RON!
LET'S TRY THAT THE OTHER WAY AROUND BLOKE!
BAM
POW
WOK!
GIRLS! I SAY, GIRLS HAVE ALL THE BRAINS!! YOU KNOW WHO HAS ALL THE BRAINS?
GIRLS!
WHAT GIRLS?
SMAK!
POK!
CRAK!
WAP
6
THE END

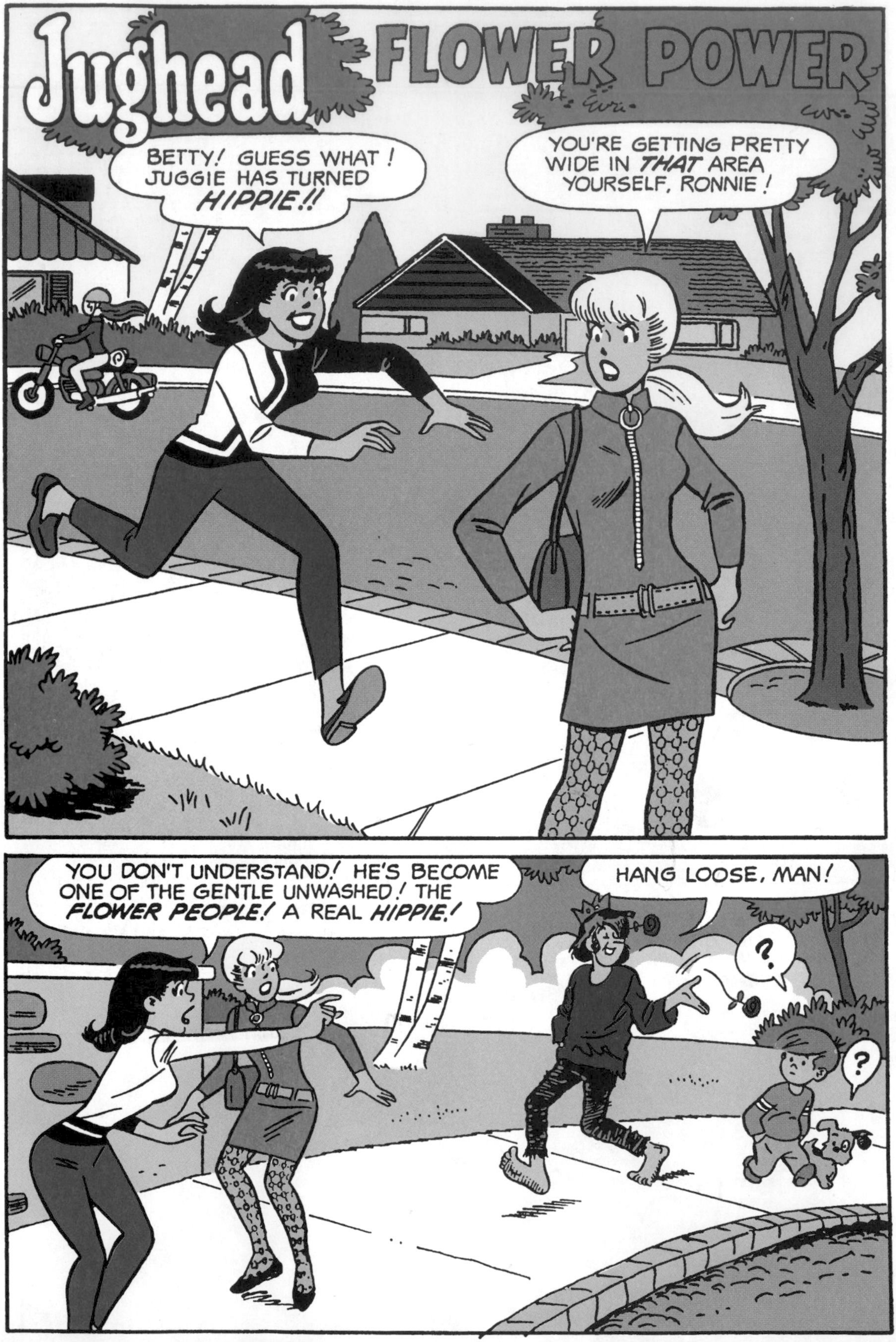
Jughead
FLOWER POWER
BETTY! GUESS WHAT! JUGGIE HAS TURNED HIPPIE!!
YOU'RE GETTING PRETTY WIDE IN THAT AREA YOURSELF, RONNIE!
YOU DON'T UNDERSTAND! HE'S BECOME ONE OF THE GENTLE UNWASHED! THE FLOWER PEOPLE! A REAL HIPPIE!
HANG LOOSE, MAN!
?
?

ORIGINALLY PRESENTED IN **JUGHEAD # 154**, MARCH, 1968

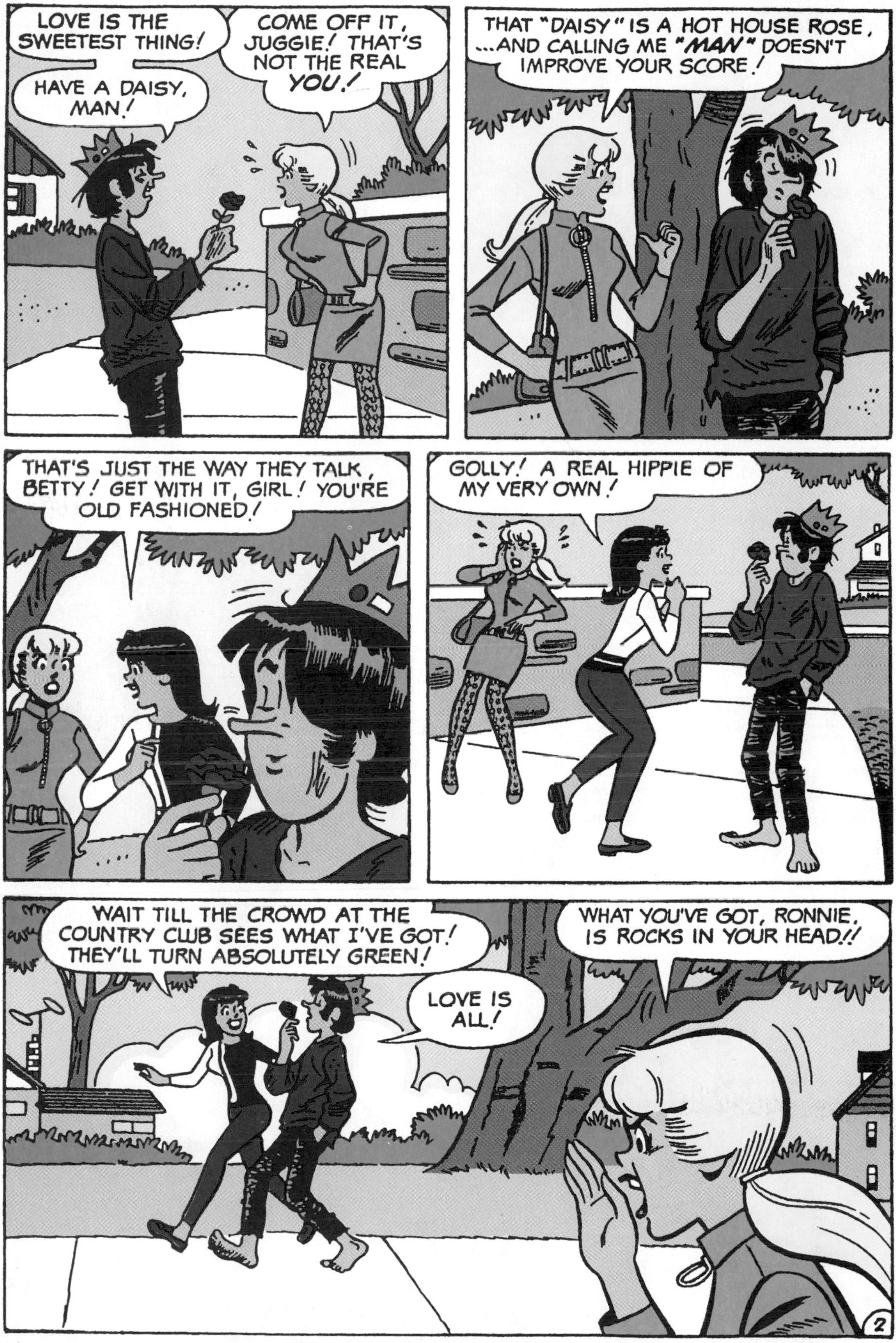
LOVE IS THE SWEETEST THING!
HAVE A DAISY, MAN!
COME OFF IT, JUGGIE! THAT'S NOT THE REAL YOU!
THAT "DAISY" IS A HOT HOUSE ROSE, ...AND CALLING ME "MAN" DOESN'T IMPROVE YOUR SCORE!
THAT'S JUST THE WAY THEY TALK, BETTY! GET WITH IT, GIRL! YOU'RE OLD FASHIONED!
GOLLY! A REAL HIPPIE OF MY VERY OWN!
WAIT TILL THE CROWD AT THE COUNTRY CLUB SEES WHAT I'VE GOT! THEY'LL TURN ABSOLUTELY GREEN!
LOVE IS ALL!
WHAT YOU'VE GOT, RONNIE, IS ROCKS IN YOUR HEAD!!
2

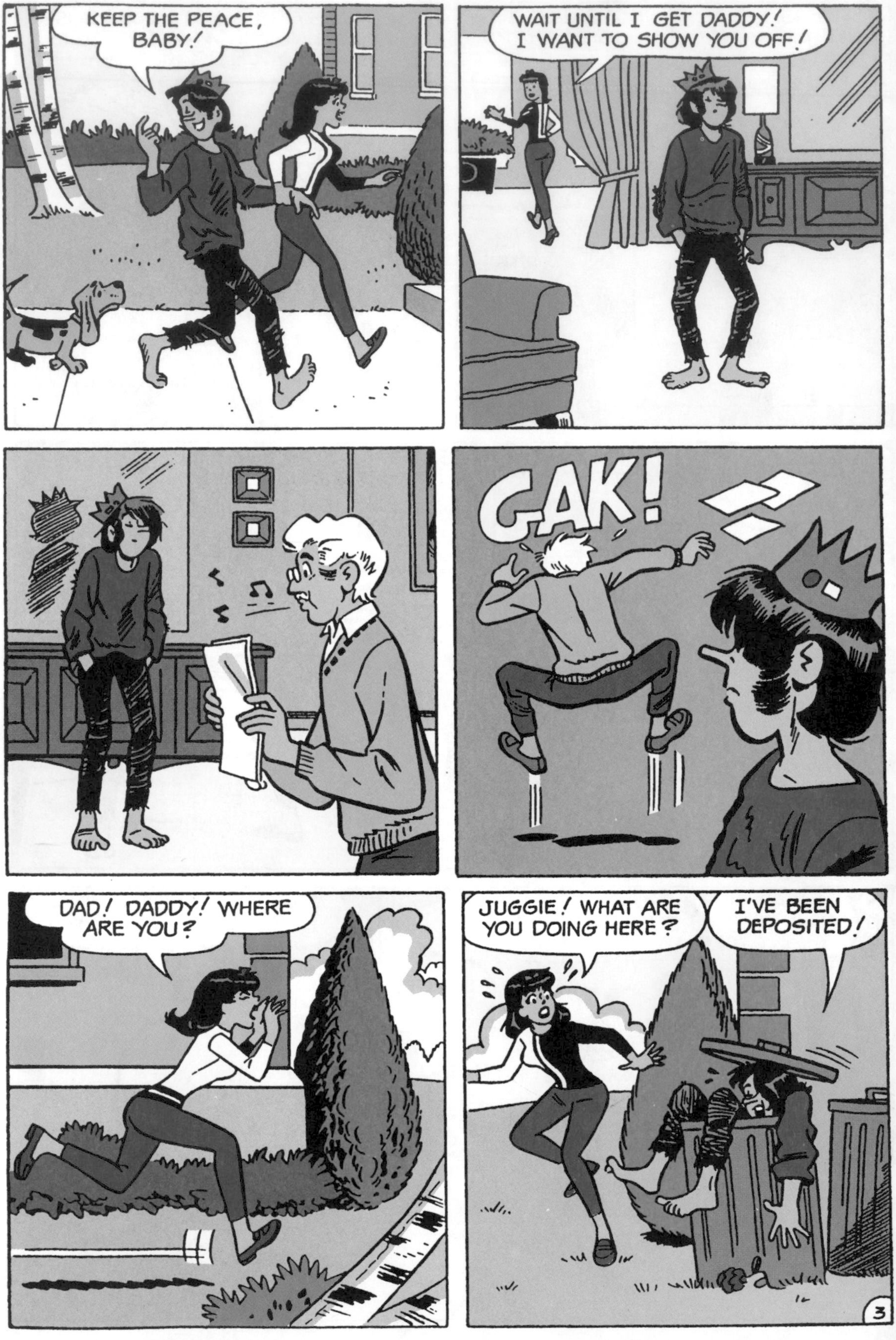
KEEP THE PEACE, BABY!
WAIT UNTIL I GET DADDY! I WANT TO SHOW YOU OFF!
GAK!
DAD! DADDY! WHERE ARE YOU?
JUGGIE! WHAT ARE YOU DOING HERE?
I'VE BEEN DEPOSITED!
3

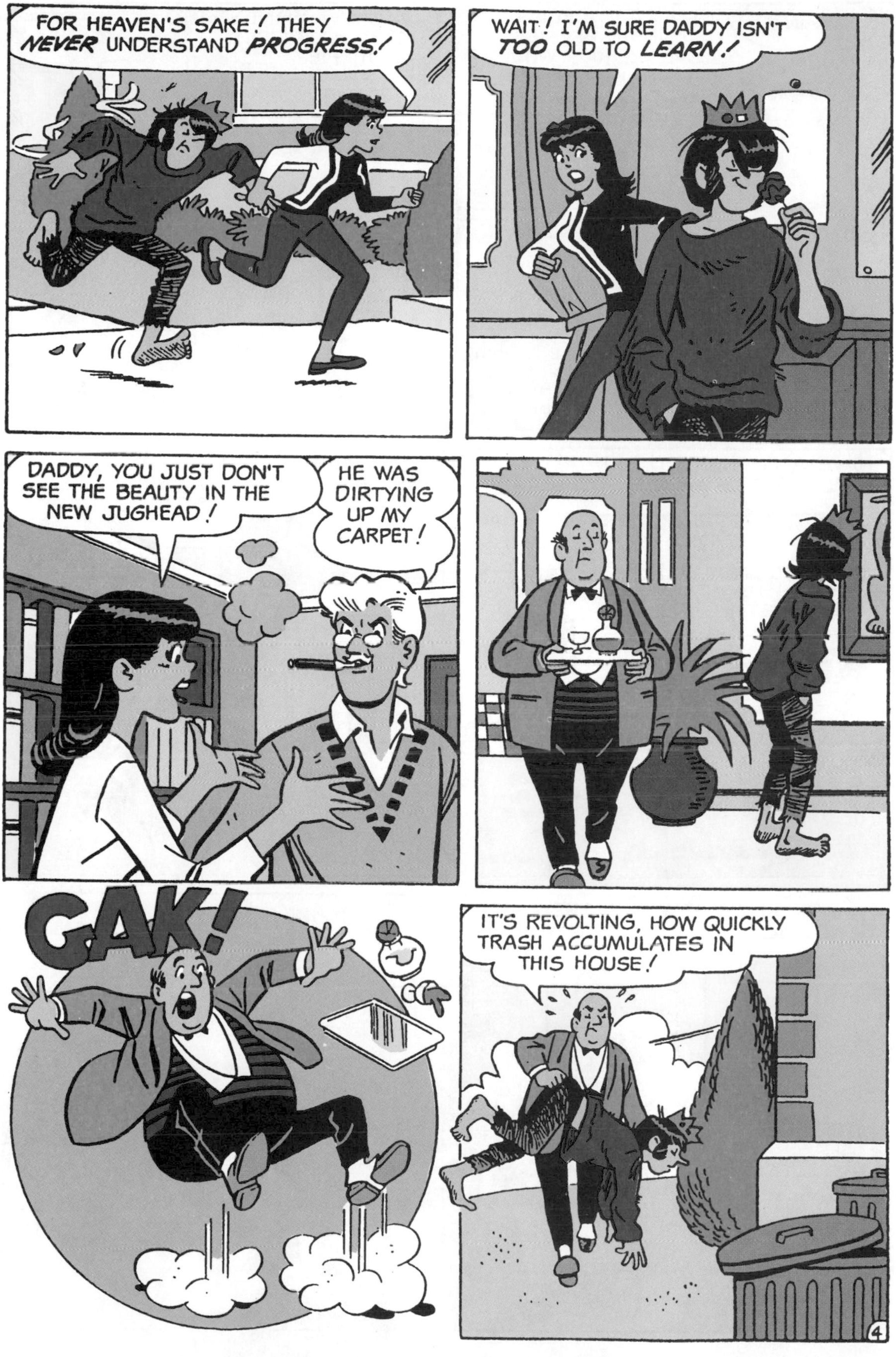
FOR HEAVEN'S SAKE! THEY NEVER UNDERSTAND PROGRESS!
WAIT! I'M SURE DADDY ISN'T TOO OLD TO LEARN!
DADDY, YOU JUST DON'T SEE THE BEAUTY IN THE NEW JUGHEAD!
HE WAS DIRTYING UP MY CARPET!
GAK!
IT'S REVOLTING, HOW QUICKLY TRASH ACCUMULATES IN THIS HOUSE!
4

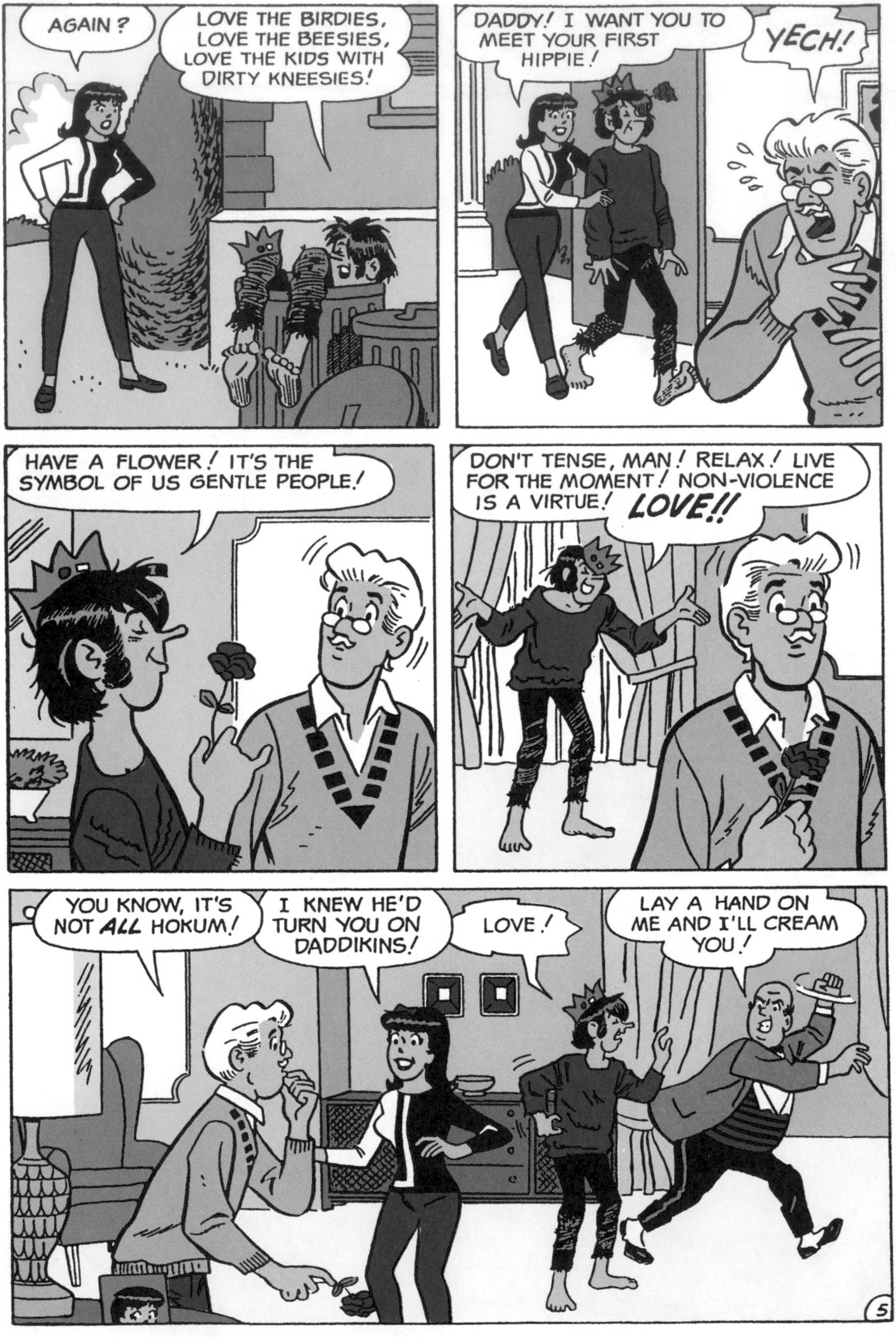
AGAIN ?
LOVE THE BIRDIES, LOVE THE BEESIES, LOVE THE KIDS WITH DIRTY KNEESIES!
DADDY! I WANT YOU TO MEET YOUR FIRST HIPPIE!
YECH!
HAVE A FLOWER! IT'S THE SYMBOL OF US GENTLE PEOPLE!
DON'T TENSE, MAN! RELAX! LIVE FOR THE MOMENT! NON-VIOLENCE IS A VIRTUE! LOVE!!
YOU KNOW, IT'S NOT ALL HOKUM!
I KNEW HE'D TURN YOU ON DADDIKINS!
LOVE!
LAY A HAND ON ME AND I'LL CREAM YOU!
5

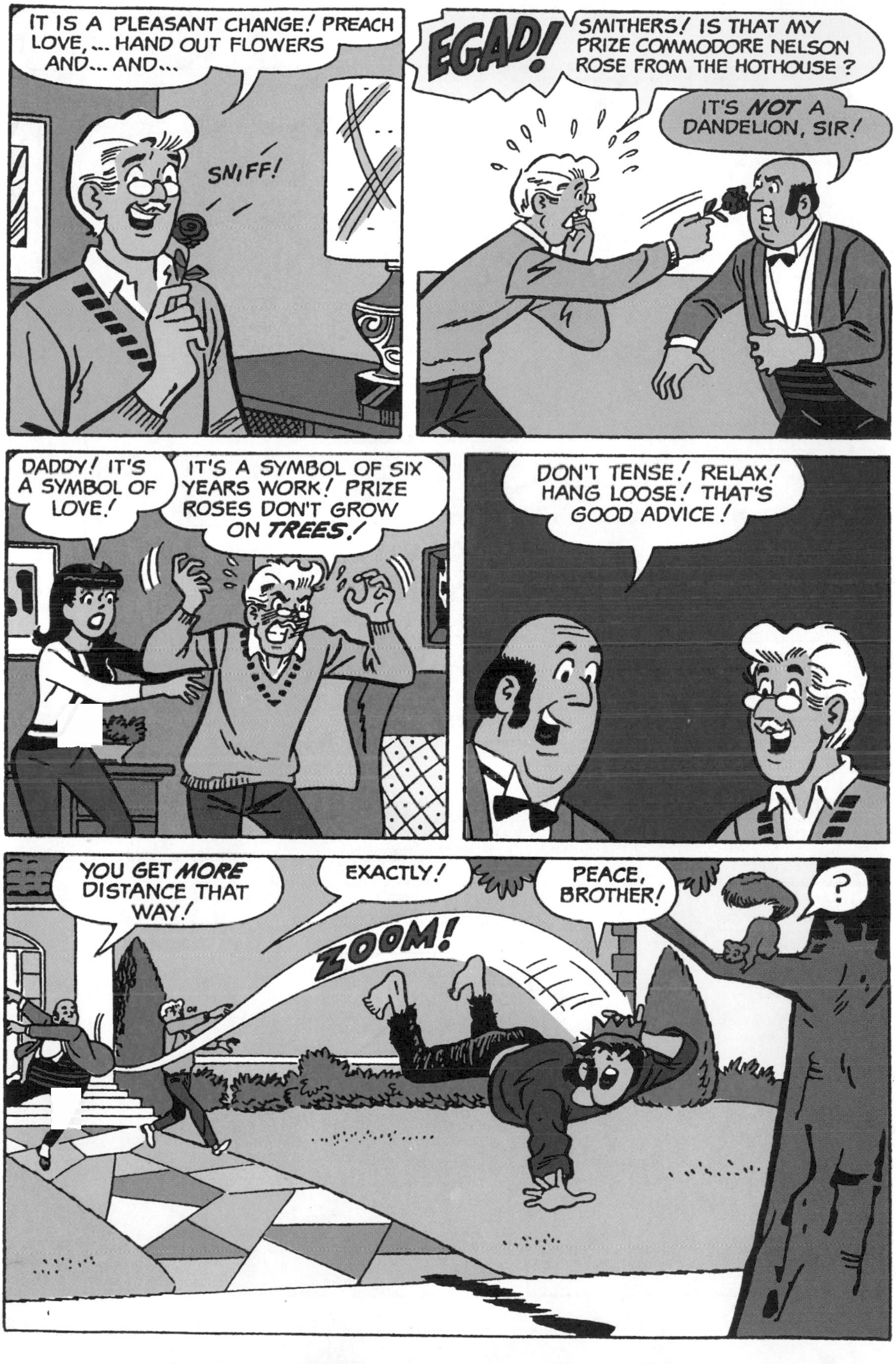
IT IS A PLEASANT CHANGE! PREACH LOVE, ... HAND OUT FLOWERS AND... AND...
SNIFF!
EGAD!
SMITHERS! IS THAT MY PRIZE COMMODORE NELSON ROSE FROM THE HOTHOUSE?
IT'S NOT A DANDELION, SIR!
DADDY! IT'S A SYMBOL OF LOVE!
IT'S A SYMBOL OF SIX YEARS WORK! PRIZE ROSES DON'T GROW ON TREES!
DON'T TENSE! RELAX! HANG LOOSE! THAT'S GOOD ADVICE!
YOU GET MORE DISTANCE THAT WAY!
EXACTLY!
PEACE, BROTHER!
?
ZOOM!

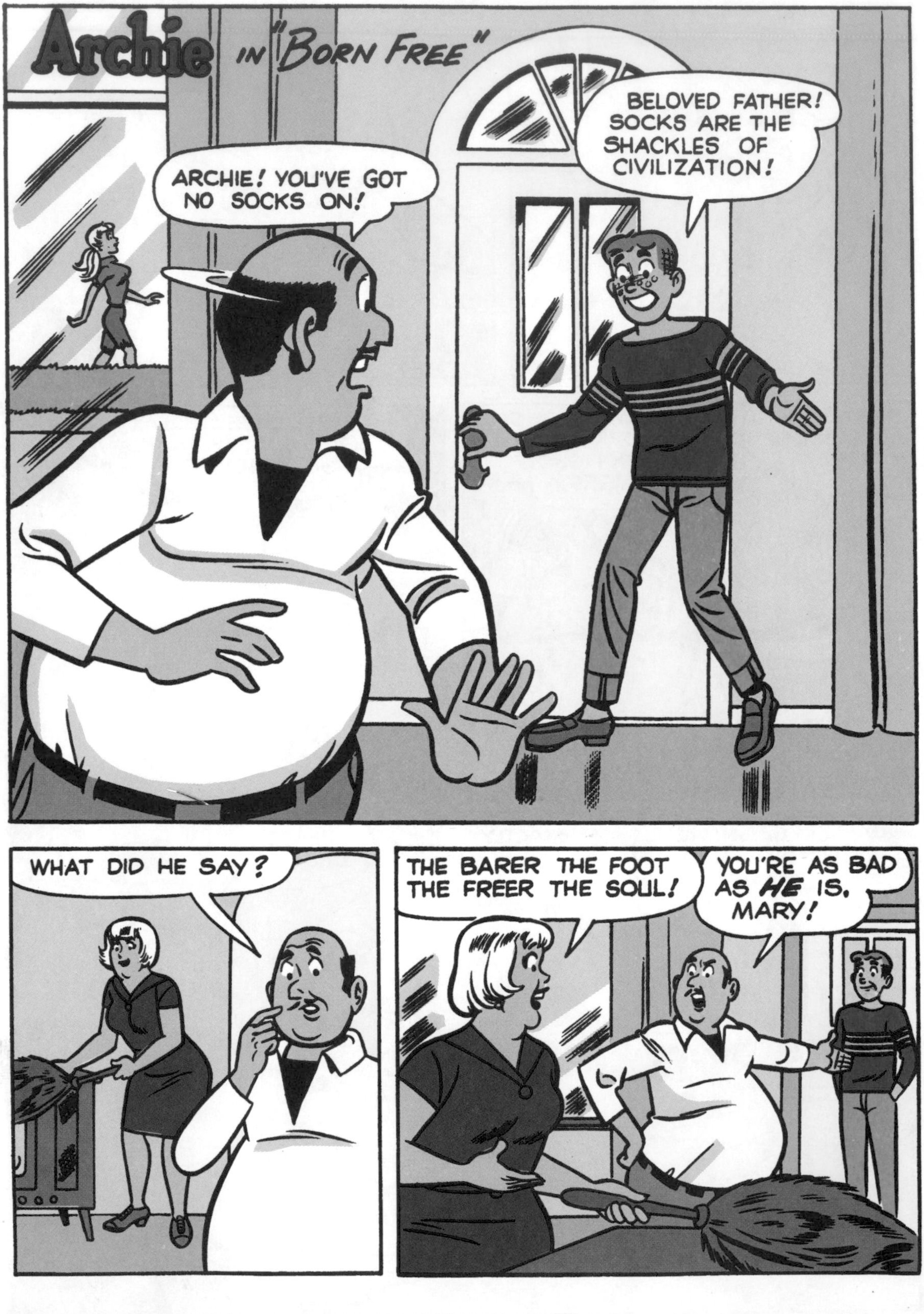
Archie IN "BORN FREE"
ARCHIE! YOU'VE GOT NO SOCKS ON!
BELOVED FATHER! SOCKS ARE THE SHACKLES OF CIVILIZATION!
WHAT DID HE SAY?
THE BARER THE FOOT THE FREER THE SOUL!
YOU'RE AS BAD AS HE IS, MARY!

ORIGINALLY PRESENTED IN **PEP #219**, JULY, 1968

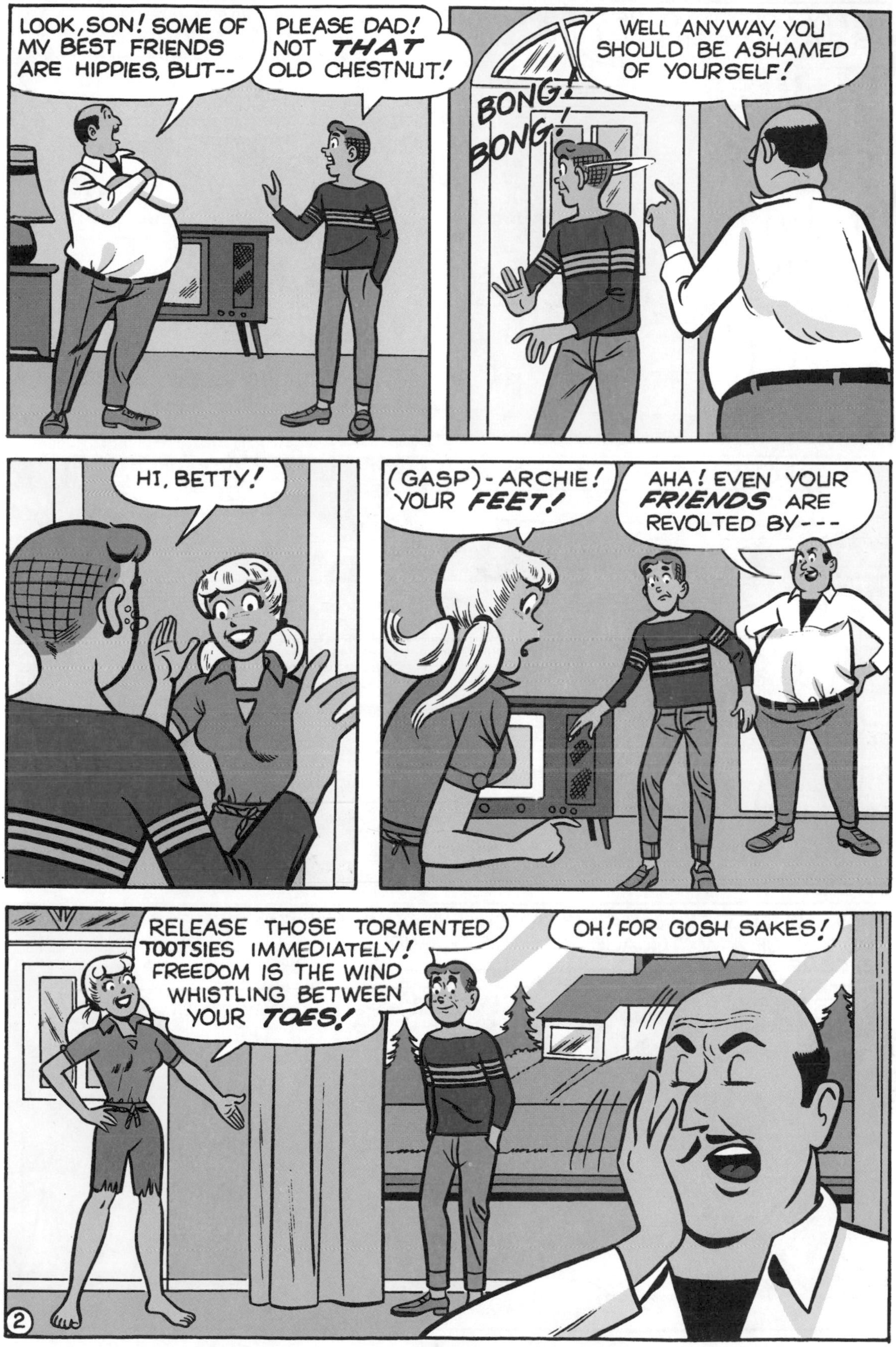
LOOK, SON! SOME OF MY BEST FRIENDS ARE HIPPIES, BUT--
PLEASE DAD! NOT THAT OLD CHESTNUT!
BONG! BONG!
WELL ANYWAY, YOU SHOULD BE ASHAMED OF YOURSELF!
HI, BETTY!
(GASP)-ARCHIE! YOUR FEET!
AHA! EVEN YOUR FRIENDS ARE REVOLTED BY---
RELEASE THOSE TORMENTED TOOTSIES IMMEDIATELY! FREEDOM IS THE WIND WHISTLING BETWEEN YOUR TOES!
OH! FOR GOSH SAKES!
2

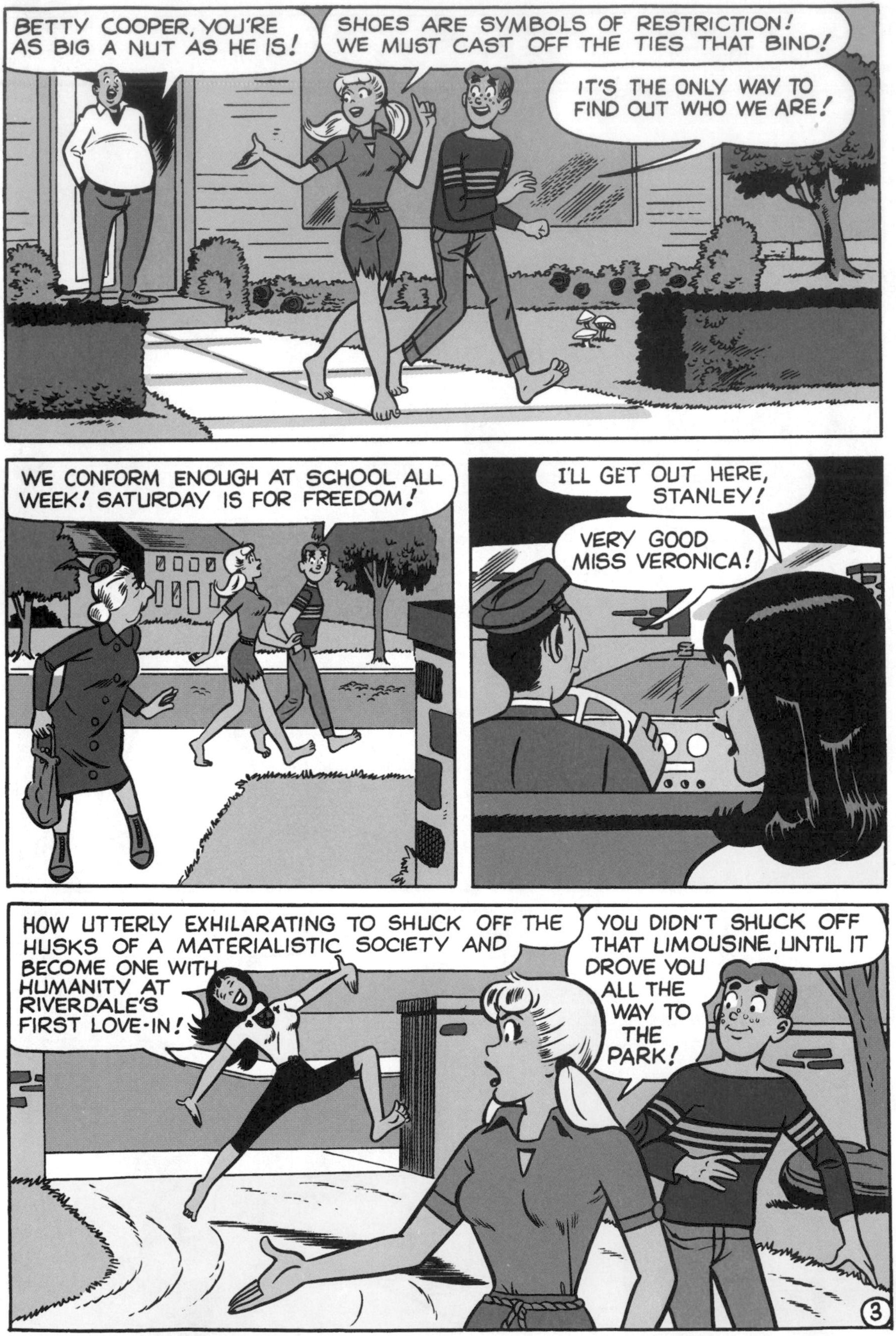
BETTY COOPER, YOU'RE AS BIG A NUT AS HE IS!
SHOES ARE SYMBOLS OF RESTRICTION! WE MUST CAST OFF THE TIES THAT BIND!
IT'S THE ONLY WAY TO FIND OUT WHO WE ARE!
WE CONFORM ENOUGH AT SCHOOL ALL WEEK! SATURDAY IS FOR FREEDOM!
I'LL GET OUT HERE, STANLEY!
VERY GOOD MISS VERONICA!
HOW UTTERLY EXHILARATING TO SHUCK OFF THE HUSKS OF A MATERIALISTIC SOCIETY AND BECOME ONE WITH HUMANITY AT RIVERDALE'S FIRST LOVE-IN!
YOU DIDN'T SHUCK OFF THAT LIMOUSINE, UNTIL IT DROVE YOU ALL THE WAY TO THE PARK!
3

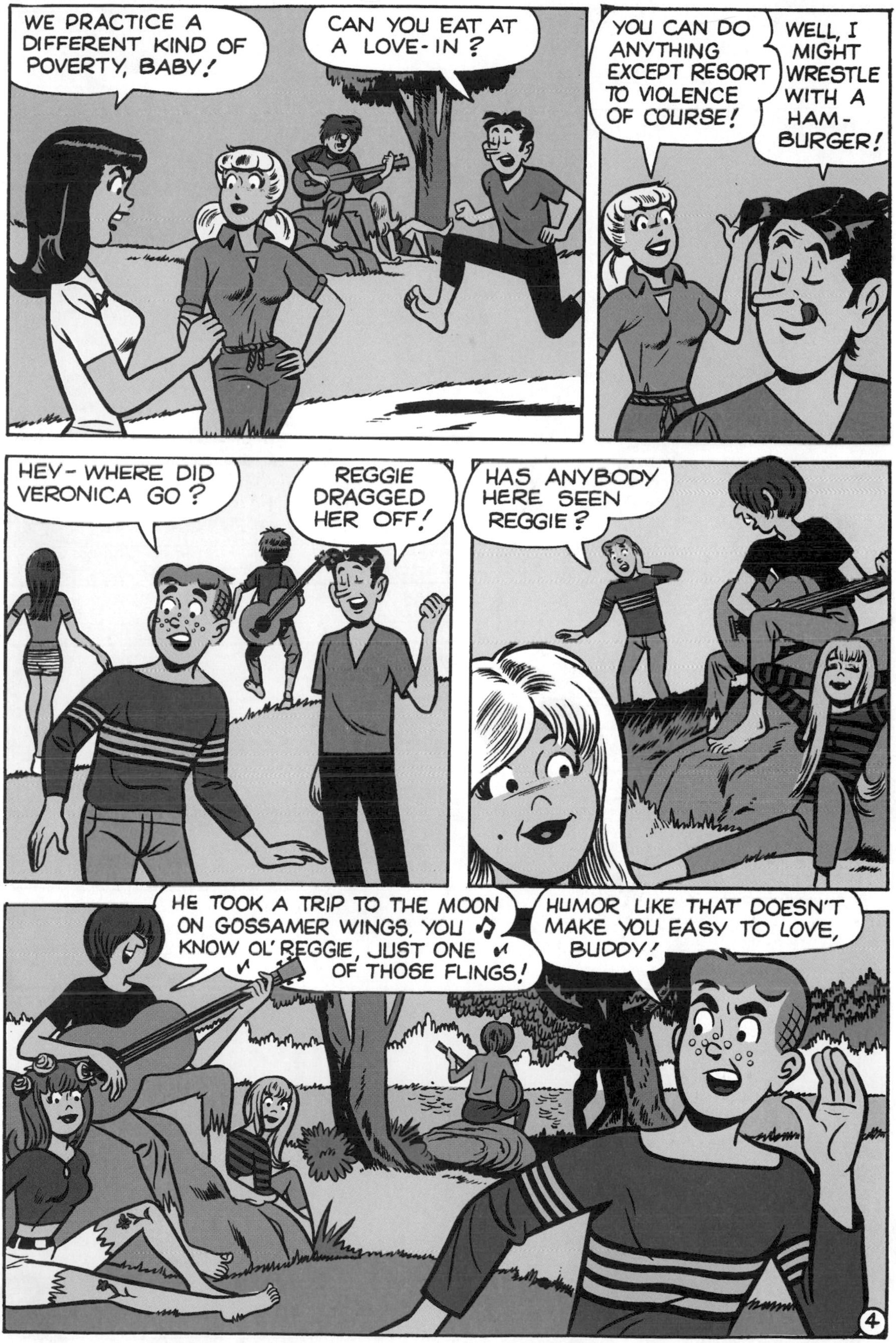
WE PRACTICE A DIFFERENT KIND OF POVERTY, BABY!
CAN YOU EAT AT A LOVE-IN?
YOU CAN DO ANYTHING EXCEPT RESORT TO VIOLENCE OF COURSE!
WELL, I MIGHT WRESTLE WITH A HAM-BURGER!
HEY- WHERE DID VERONICA GO?
REGGIE DRAGGED HER OFF!
HAS ANYBODY HERE SEEN REGGIE?
HE TOOK A TRIP TO THE MOON ON GOSSAMER WINGS. YOU KNOW OL' REGGIE, JUST ONE OF THOSE FLINGS!
HUMOR LIKE THAT DOESN'T MAKE YOU EASY TO LOVE, BUDDY!
4

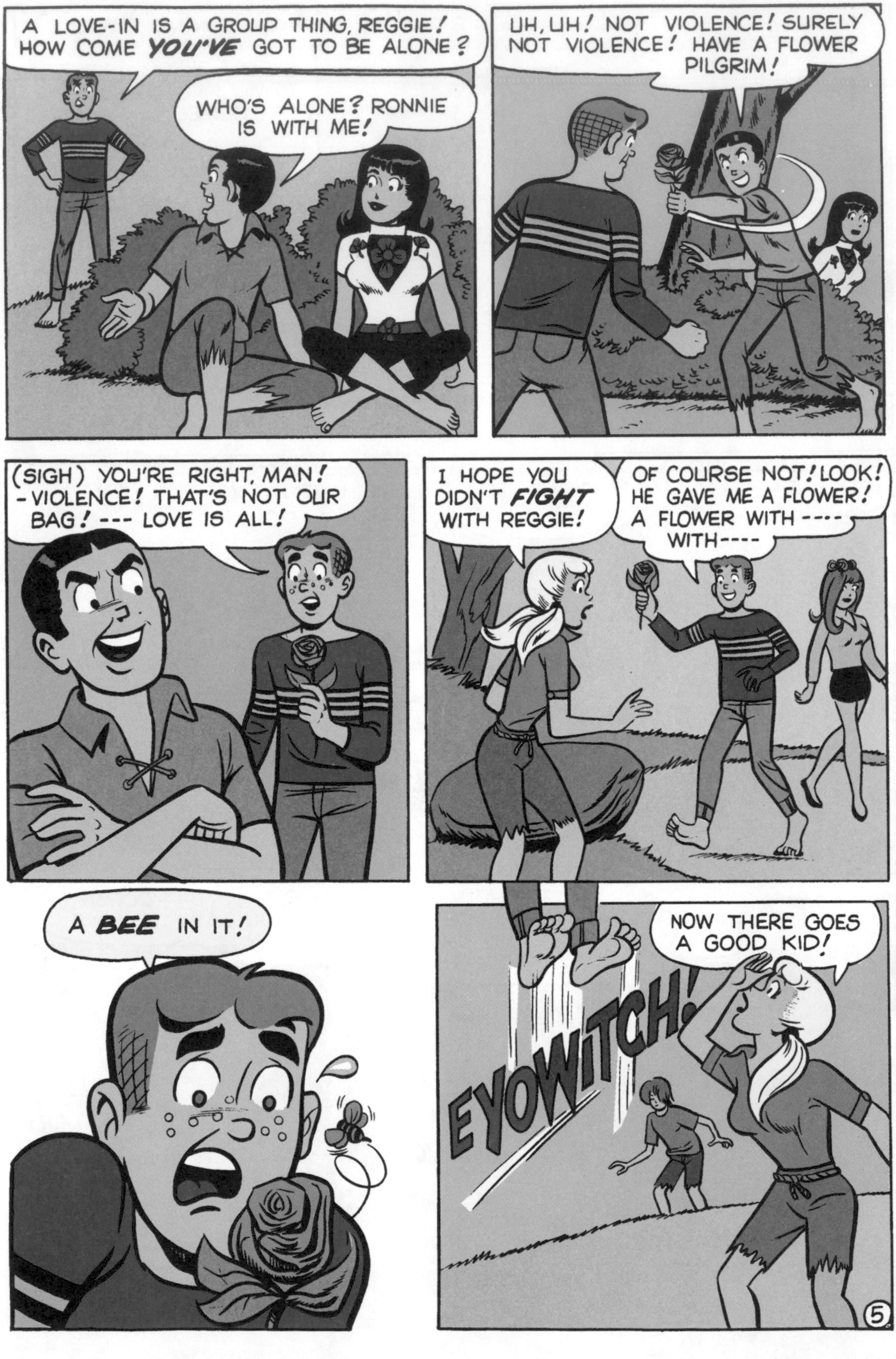
A LOVE-IN IS A GROUP THING, REGGIE! HOW COME YOU'VE GOT TO BE ALONE?
WHO'S ALONE? RONNIE IS WITH ME!
UH, UH! NOT VIOLENCE! SURELY NOT VIOLENCE! HAVE A FLOWER PILGRIM!
(SIGH) YOU'RE RIGHT, MAN! -VIOLENCE! THAT'S NOT OUR BAG! --- LOVE IS ALL!
I HOPE YOU DIDN'T FIGHT WITH REGGIE!
OF COURSE NOT! LOOK! HE GAVE ME A FLOWER! A FLOWER WITH ---- WITH----
A BEE IN IT!
NOW THERE GOES A GOOD KID!
EYOWITCH!
5

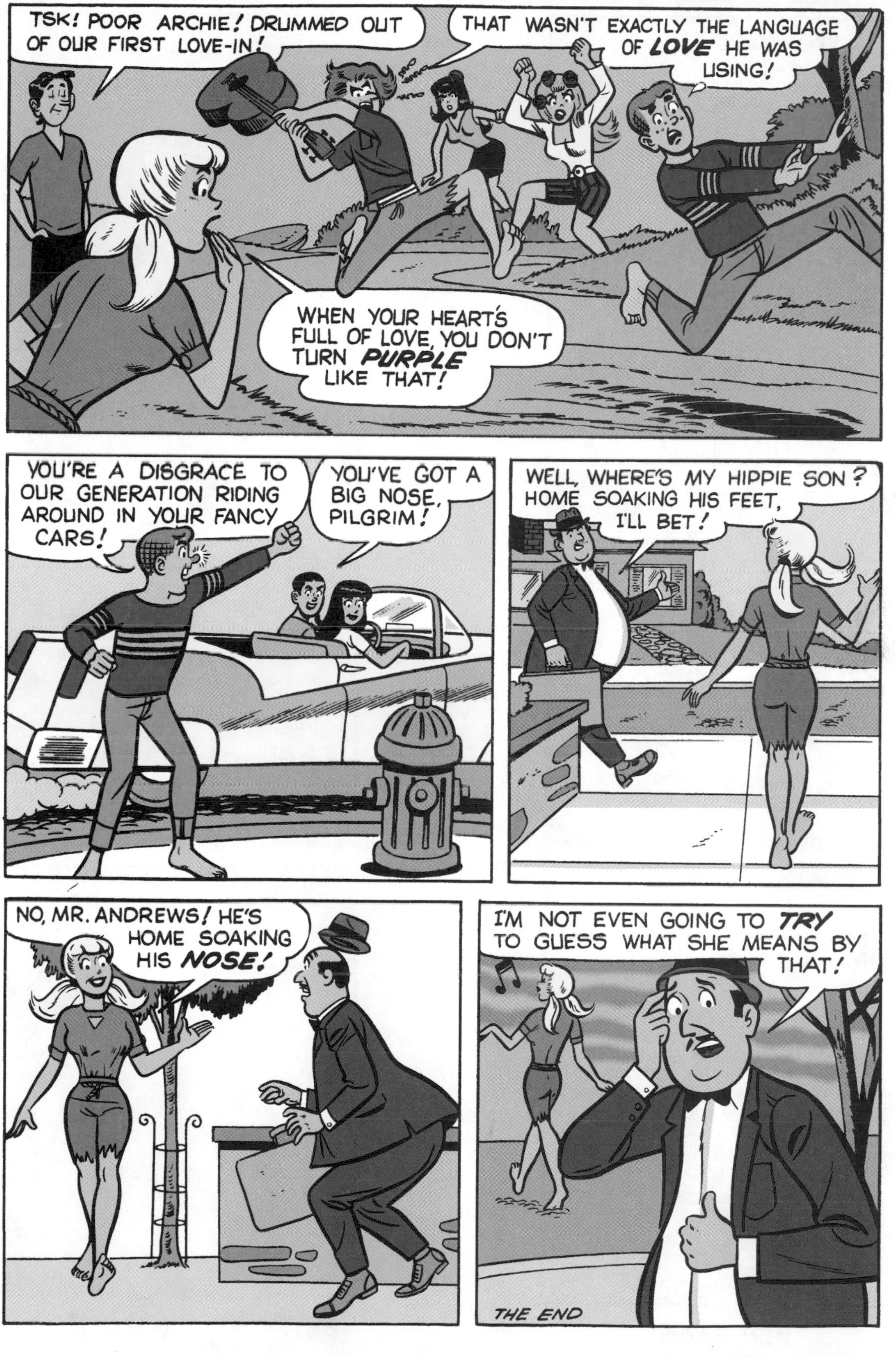
TSK! POOR ARCHIE! DRUMMED OUT OF OUR FIRST LOVE-IN!
THAT WASN'T EXACTLY THE LANGUAGE OF LOVE HE WAS USING!
WHEN YOUR HEART'S FULL OF LOVE, YOU DON'T TURN PURPLE LIKE THAT!
YOU'RE A DISGRACE TO OUR GENERATION RIDING AROUND IN YOUR FANCY CARS!
YOU'VE GOT A BIG NOSE, PILGRIM!
WELL, WHERE'S MY HIPPIE SON? HOME SOAKING HIS FEET, I'LL BET!
NO, MR. ANDREWS! HE'S HOME SOAKING HIS NOSE!
I'M NOT EVEN GOING TO TRY TO GUESS WHAT SHE MEANS BY THAT!
THE END

A GALLERY OF CLASSIC 60'S COVER GAGS

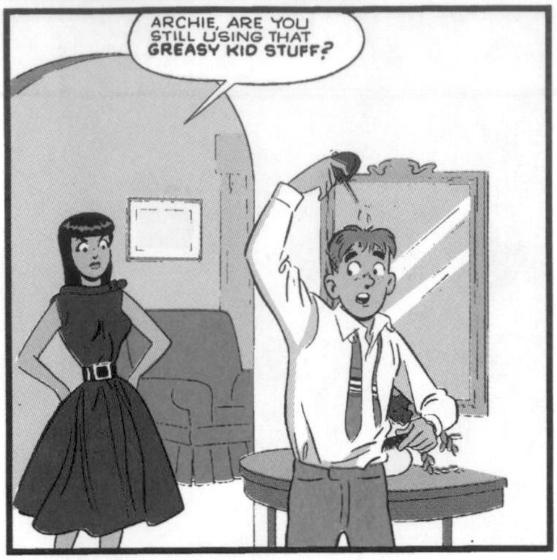
ARCHIE, ARE YOU STILL USING THAT GREASY KID STUFF?

ARCHIE #138
JULY, 1963

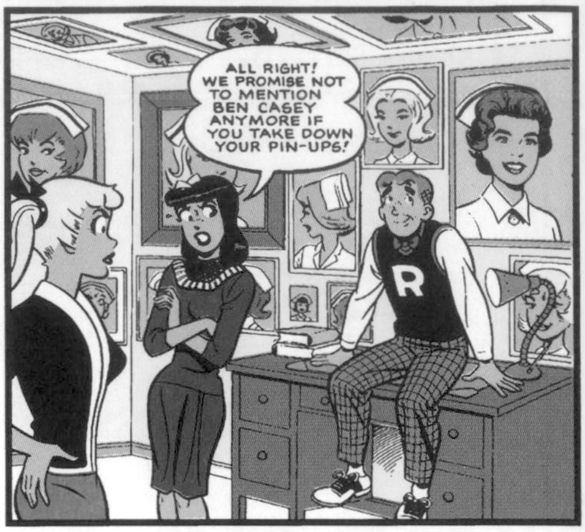
ALL RIGHT! WE PROMISE NOT TO MENTION BEN CASEY ANYMORE IF YOU TAKE DOWN YOUR PIN-UPS!
R

PALS'N-GALS
SPRING, 1963

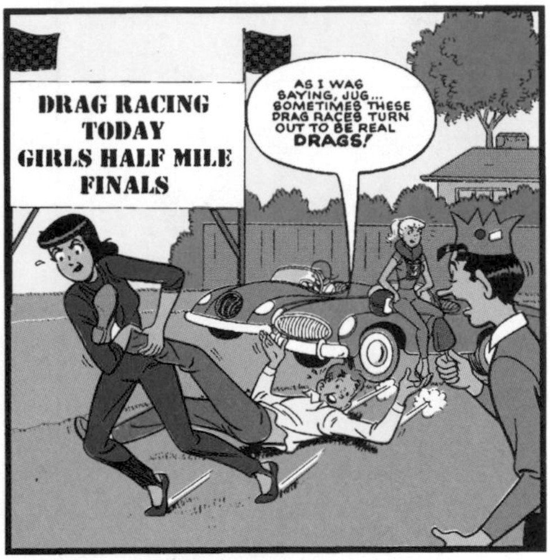
DRAG RACING TODAY GIRLS HALF MILE FINALS
AS I WAS SAYING, JUG... SOMETIMES THESE DRAG RACES TURN OUT TO BE REAL DRAGS!

ARCHIE #148
AUG., 1964

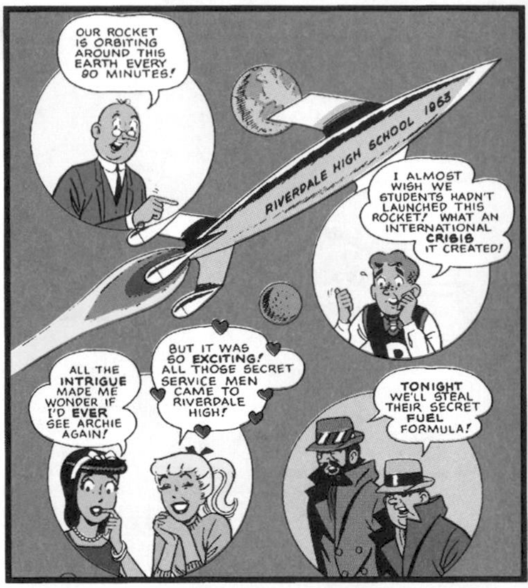
OUR ROCKET IS ORBITING AROUND THIS EARTH EVERY 80 MINUTES!
RIVERDALE HIGH SCHOOL 1963
I ALMOST WISH WE STUDENTS HADN'T LAUNCHED THIS ROCKET! WHAT AN INTERNATIONAL CRISIS IT CREATED!
ALL THE INTRIGUE MADE ME WONDER IF I'D EVER SEE ARCHIE AGAIN!
BUT IT WAS SO EXCITING! ALL THOSE SECRET SERVICE MEN CAME TO RIVERDALE HIGH!
TONIGHT WE'LL STEAL THEIR SECRET FUEL FORMULA!

LIFE WITH ARCHIE #19
MARCH, 1963

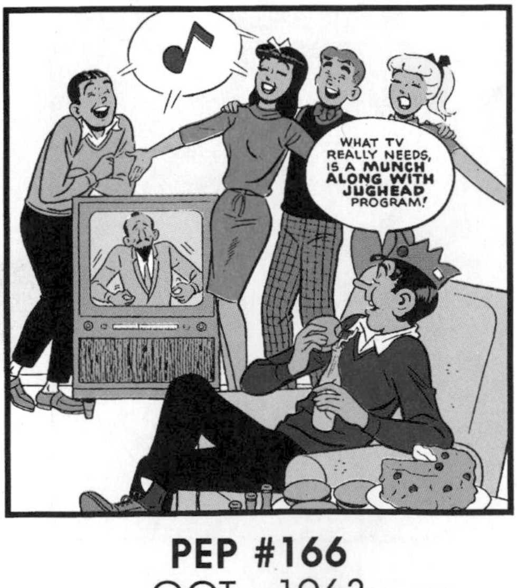
WHAT TV REALLY NEEDS, IS A MUNCH ALONG WITH JUGHEAD PROGRAM!

PEP #166
OCT., 1963

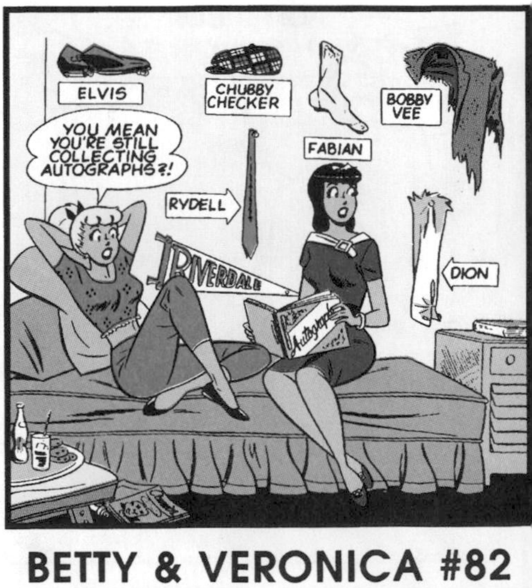
ELVIS
CHUBBY CHECKER
BOBBY VEE
FABIAN
YOU MEAN YOU'RE STILL COLLECTING AUTOGRAPHS?!
RYDELL
DION
RIVERDALE
Autographs

BETTY & VERONICA #82
OCT., 1964

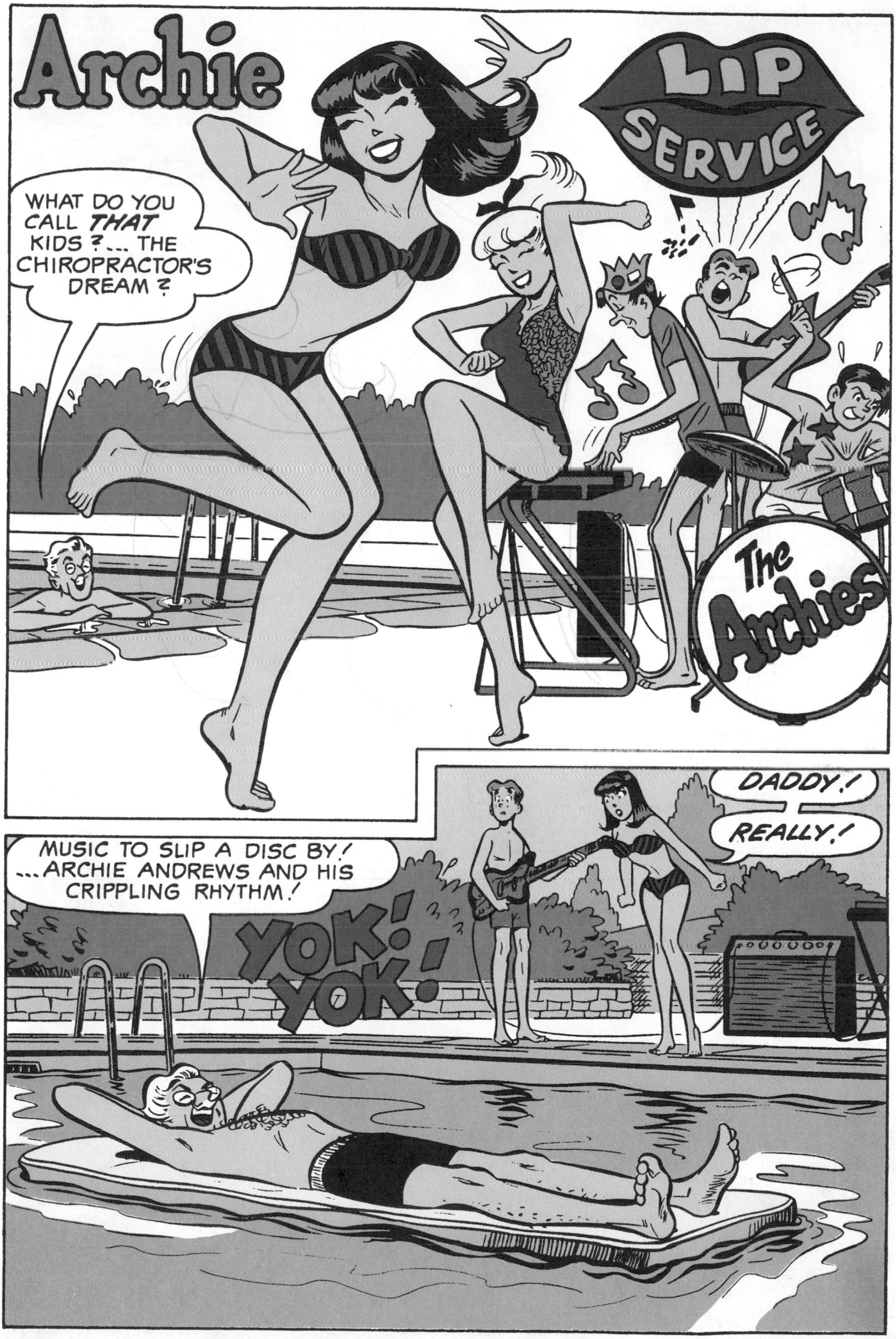
Archie
LIP SERVICE
WHAT DO YOU CALL THAT KIDS ?... THE CHIROPRACTOR'S DREAM ?
The Archies
MUSIC TO SLIP A DISC BY! ...ARCHIE ANDREWS AND HIS CRIPPLING RHYTHM!
DADDY!
REALLY!
YOK! YOK!

ORIGINALLY PRESENTED IN **LIFE WITH ARCHIE #78**, OCTOBER, 1968

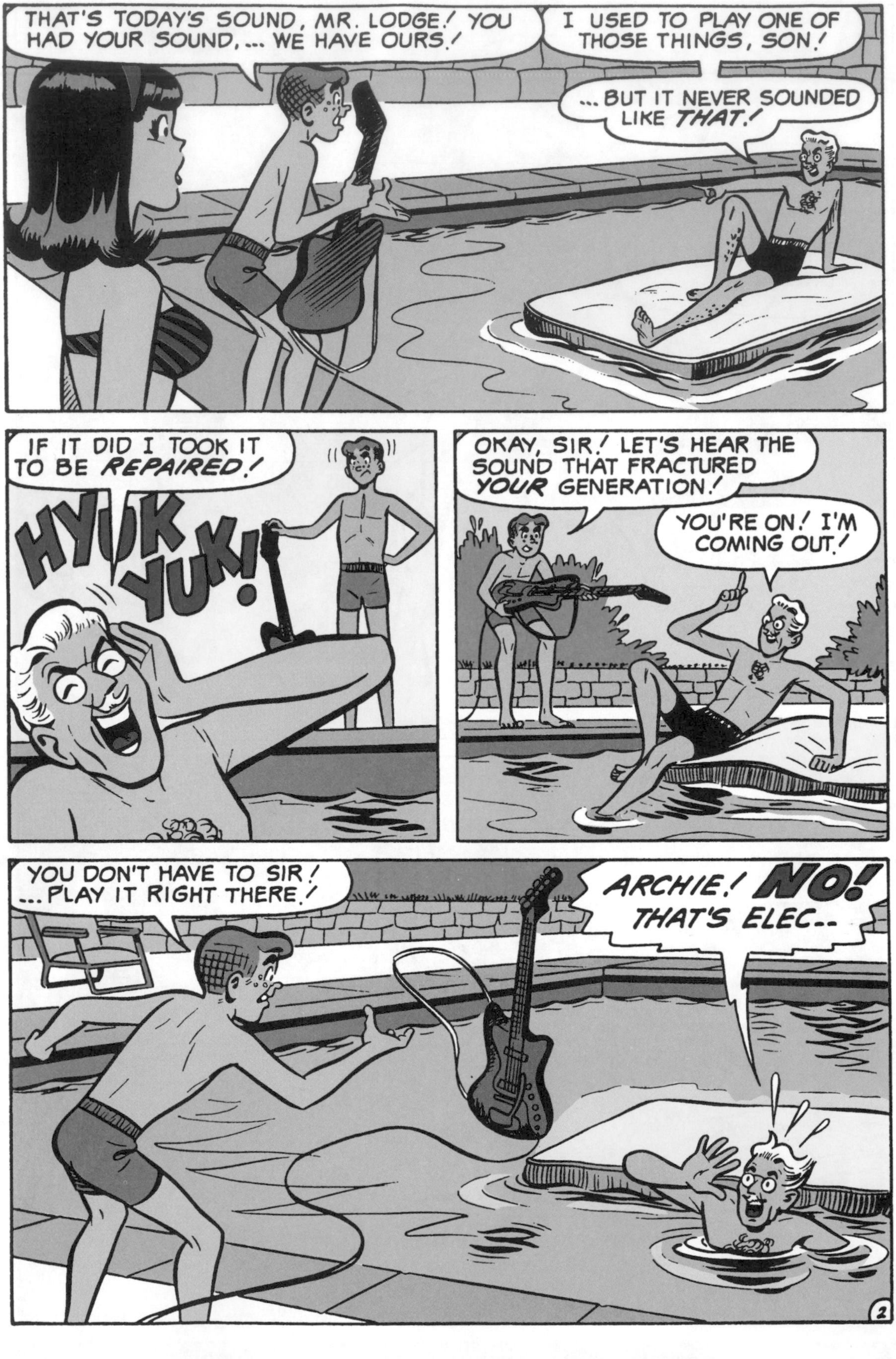
THAT'S TODAY'S SOUND, MR. LODGE! YOU HAD YOUR SOUND, ... WE HAVE OURS!
I USED TO PLAY ONE OF THOSE THINGS, SON!
... BUT IT NEVER SOUNDED LIKE THAT!
IF IT DID I TOOK IT TO BE REPAIRED!
HYUK YUK!
OKAY, SIR! LET'S HEAR THE SOUND THAT FRACTURED YOUR GENERATION!
YOU'RE ON! I'M COMING OUT!
YOU DON'T HAVE TO SIR! ... PLAY IT RIGHT THERE!
ARCHIE! NO! THAT'S ELEC...
2

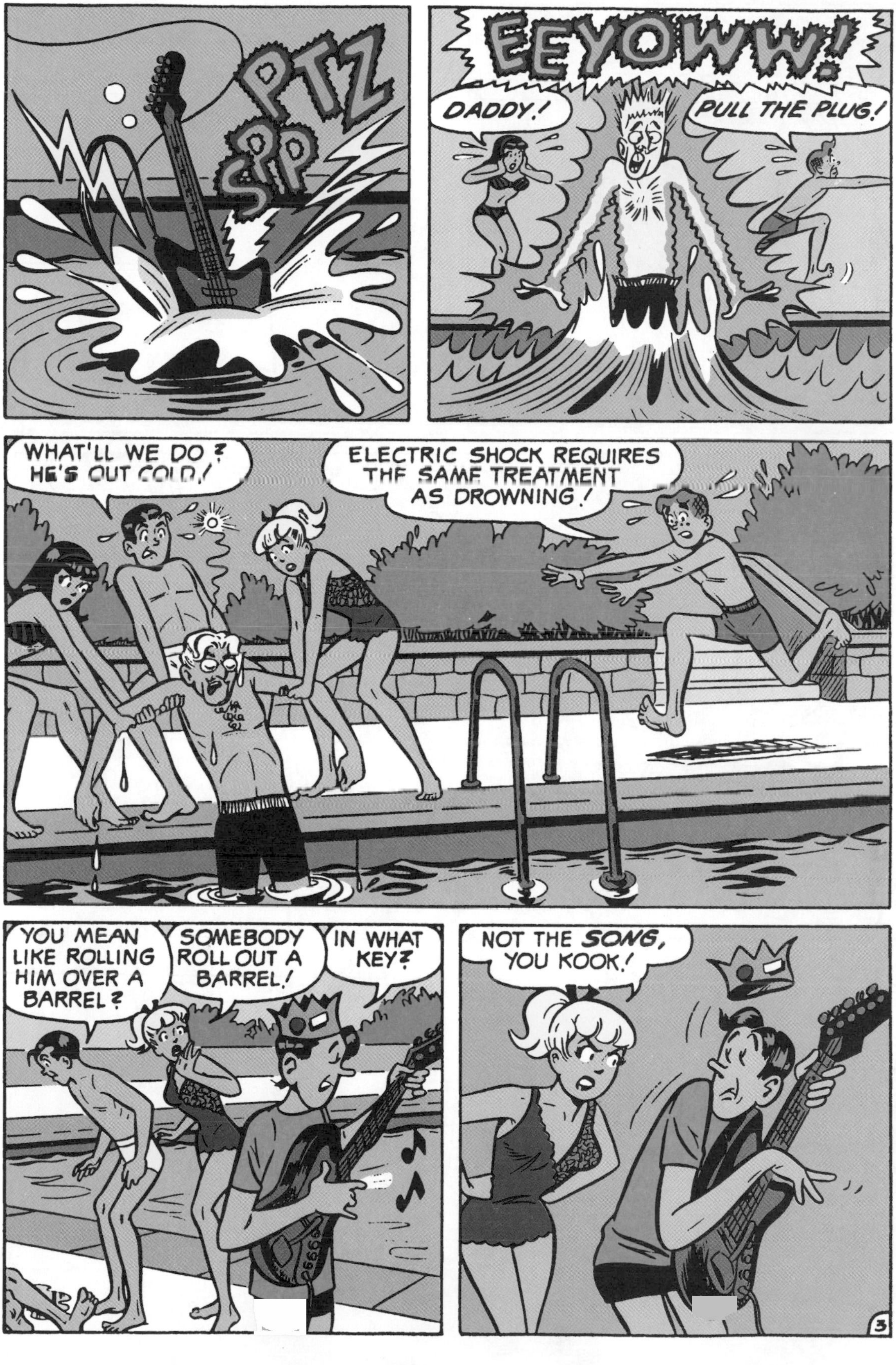
PTZ
SPP
EEYOWW!
DADDY!
PULL THE PLUG!
WHAT'LL WE DO? HE'S OUT COLD!
ELECTRIC SHOCK REQUIRES THE SAME TREATMENT AS DROWNING!
YOU MEAN LIKE ROLLING HIM OVER A BARREL?
SOMEBODY ROLL OUT A BARREL!
IN WHAT KEY?
NOT THE SONG, YOU KOOK!
3

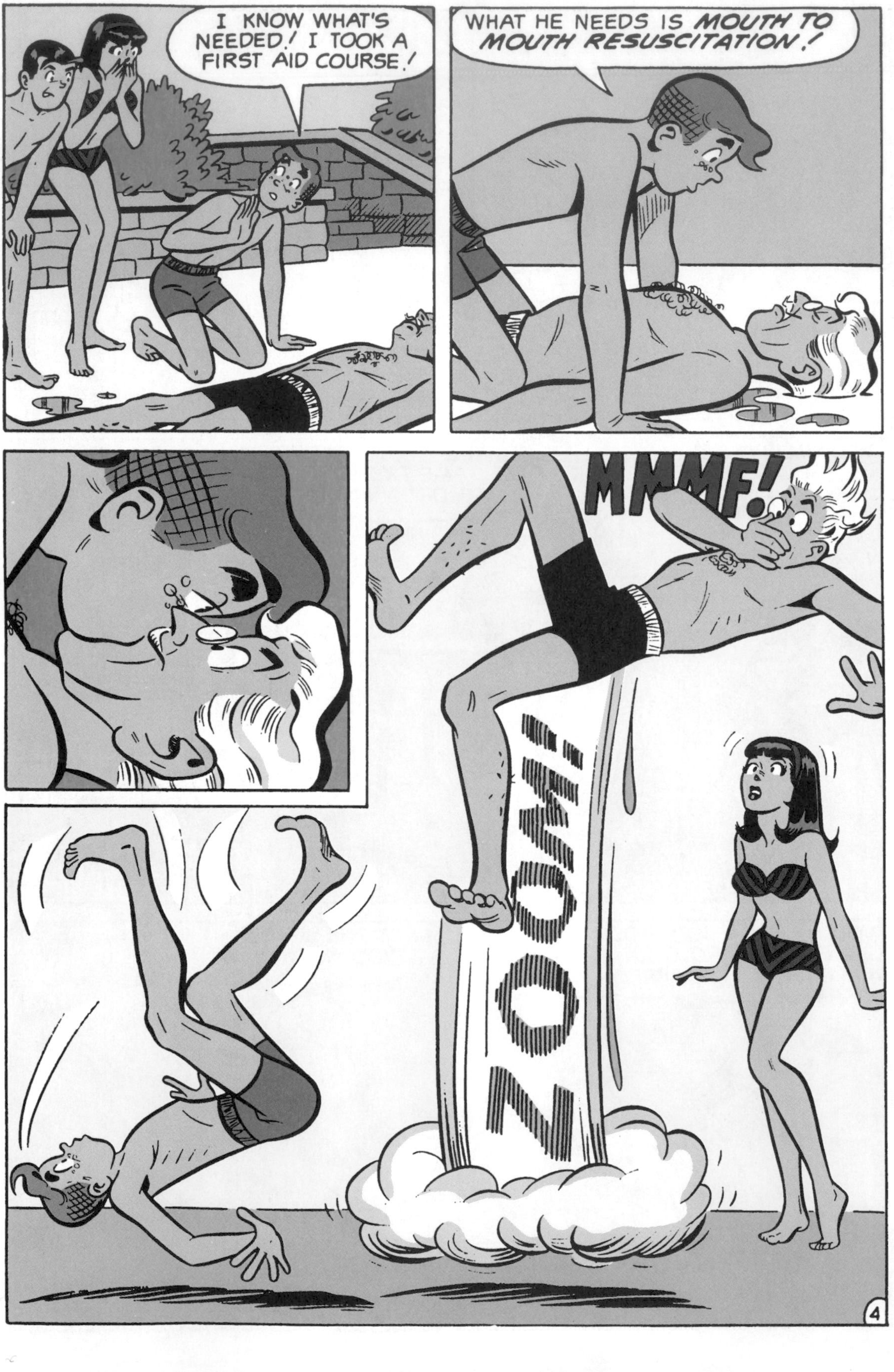
I KNOW WHAT'S NEEDED! I TOOK A FIRST AID COURSE!
WHAT HE NEEDS IS MOUTH TO MOUTH RESUSCITATION!
MMMF!
ZOOM!!
4

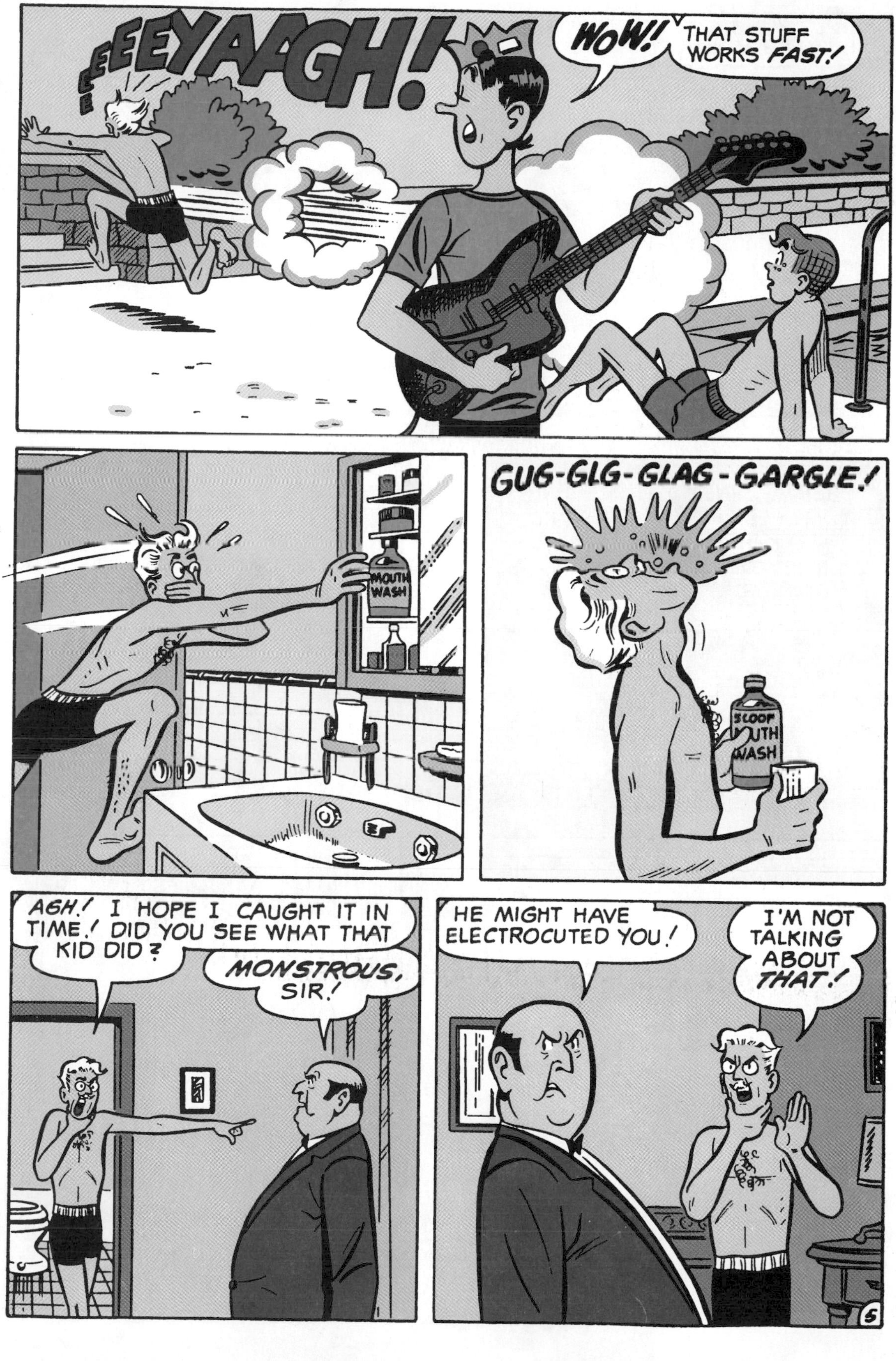
EEEYAAGH!
WOW! THAT STUFF WORKS FAST!
MOUTH WASH
GUG-GIG-GLAG-GARGLE!
AGH! I HOPE I CAUGHT IT IN TIME! DID YOU SEE WHAT THAT KID DID?
MONSTROUS, SIR!
HE MIGHT HAVE ELECTROCUTED YOU!
I'M NOT TALKING ABOUT THAT!
5

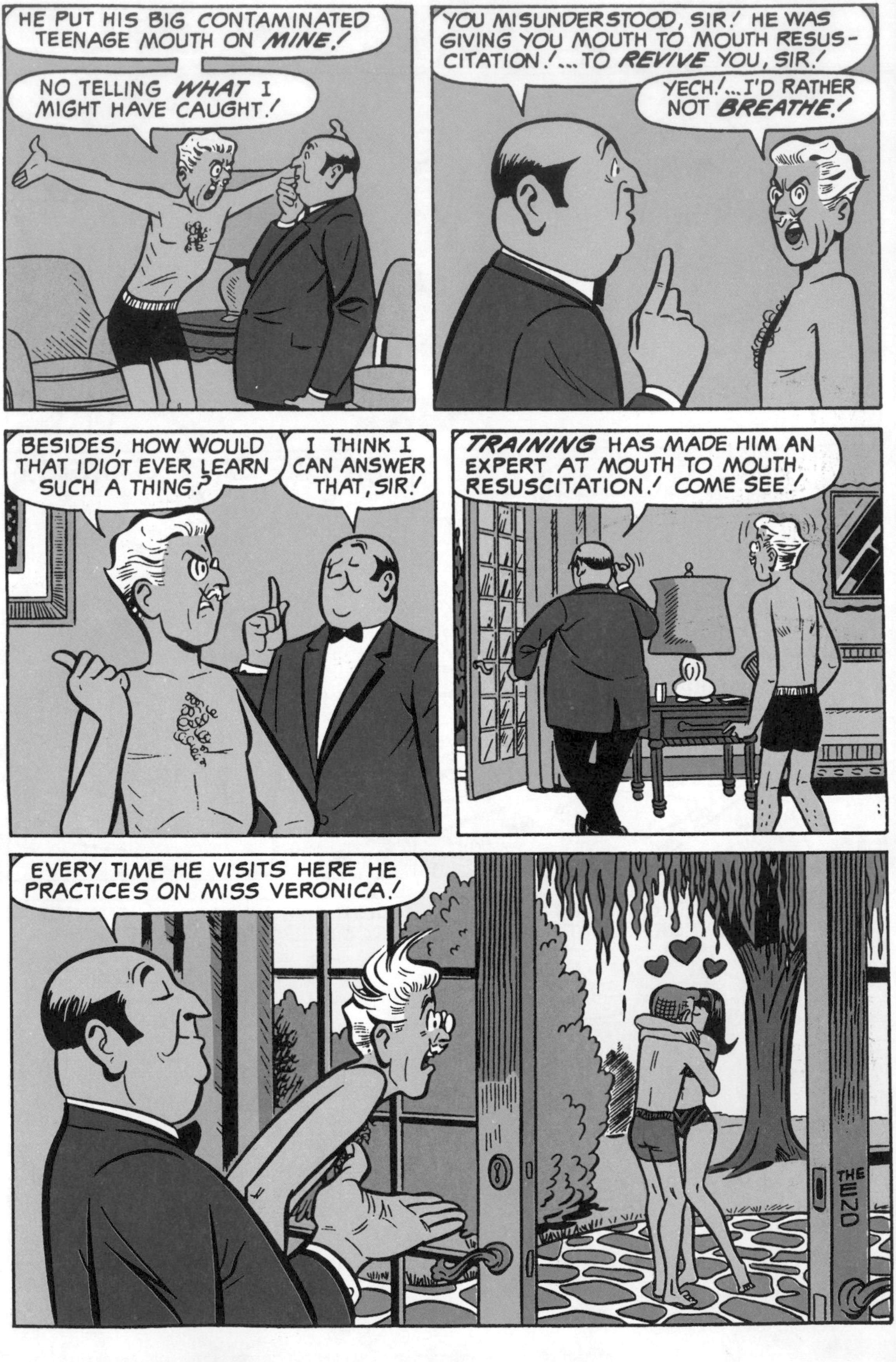
HE PUT HIS BIG CONTAMINATED TEENAGE MOUTH ON MINE!
NO TELLING WHAT I MIGHT HAVE CAUGHT!
YOU MISUNDERSTOOD, SIR! HE WAS GIVING YOU MOUTH TO MOUTH RESUSCITATION!...TO REVIVE YOU, SIR!
YECH!...I'D RATHER NOT BREATHE!
BESIDES, HOW WOULD THAT IDIOT EVER LEARN SUCH A THING?
I THINK I CAN ANSWER THAT, SIR!
TRAINING HAS MADE HIM AN EXPERT AT MOUTH TO MOUTH RESUSCITATION! COME SEE!
EVERY TIME HE VISITS HERE HE PRACTICES ON MISS VERONICA!
THE END

Betty -IN- THE TIME OF YOUR LIFE

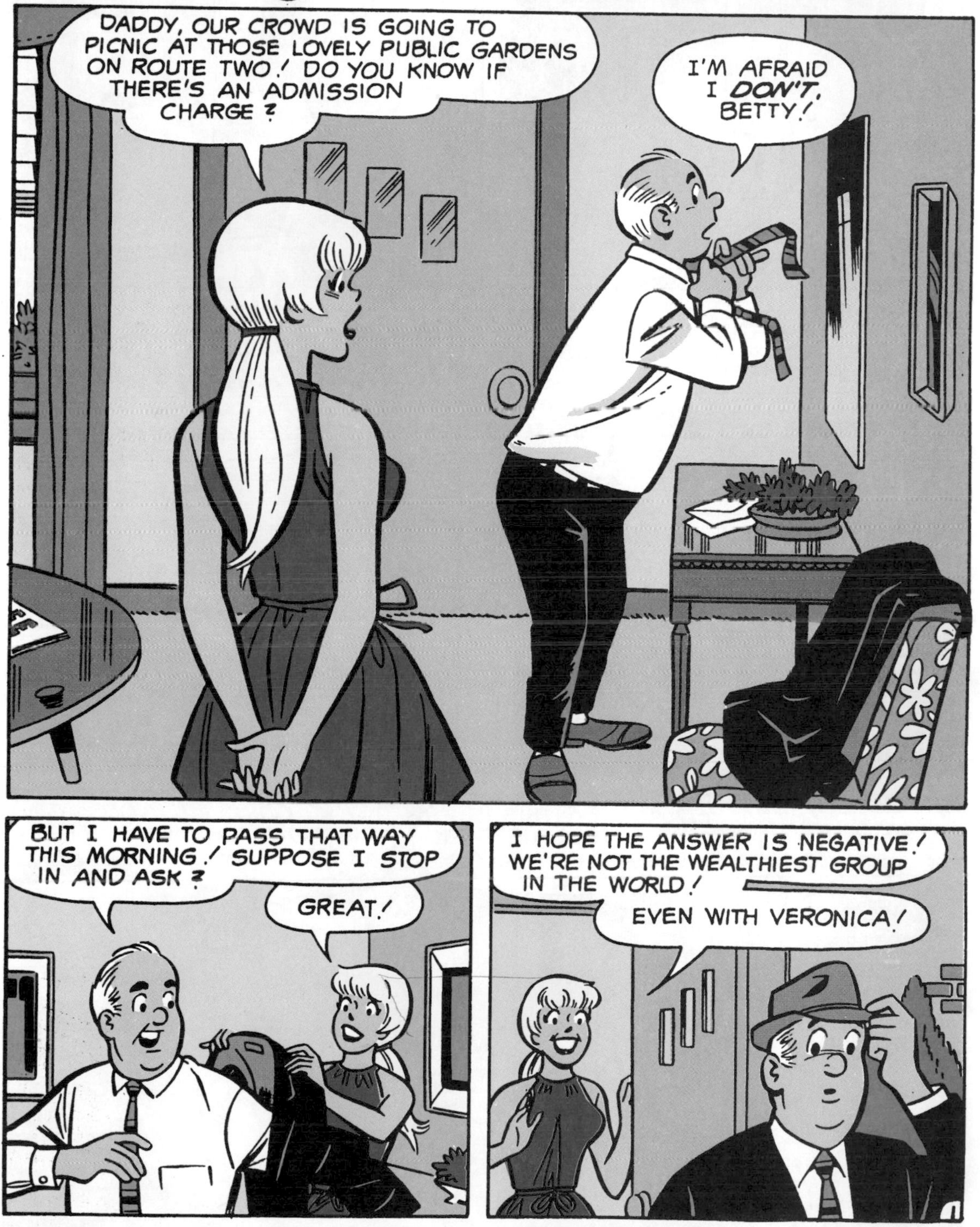
DADDY, OUR CROWD IS GOING TO PICNIC AT THOSE LOVELY PUBLIC GARDENS ON ROUTE TWO! DO YOU KNOW IF THERE'S AN ADMISSION CHARGE?
I'M AFRAID I *DON'T*, BETTY!
BUT I HAVE TO PASS THAT WAY THIS MORNING! SUPPOSE I STOP IN AND ASK?
GREAT!
I HOPE THE ANSWER IS NEGATIVE! WE'RE NOT THE WEALTHIEST GROUP IN THE WORLD!
EVEN WITH VERONICA!

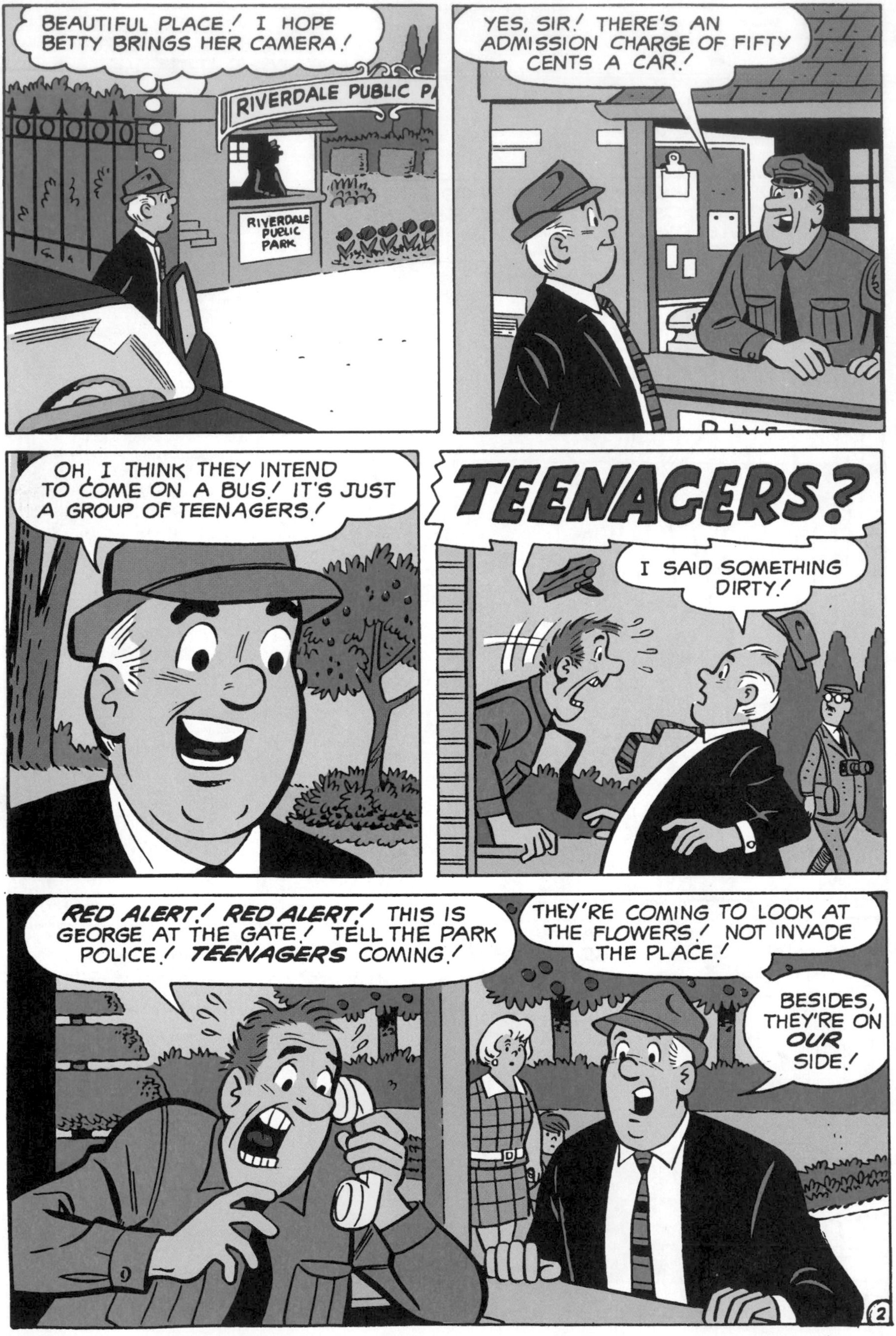
BEAUTIFUL PLACE! I HOPE BETTY BRINGS HER CAMERA!
RIVERDALE PUBLIC PA
RIVERDALE PUBLIC PARK
YES, SIR! THERE'S AN ADMISSION CHARGE OF FIFTY CENTS A CAR!
OH, I THINK THEY INTEND TO COME ON A BUS! IT'S JUST A GROUP OF TEENAGERS!
TEENAGERS?
I SAID SOMETHING DIRTY!
RED ALERT! RED ALERT! THIS IS GEORGE AT THE GATE! TELL THE PARK POLICE! TEENAGERS COMING!
THEY'RE COMING TO LOOK AT THE FLOWERS! NOT INVADE THE PLACE!
BESIDES, THEY'RE ON OUR SIDE!
2

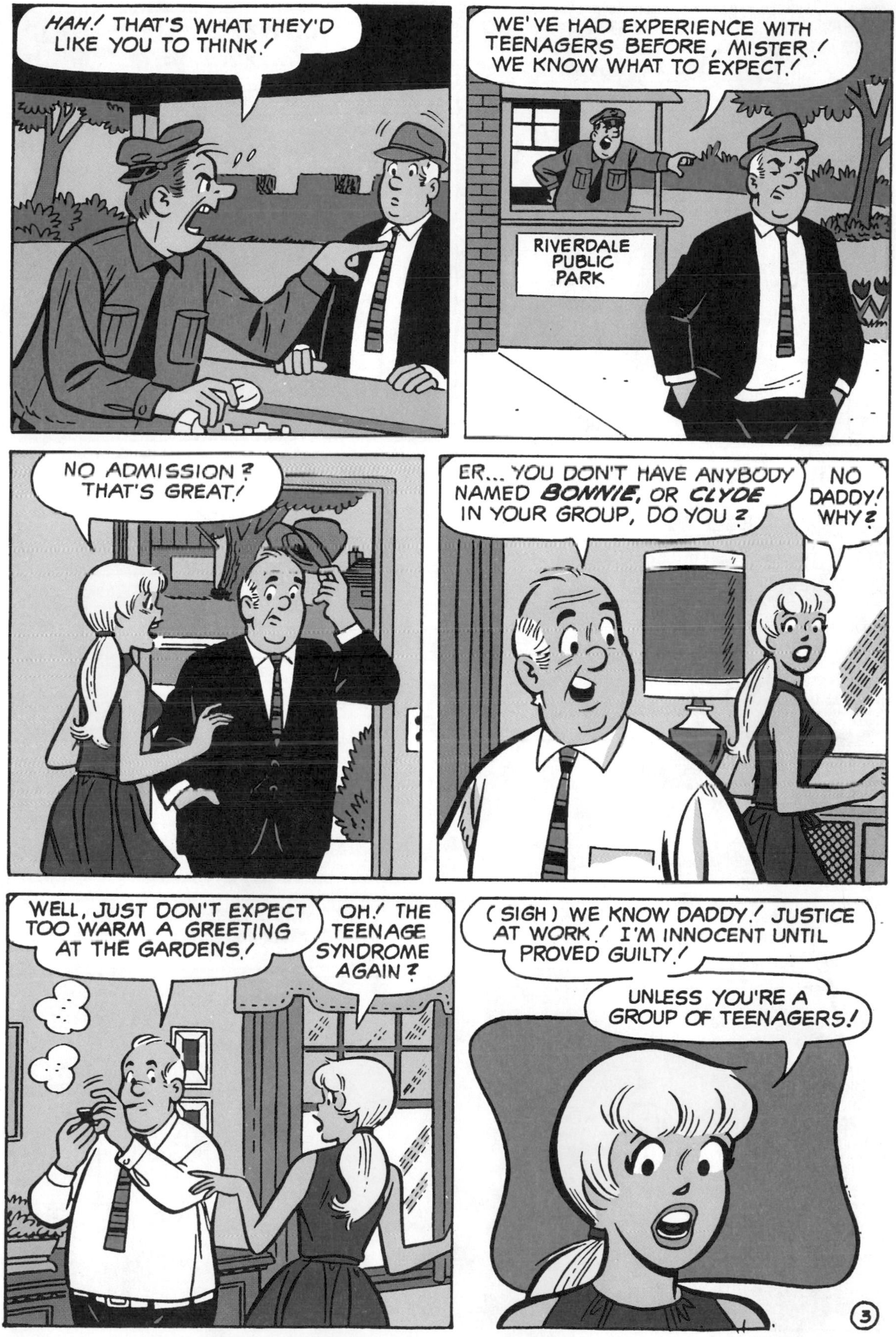
HAH! THAT'S WHAT THEY'D LIKE YOU TO THINK!
WE'VE HAD EXPERIENCE WITH TEENAGERS BEFORE, MISTER! WE KNOW WHAT TO EXPECT!
RIVERDALE PUBLIC PARK
NO ADMISSION? THAT'S GREAT!
ER... YOU DON'T HAVE ANYBODY NAMED BONNIE, OR CLYDE IN YOUR GROUP, DO YOU?
NO DADDY! WHY?
WELL, JUST DON'T EXPECT TOO WARM A GREETING AT THE GARDENS!
OH! THE TEENAGE SYNDROME AGAIN?
(SIGH) WE KNOW DADDY! JUSTICE AT WORK! I'M INNOCENT UNTIL PROVED GUILTY!
UNLESS YOU'RE A GROUP OF TEENAGERS!
3

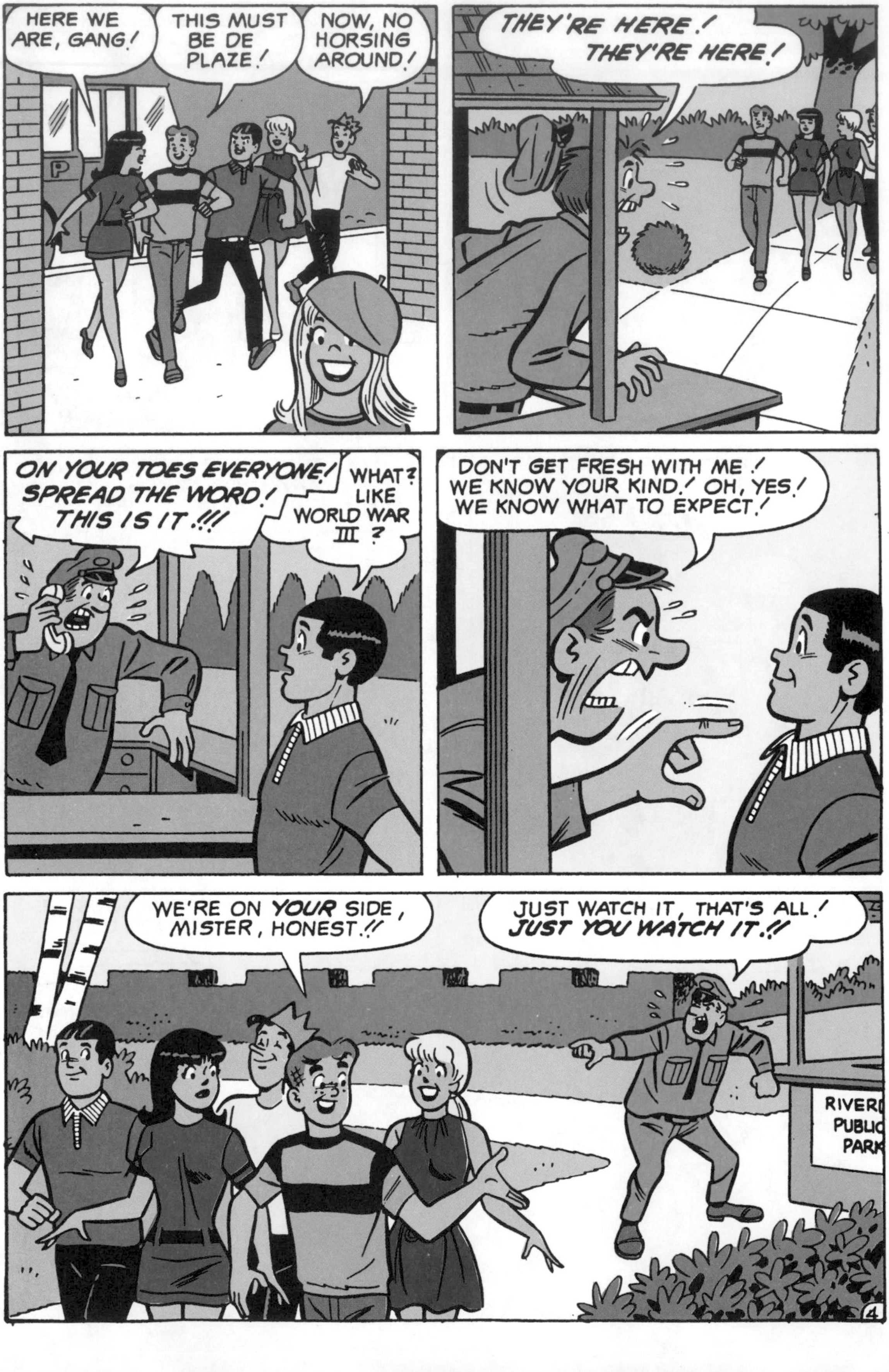
HERE WE ARE, GANG!
THIS MUST BE DE PLAZE!
NOW, NO HORSING AROUND!
THEY'RE HERE! THEY'RE HERE!
ON YOUR TOES EVERYONE! SPREAD THE WORD! THIS IS IT!!!
WHAT? LIKE WORLD WAR III?
DON'T GET FRESH WITH ME! WE KNOW YOUR KIND! OH, YES! WE KNOW WHAT TO EXPECT!
WE'RE ON YOUR SIDE, MISTER, HONEST!!
JUST WATCH IT, THAT'S ALL! JUST YOU WATCH IT!!
RIVERD PUBLIC PARK
4

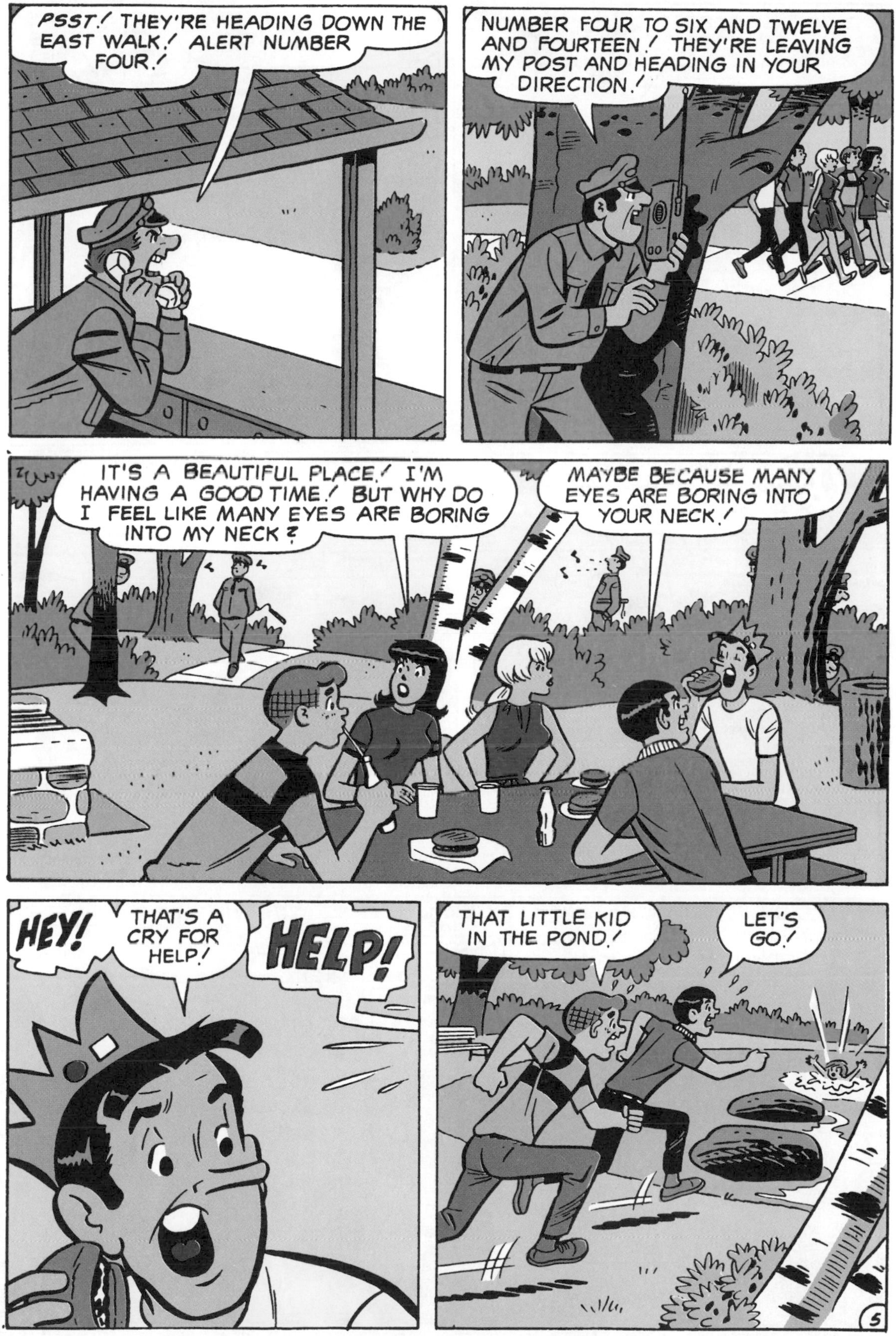
PSST! THEY'RE HEADING DOWN THE EAST WALK! ALERT NUMBER FOUR!
NUMBER FOUR TO SIX AND TWELVE AND FOURTEEN! THEY'RE LEAVING MY POST AND HEADING IN YOUR DIRECTION!
IT'S A BEAUTIFUL PLACE! I'M HAVING A GOOD TIME! BUT WHY DO I FEEL LIKE MANY EYES ARE BORING INTO MY NECK?
MAYBE BECAUSE MANY EYES ARE BORING INTO YOUR NECK!
HEY!
THAT'S A CRY FOR HELP!
HELP!
THAT LITTLE KID IN THE POND!
LET'S GO!
5

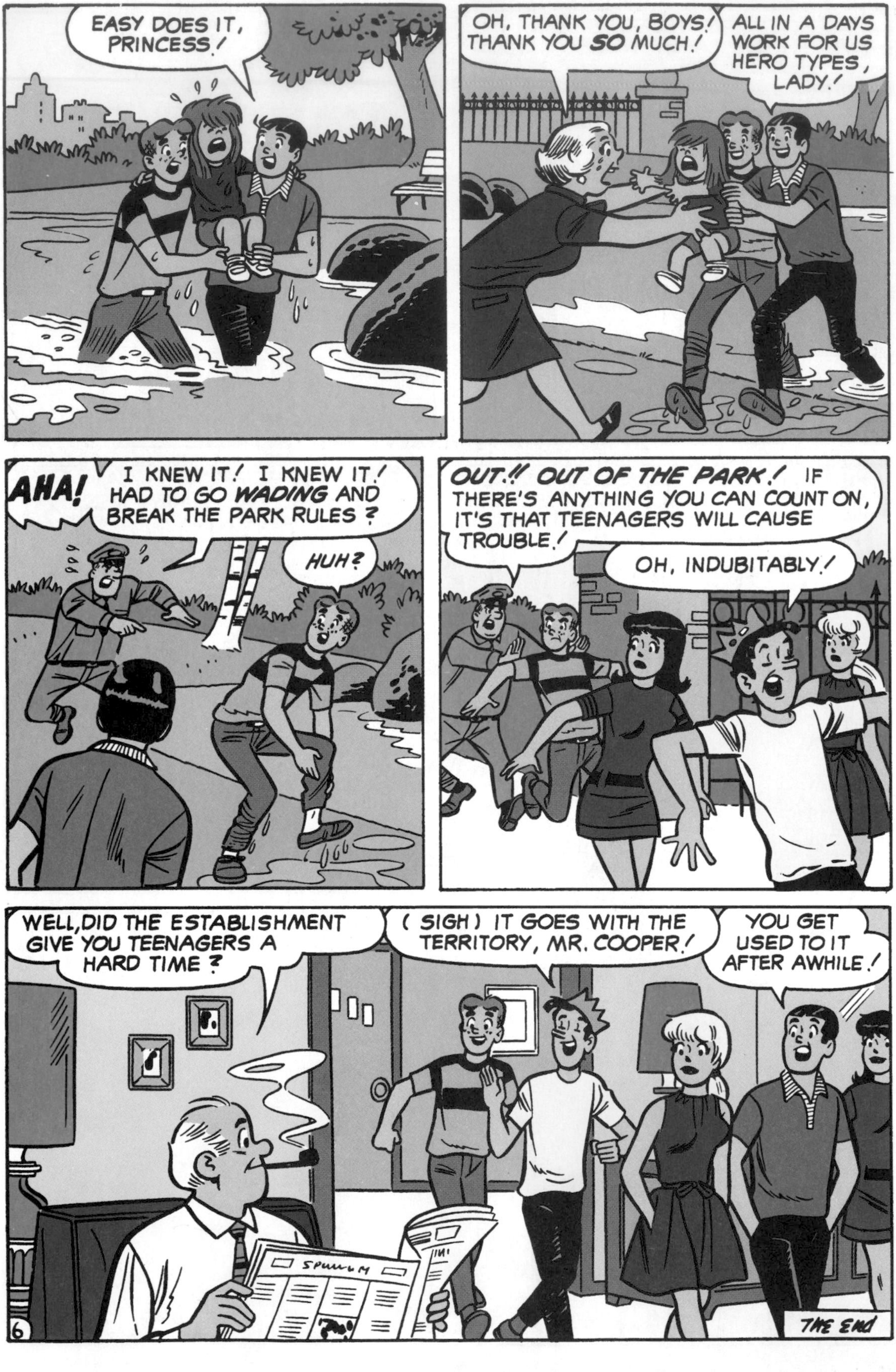
EASY DOES IT, PRINCESS!
OH, THANK YOU, BOYS! THANK YOU SO MUCH!
ALL IN A DAYS WORK FOR US HERO TYPES, LADY!
AHA!
I KNEW IT! I KNEW IT! HAD TO GO WADING AND BREAK THE PARK RULES?
HUH?
OUT!! OUT OF THE PARK! IF THERE'S ANYTHING YOU CAN COUNT ON, IT'S THAT TEENAGERS WILL CAUSE TROUBLE!
OH, INDUBITABLY!
WELL, DID THE ESTABLISHMENT GIVE YOU TEENAGERS A HARD TIME?
(SIGH) IT GOES WITH THE TERRITORY, MR. COOPER!
YOU GET USED TO IT AFTER AWHILE!
6
THE END

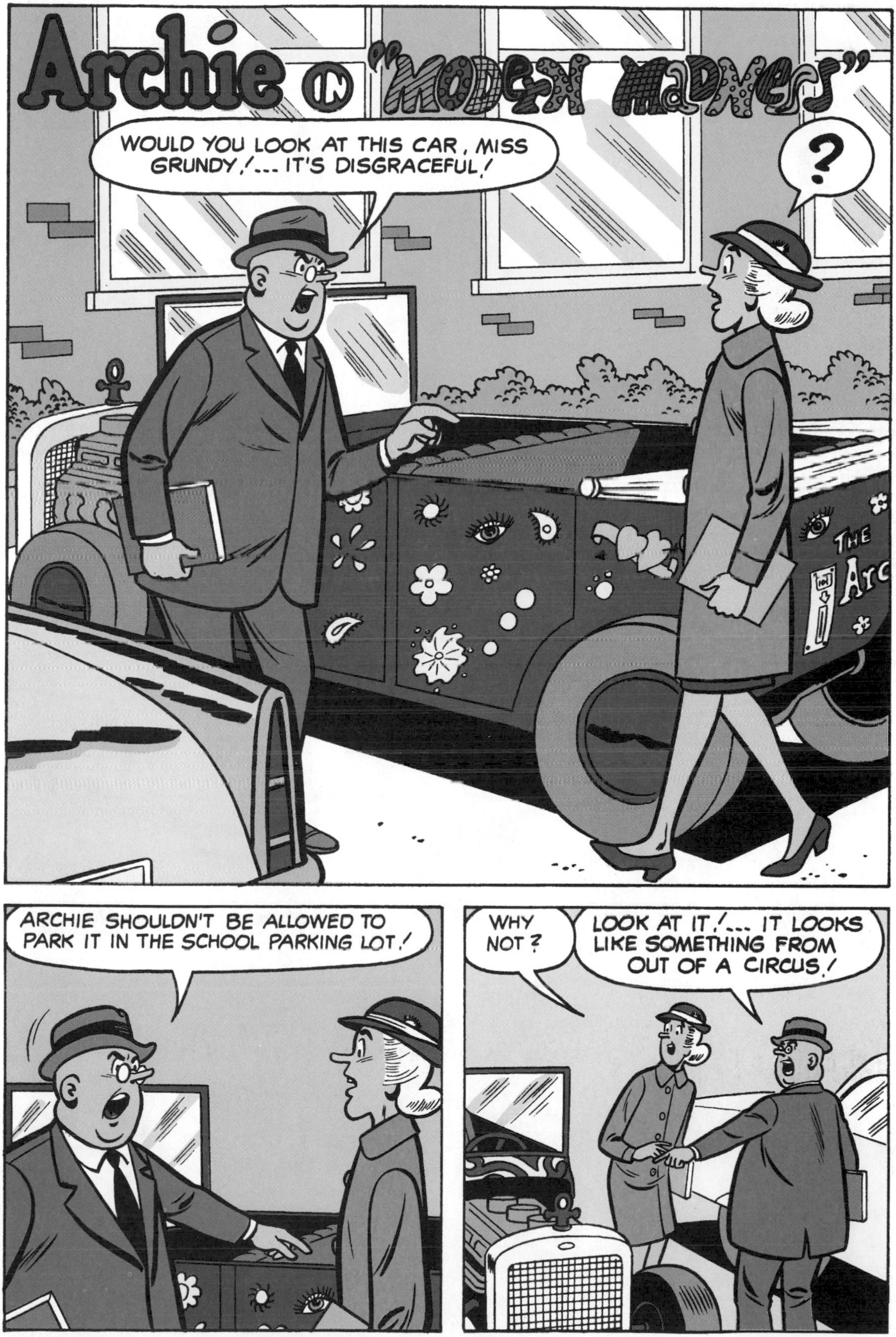
Archie IN "MODERN MADNESS"
WOULD YOU LOOK AT THIS CAR, MISS GRUNDY!... IT'S DISGRACEFUL!
?
ARCHIE SHOULDN'T BE ALLOWED TO PARK IT IN THE SCHOOL PARKING LOT!
WHY NOT?
LOOK AT IT!... IT LOOKS LIKE SOMETHING FROM OUT OF A CIRCUS!

ORIGINALLY PRESENTED IN **LIFE WITH ARCHIE #84**, APRIL, 1969

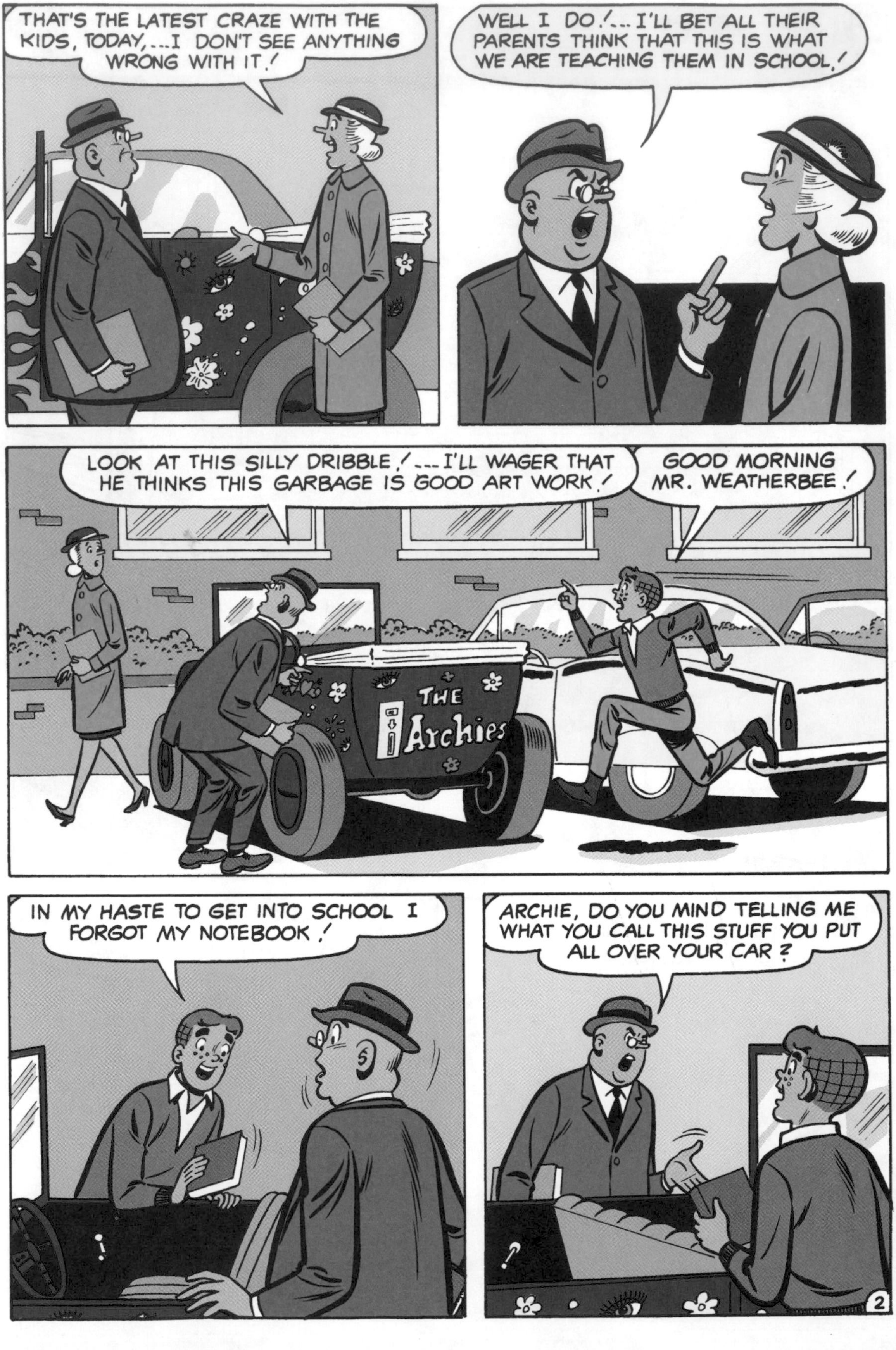
THAT'S THE LATEST CRAZE WITH THE KIDS, TODAY,...I DON'T SEE ANYTHING WRONG WITH IT.!
WELL I DO.!...I'LL BET ALL THEIR PARENTS THINK THAT THIS IS WHAT WE ARE TEACHING THEM IN SCHOOL.!
LOOK AT THIS SILLY DRIBBLE.!...I'LL WAGER THAT HE THINKS THIS GARBAGE IS GOOD ART WORK.!
GOOD MORNING MR. WEATHERBEE.!
THE Archies
IN MY HASTE TO GET INTO SCHOOL I FORGOT MY NOTEBOOK.!
ARCHIE, DO YOU MIND TELLING ME WHAT YOU CALL THIS STUFF YOU PUT ALL OVER YOUR CAR?

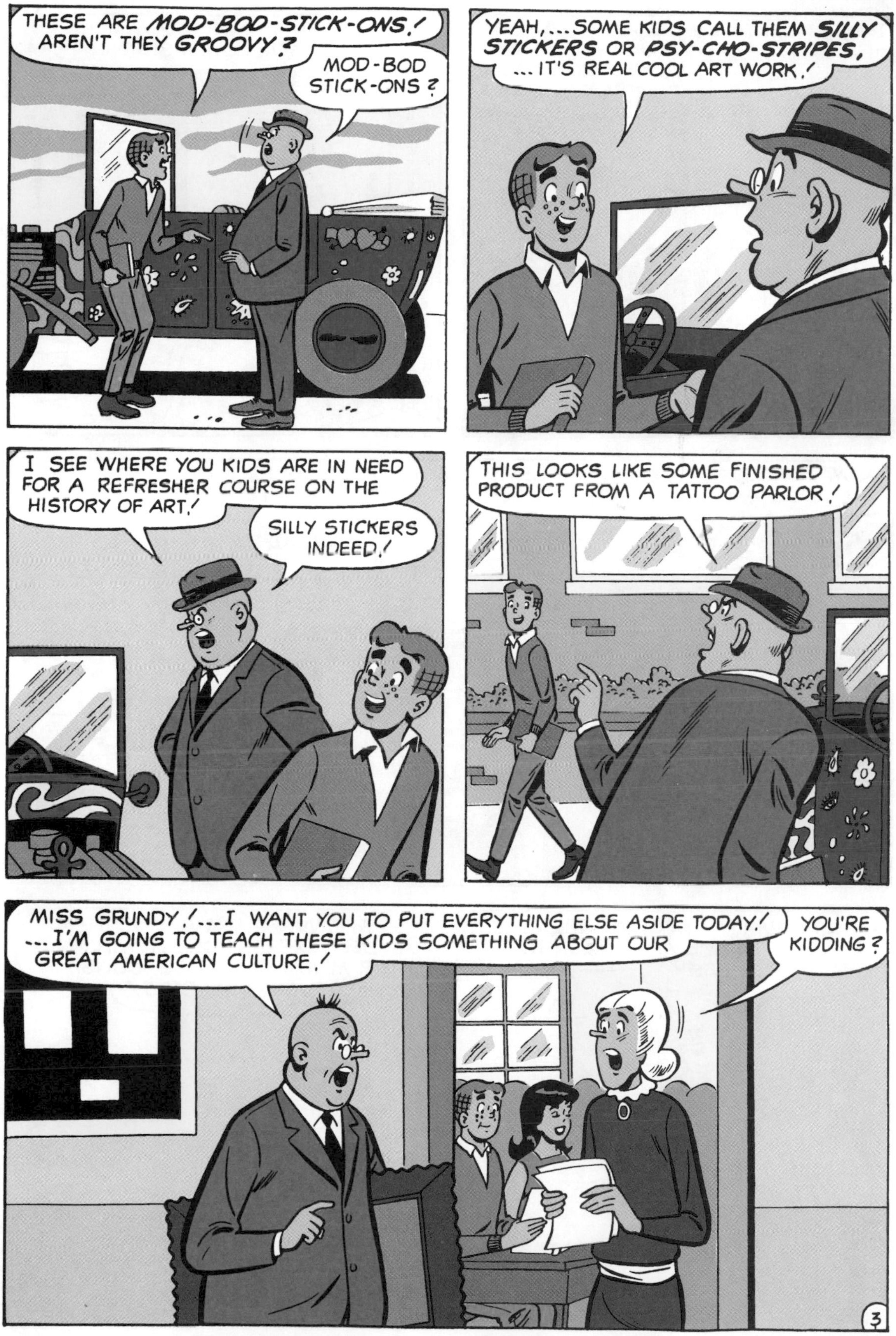
THESE ARE MOD-BOD-STICK-ONS.! AREN'T THEY GROOVY?
MOD-BOD STICK-ONS?
YEAH,...SOME KIDS CALL THEM SILLY STICKERS OR PSY-CHO-STRIPES, ...IT'S REAL COOL ART WORK.!
I SEE WHERE YOU KIDS ARE IN NEED FOR A REFRESHER COURSE ON THE HISTORY OF ART.!
SILLY STICKERS INDEED.!
THIS LOOKS LIKE SOME FINISHED PRODUCT FROM A TATTOO PARLOR.!
MISS GRUNDY.!...I WANT YOU TO PUT EVERYTHING ELSE ASIDE TODAY.! ...I'M GOING TO TEACH THESE KIDS SOMETHING ABOUT OUR GREAT AMERICAN CULTURE.!
YOU'RE KIDDING?
3

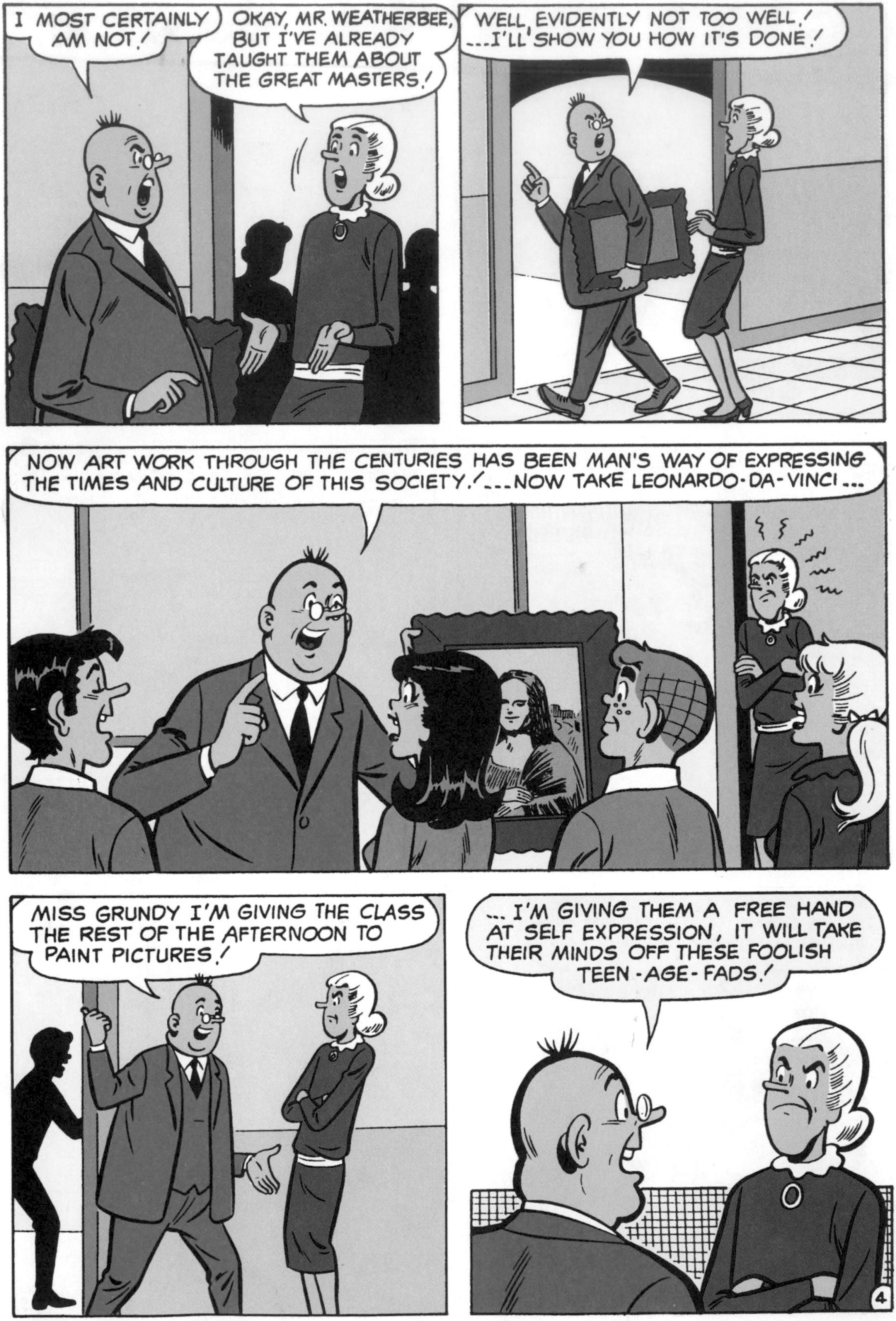
I MOST CERTAINLY AM NOT!
OKAY, MR. WEATHERBEE, BUT I'VE ALREADY TAUGHT THEM ABOUT THE GREAT MASTERS!
WELL, EVIDENTLY NOT TOO WELL! ...I'LL SHOW YOU HOW IT'S DONE!
NOW ART WORK THROUGH THE CENTURIES HAS BEEN MAN'S WAY OF EXPRESSING THE TIMES AND CULTURE OF THIS SOCIETY! ...NOW TAKE LEONARDO-DA-VINCI...
MISS GRUNDY I'M GIVING THE CLASS THE REST OF THE AFTERNOON TO PAINT PICTURES!
...I'M GIVING THEM A FREE HAND AT SELF EXPRESSION, IT WILL TAKE THEIR MINDS OFF THESE FOOLISH TEEN-AGE-FADS!
4

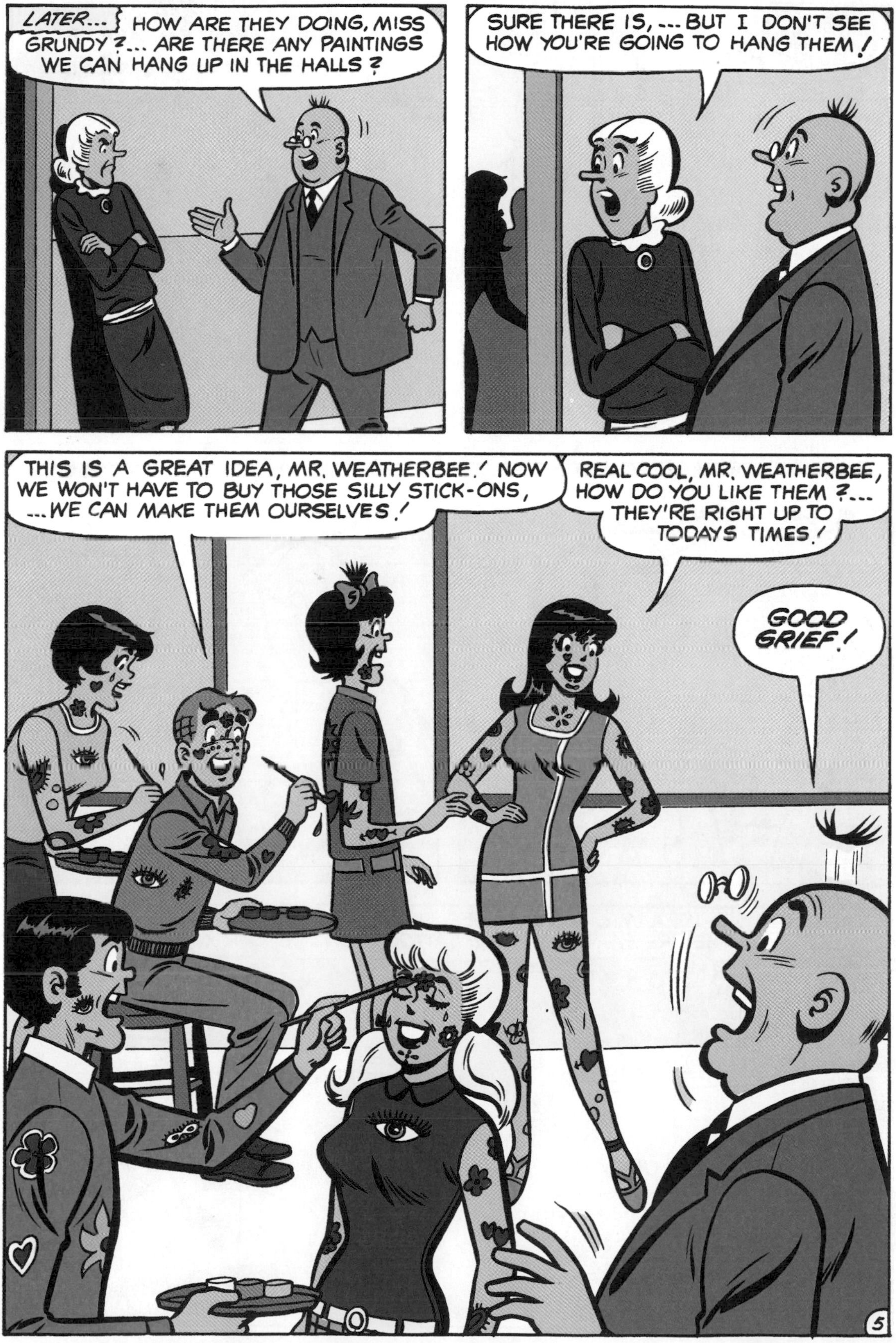
LATER...
HOW ARE THEY DOING, MISS GRUNDY?... ARE THERE ANY PAINTINGS WE CAN HANG UP IN THE HALLS?
SURE THERE IS, --- BUT I DON'T SEE HOW YOU'RE GOING TO HANG THEM!
THIS IS A GREAT IDEA, MR. WEATHERBEE! NOW WE WON'T HAVE TO BUY THOSE SILLY STICK-ONS, ...WE CAN MAKE THEM OURSELVES!
REAL COOL, MR. WEATHERBEE, HOW DO YOU LIKE THEM?... THEY'RE RIGHT UP TO TODAYS TIMES!
GOOD GRIEF!
5

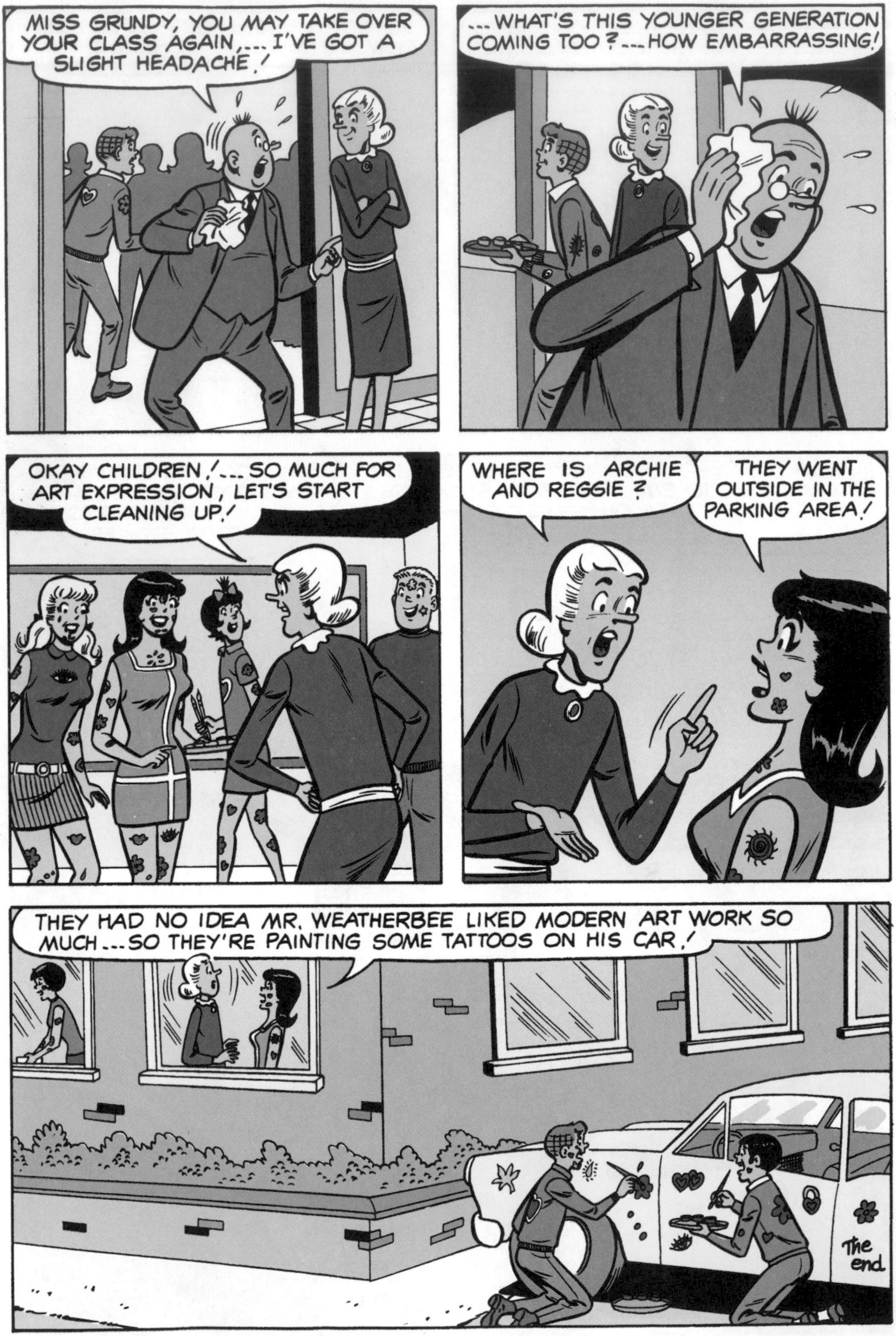
MISS GRUNDY, YOU MAY TAKE OVER YOUR CLASS AGAIN,... I'VE GOT A SLIGHT HEADACHE!
...WHAT'S THIS YOUNGER GENERATION COMING TOO?... HOW EMBARRASSING!
OKAY CHILDREN!... SO MUCH FOR ART EXPRESSION, LET'S START CLEANING UP!
WHERE IS ARCHIE AND REGGIE?
THEY WENT OUTSIDE IN THE PARKING AREA!
THEY HAD NO IDEA MR. WEATHERBEE LIKED MODERN ART WORK SO MUCH... SO THEY'RE PAINTING SOME TATTOOS ON HIS CAR!
The end

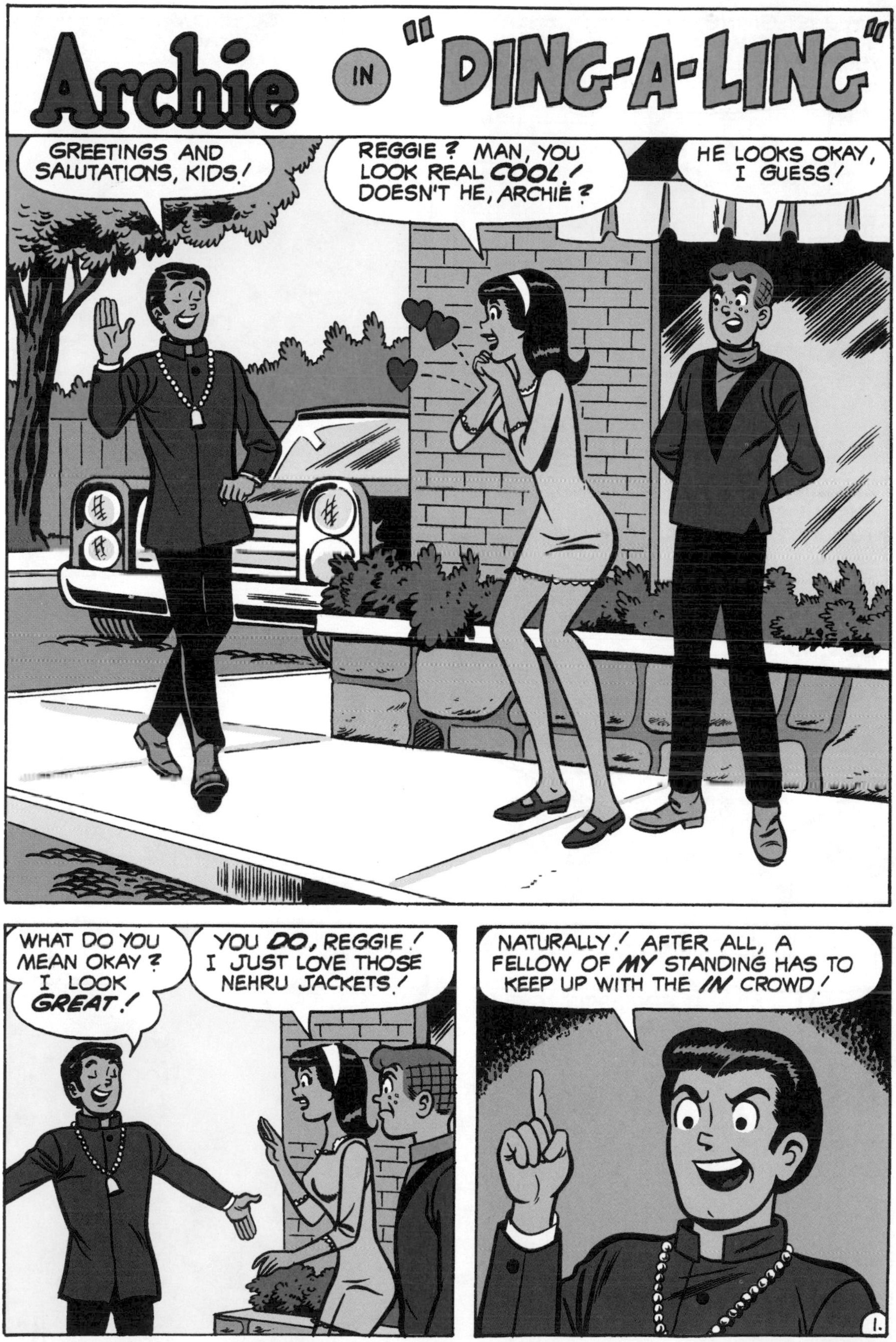
Archie IN "DING-A-LING"
GREETINGS AND SALUTATIONS, KIDS!
REGGIE? MAN, YOU LOOK REAL COOL! DOESN'T HE, ARCHIE?
HE LOOKS OKAY, I GUESS!
WHAT DO YOU MEAN OKAY? I LOOK GREAT!
YOU DO, REGGIE! I JUST LOVE THOSE NEHRU JACKETS!
NATURALLY! AFTER ALL, A FELLOW OF MY STANDING HAS TO KEEP UP WITH THE IN CROWD!
1.

ORIGINALLY PRESENTED IN **PEP #225**, JANUARY, 1969

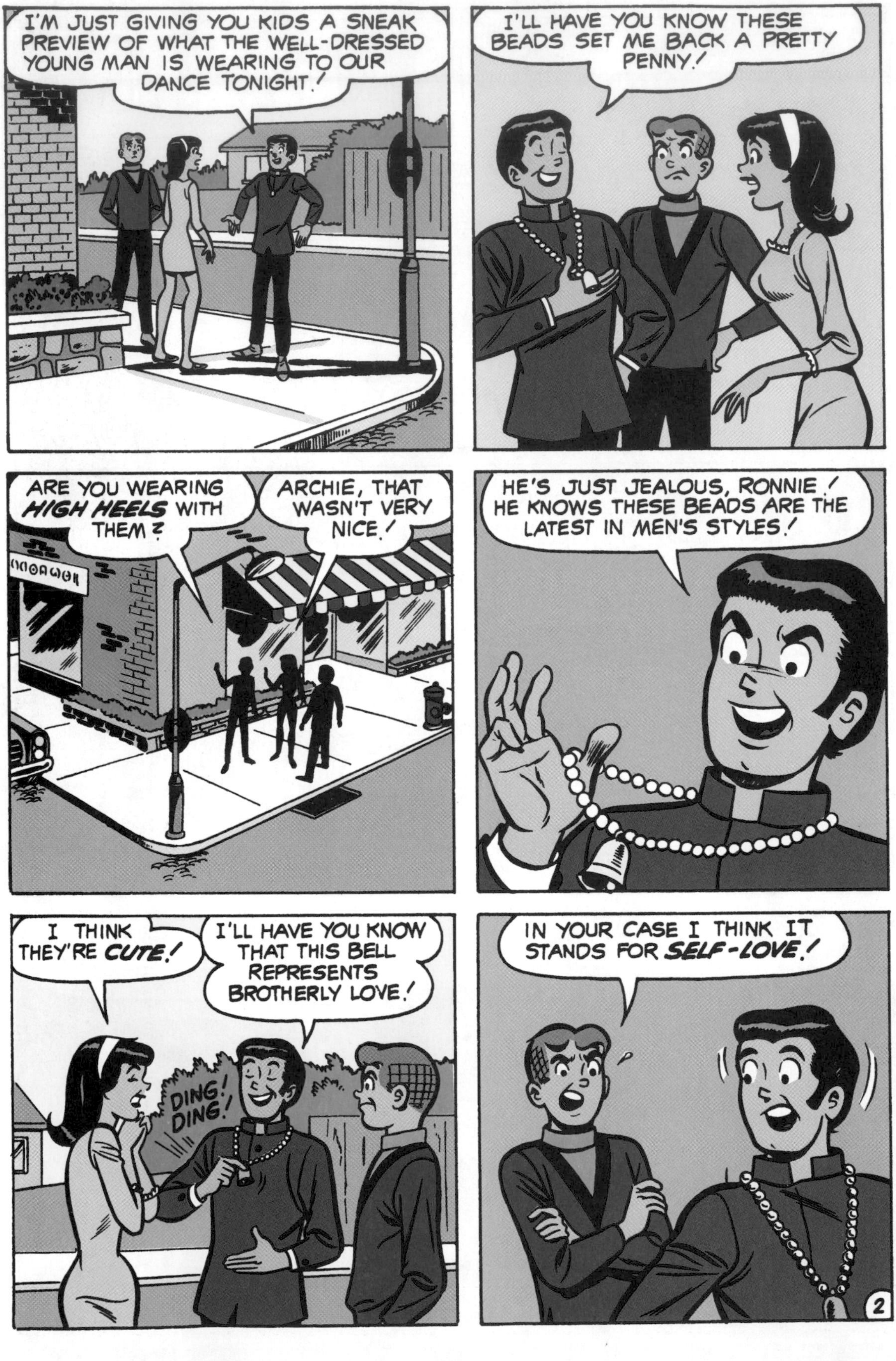
I'M JUST GIVING YOU KIDS A SNEAK PREVIEW OF WHAT THE WELL-DRESSED YOUNG MAN IS WEARING TO OUR DANCE TONIGHT!
I'LL HAVE YOU KNOW THESE BEADS SET ME BACK A PRETTY PENNY!
ARE YOU WEARING HIGH HEELS WITH THEM?
ARCHIE, THAT WASN'T VERY NICE!
HE'S JUST JEALOUS, RONNIE! HE KNOWS THESE BEADS ARE THE LATEST IN MEN'S STYLES!
I THINK THEY'RE CUTE!
I'LL HAVE YOU KNOW THAT THIS BELL REPRESENTS BROTHERLY LOVE!
DING! DING!
IN YOUR CASE I THINK IT STANDS FOR SELF-LOVE!
2

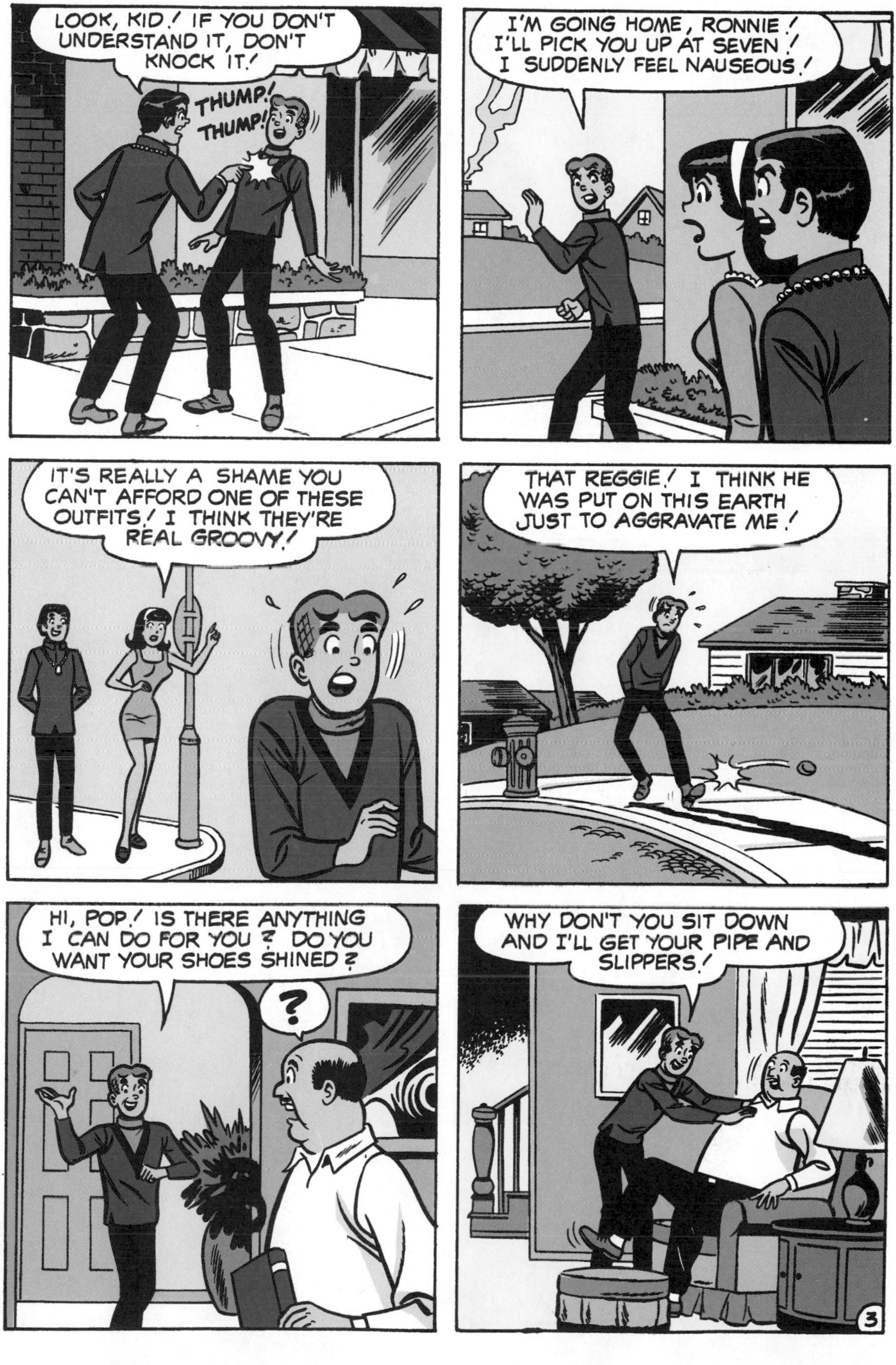
LOOK, KID! IF YOU DON'T UNDERSTAND IT, DON'T KNOCK IT!
THUMP! THUMP!
I'M GOING HOME, RONNIE! I'LL PICK YOU UP AT SEVEN! I SUDDENLY FEEL NAUSEOUS!
IT'S REALLY A SHAME YOU CAN'T AFFORD ONE OF THESE OUTFITS! I THINK THEY'RE REAL GROOVY!
THAT REGGIE! I THINK HE WAS PUT ON THIS EARTH JUST TO AGGRAVATE ME!
HI, POP! IS THERE ANYTHING I CAN DO FOR YOU? DO YOU WANT YOUR SHOES SHINED?
?
WHY DON'T YOU SIT DOWN AND I'LL GET YOUR PIPE AND SLIPPERS!
3

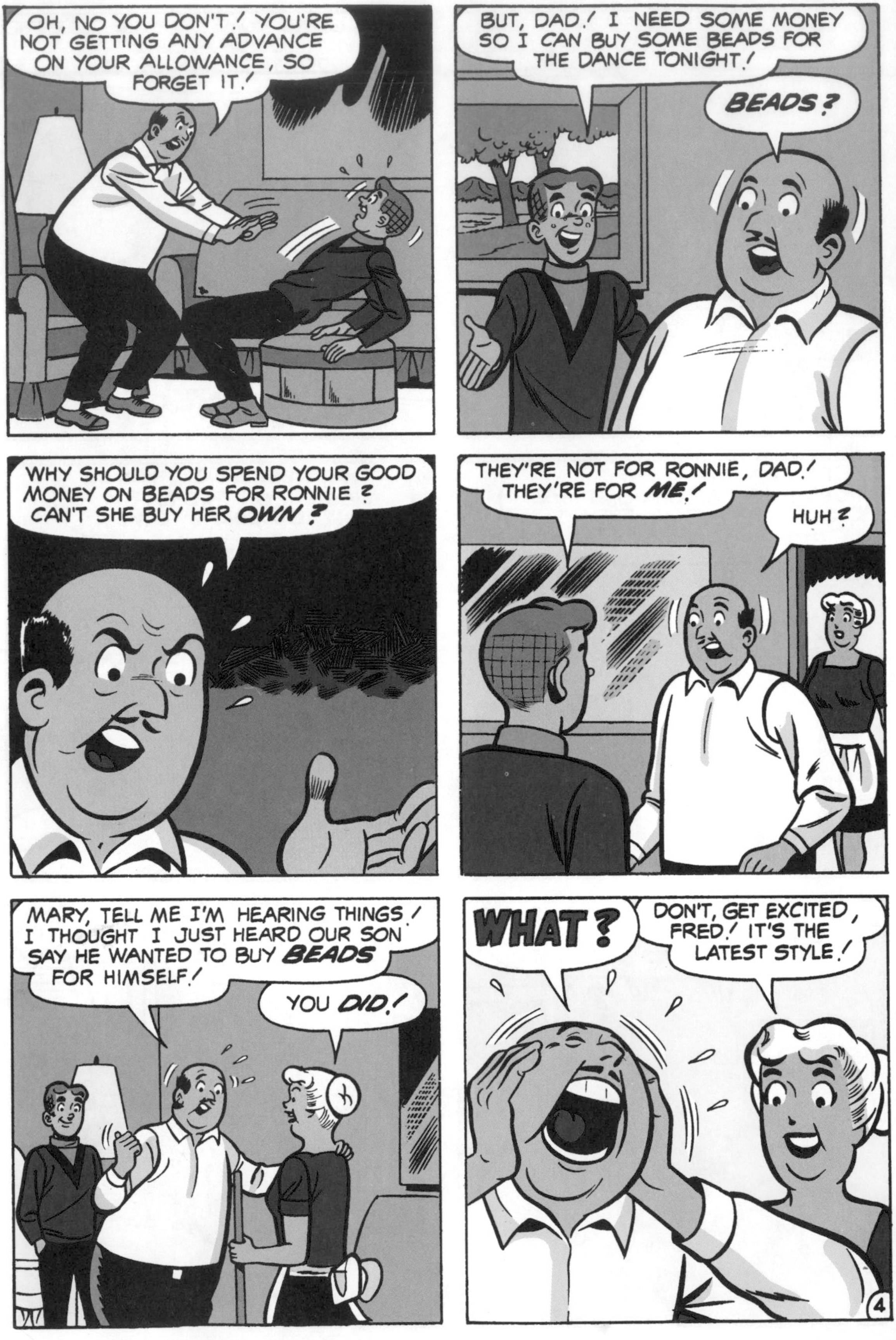
OH, NO YOU DON'T! YOU'RE NOT GETTING ANY ADVANCE ON YOUR ALLOWANCE, SO FORGET IT!
BUT, DAD! I NEED SOME MONEY SO I CAN BUY SOME BEADS FOR THE DANCE TONIGHT!
BEADS?
WHY SHOULD YOU SPEND YOUR GOOD MONEY ON BEADS FOR RONNIE? CAN'T SHE BUY HER OWN?
THEY'RE NOT FOR RONNIE, DAD! THEY'RE FOR ME!
HUH?
MARY, TELL ME I'M HEARING THINGS! I THOUGHT I JUST HEARD OUR SON SAY HE WANTED TO BUY BEADS FOR HIMSELF!
YOU DID!
WHAT?
DON'T, GET EXCITED, FRED! IT'S THE LATEST STYLE!
4

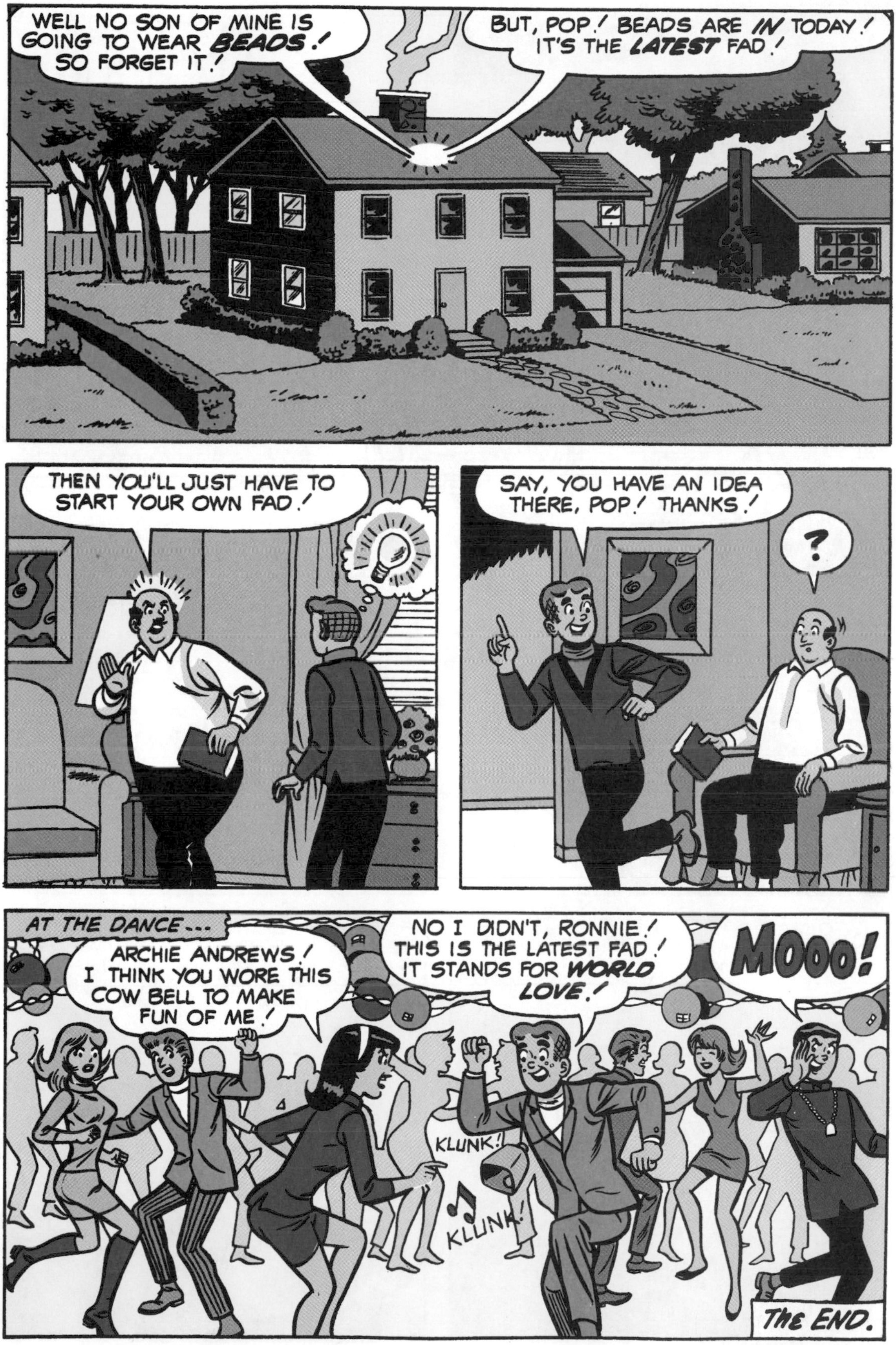
WELL NO SON OF MINE IS GOING TO WEAR BEADS! SO FORGET IT!
BUT, POP! BEADS ARE IN TODAY! IT'S THE LATEST FAD!
THEN YOU'LL JUST HAVE TO START YOUR OWN FAD!
SAY, YOU HAVE AN IDEA THERE, POP! THANKS!
?
AT THE DANCE...
ARCHIE ANDREWS! I THINK YOU WORE THIS COW BELL TO MAKE FUN OF ME!
NO I DIDN'T, RONNIE! THIS IS THE LATEST FAD! IT STANDS FOR WORLD LOVE!
MOOO!
KLUNK!
KLUNK!
THE END.

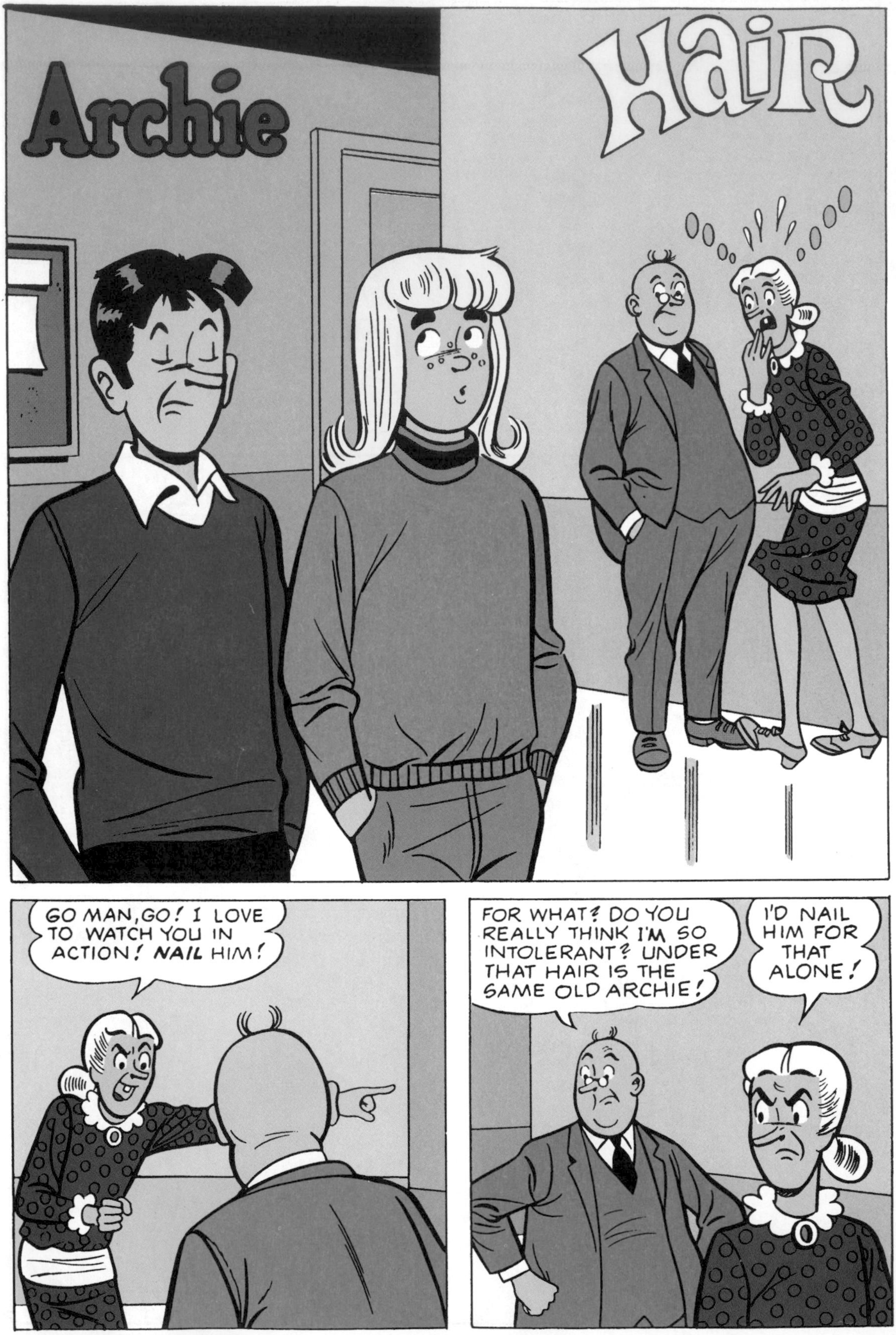
Archie
HAIR
GO MAN, GO! I LOVE TO WATCH YOU IN ACTION! **NAIL** HIM!
FOR WHAT? DO YOU REALLY THINK I'M SO INTOLERANT? UNDER THAT HAIR IS THE SAME OLD ARCHIE!
I'D NAIL HIM FOR THAT ALONE!

ORIGINALLY PRESENTED IN **PEP #229**, MAY, 1969

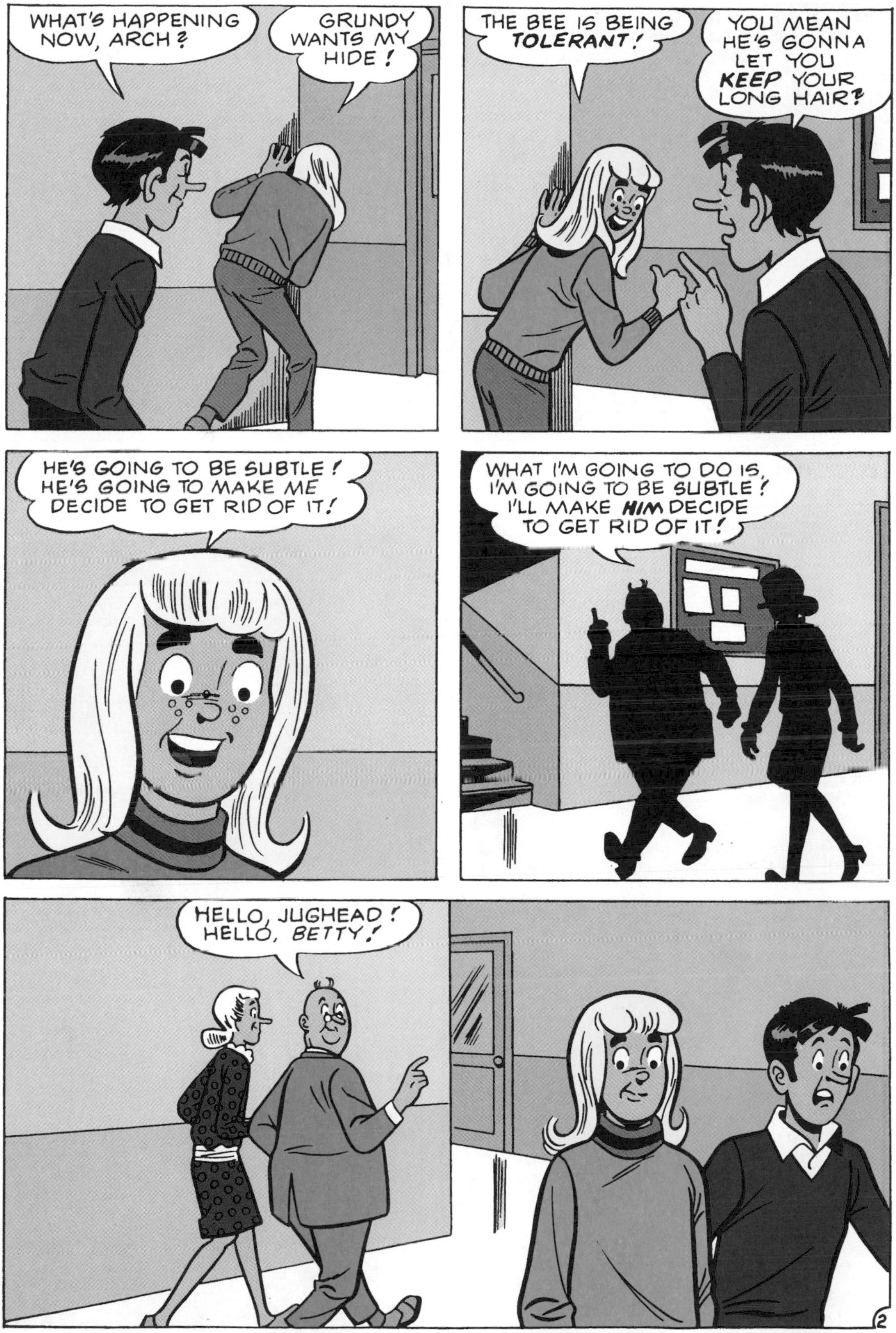
WHAT'S HAPPENING NOW, ARCH?
GRUNDY WANTS MY HIDE!
THE BEE IS BEING TOLERANT!
YOU MEAN HE'S GONNA LET YOU KEEP YOUR LONG HAIR?
HE'S GOING TO BE SUBTLE! HE'S GOING TO MAKE ME DECIDE TO GET RID OF IT!
WHAT I'M GOING TO DO IS, I'M GOING TO BE SUBTLE! I'LL MAKE HIM DECIDE TO GET RID OF IT!
HELLO, JUGHEAD! HELLO, BETTY!
2

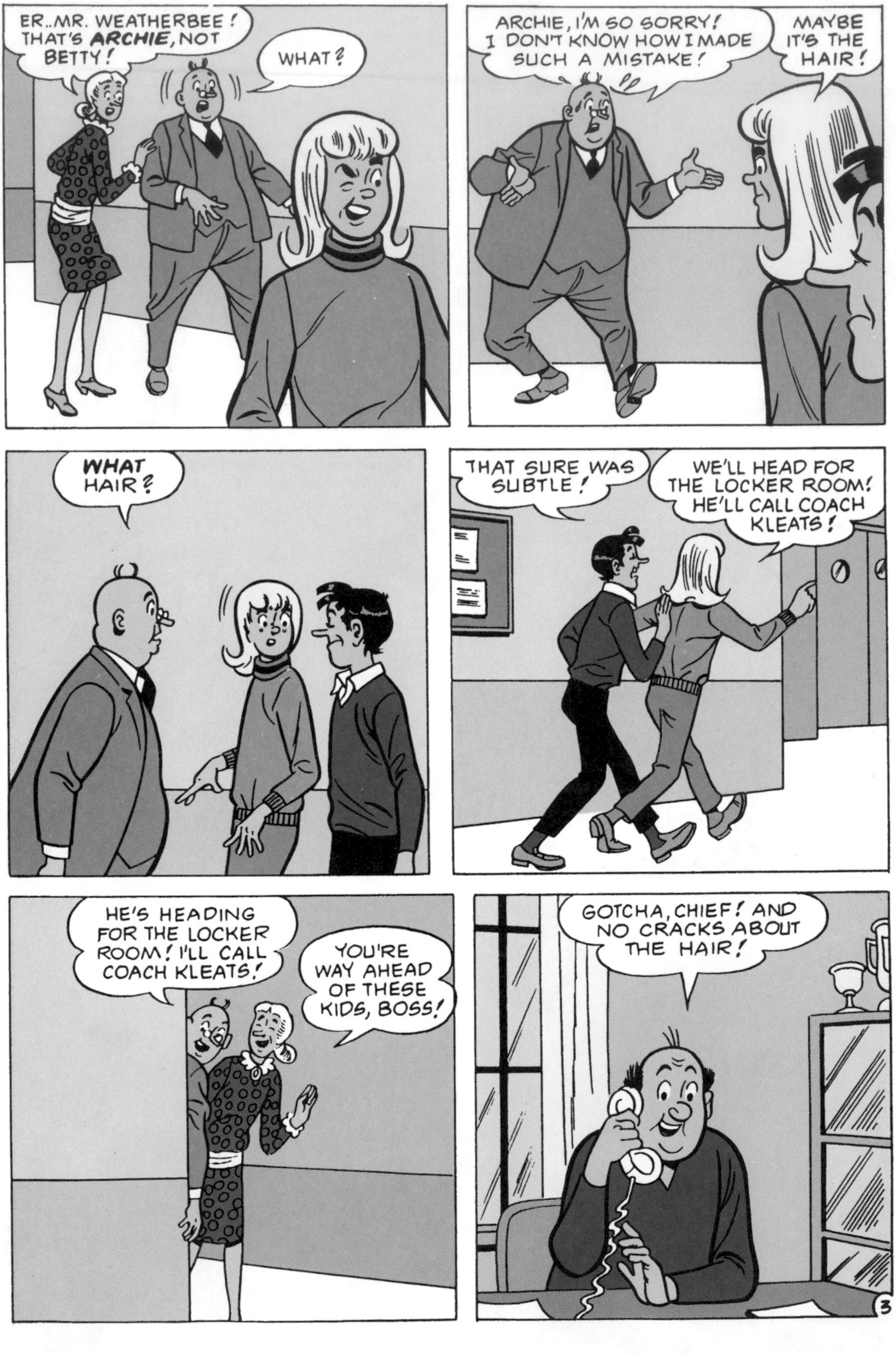
ER..MR. WEATHERBEE! THAT'S ARCHIE, NOT BETTY!
WHAT?
ARCHIE, I'M SO SORRY! I DON'T KNOW HOW I MADE SUCH A MISTAKE!
MAYBE IT'S THE HAIR!
WHAT HAIR?
THAT SURE WAS SUBTLE!
WE'LL HEAD FOR THE LOCKER ROOM! HE'LL CALL COACH KLEATS!
HE'S HEADING FOR THE LOCKER ROOM! I'LL CALL COACH KLEATS!
YOU'RE WAY AHEAD OF THESE KIDS, BOSS!
GOTCHA, CHIEF! AND NO CRACKS ABOUT THE HAIR!
3

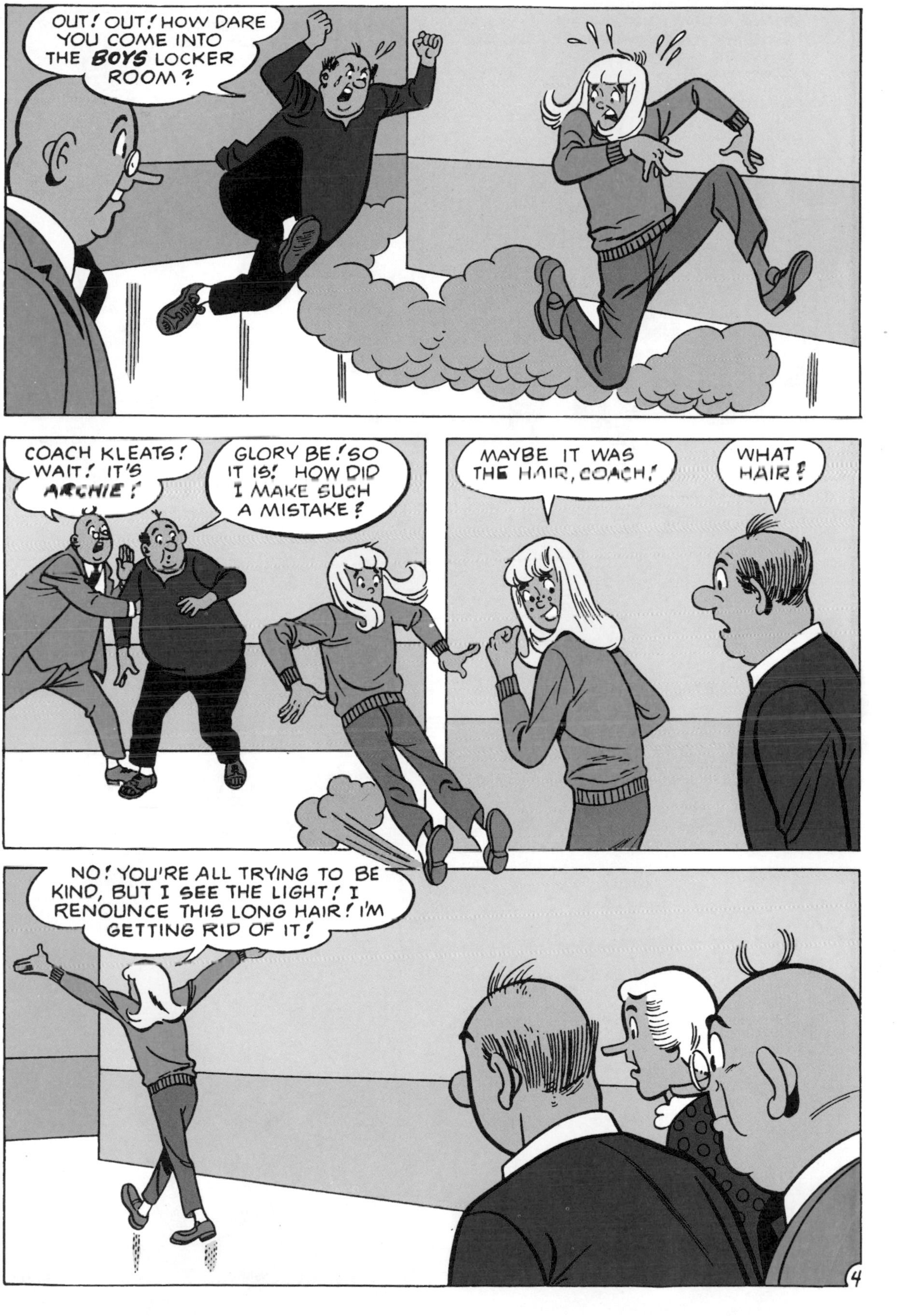
OUT! OUT! HOW DARE YOU COME INTO THE BOYS LOCKER ROOM?
COACH KLEATS! WAIT! IT'S ARCHIE!
GLORY BE! SO IT IS! HOW DID I MAKE SUCH A MISTAKE?
MAYBE IT WAS THE HAIR, COACH!
WHAT HAIR?
NO! YOU'RE ALL TRYING TO BE KIND, BUT I SEE THE LIGHT! I RENOUNCE THIS LONG HAIR! I'M GETTING RID OF IT!
4

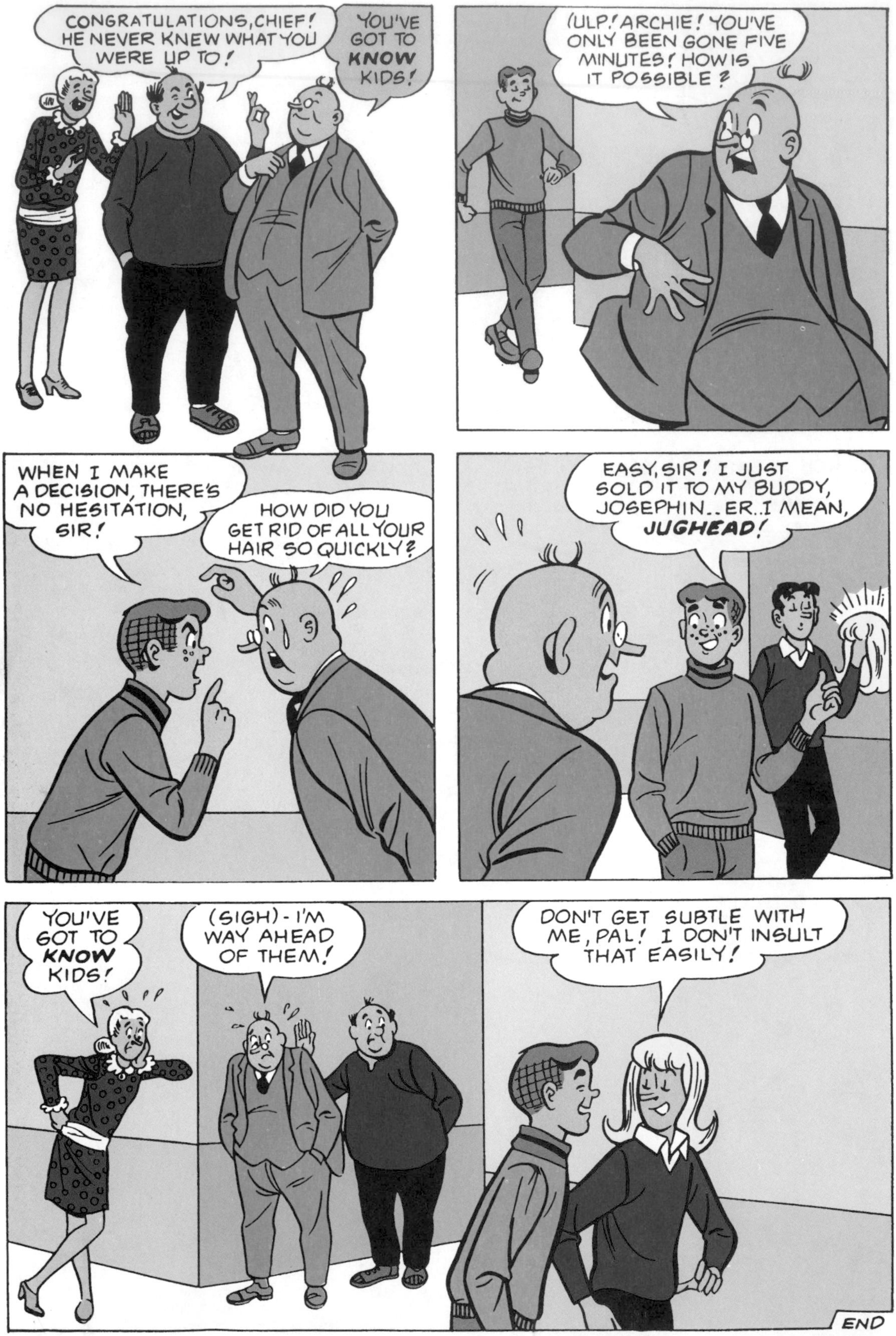
CONGRATULATIONS, CHIEF! HE NEVER KNEW WHAT YOU WERE UP TO!
YOU'VE GOT TO **KNOW** KIDS!
(ULP! ARCHIE! YOU'VE ONLY BEEN GONE FIVE MINUTES! HOW IS IT POSSIBLE?
WHEN I MAKE A DECISION, THERE'S NO HESITATION, SIR!
HOW DID YOU GET RID OF ALL YOUR HAIR SO QUICKLY?
EASY, SIR! I JUST SOLD IT TO MY BUDDY, JOSEPHIN.. ER..I MEAN, **JUGHEAD**!
YOU'VE GOT TO **KNOW** KIDS!
(SIGH) - I'M WAY AHEAD OF THEM!
DON'T GET SUBTLE WITH ME, PAL! I DON'T INSULT THAT EASILY!
END